Salvation for the Sinned-Against

Missional Church, Public Theology, World Christianity

Stephen Bevans, Paul S. Chung, Veli-Matti Kärkkäinen
and Craig L. Nessan, Series Editors

IN THE MIDST OF globalization there is crisis as well as opportunity. A model of God's mission is of special significance for ecclesiology and public theology when explored in diverse perspectives and frameworks in the postcolonial context of World Christianity. In the face of the new, complex global civilization characterized by the Second Axial Age, the theology of mission, missional ecclesiology, and public ethics endeavor to provide a larger framework for missiology. It does so in interaction with our social, multicultural, political, economic, and intercivilizational situation. These fields create ways to refurbish mission as constructive theology in critical and creative engagement with cultural anthropology, world religions, prophetic theology, postcolonial hermeneutics, and contextual theologies of World Christianity. Such endeavors play a critical role in generating theological, missional, social-ethical alternatives to the reality of Empire—a reality characterized by civilizational conflict, and by the complex system of a colonized lifeworld that is embedded within practices of greed, dominion, and ecological devastation. This series—Missional Church, Public Theology, World Christianity—invites scholars to promote alternative church practices for life-enhancing culture and for evangelization as telling the truth in the public sphere, especially in solidarity with those on the margins and in ecological stewardship for the lifeworld.

Salvation for the Sinned-Against
Han and Schillebeeckx in Intercultural Dialogue

Kevin P. Considine

Foreword by
Robert J. Schreiter

☙PICKWICK *Publications* · Eugene, Oregon

SALVATION FOR THE SINNED-AGAINST
Han and Schillebeeckx in Intercultural Dialogue

Missional Church, Public Theology, World Christianity 5

Copyright © 2015 Kevin P. Considine. All rights reserved. Except for brief quotations in critical publications or reviews, no part of this book may be reproduced in any manner without prior written permission from the publisher. Write: Permissions, Wipf and Stock Publishers, 199 W. 8th Ave., Suite 3, Eugene, OR 97401.

Pickwick Publications
An Imprint of Wipf and Stock Publishers
199 W. 8th Ave., Suite 3
Eugene, OR 97401

www.wipfandstock.com

ISBN 13: 978-1-62564-862-4

Cataloging-in-Publication data:

Considine, Kevin P.

    Salvation for the sinned-against : han and Schillebeeckx in intercultural dialogue / Kevin P. Considine ; foreword by Robert J. Schreiter.

    xxiv + 214 p. ; 23 cm. —Includes bibliographical references and indexes.

    ISBN 13: 978-1-62564-862-4

    Missional Church, Public Theology, World Christianity 5

    1. Schillebeeckx, Edward, 1914–2009. 2. Minjung theology. 3. Salvation—Catholic Church. 4. Han (Psychology). 5. Sin. 6. Victims—religious life. I. Schreiter, Robert J. II. Title. III. Series.

BT715 .C66 2015

Manufactured in the U.S.A.   01/22/2015

To Kiae, Liam, and Elias

If one does not hear the sighs of the *han* of the *minjung*,
one cannot hear the voice of Christ knocking on our doors.
—SUH NAM-DONG

God does not want humankind to suffer.
—EDWARD SCHILLEBEECKX, OP

Contents

Foreword by Robert J. Schreiter | ix
Acknowledgments | xiii
Short Glossary of Korean and Chinese Terms | xv
Introduction: Re-envisioning Roman Catholic Soteriology | xvii

1. *Gaudium et spes*: A Relatively Inadequate Soteriology for the Sinned-Against Creature | 1
2. The Bridge: The Soteriology of Edward Schillebeeckx | 29
3. Theological Method: Intercultural Hermeneutics and the Semiotics of Culture | 66
4. An Outer-Hearer's Understanding of Korean-American Theologies of *Han* | 97
5. Intercultural Dialogue: Toward a Roman Catholic Soteriology for the Sinned-Against | 162

Bibliography | 199
Index of Authors | 211

Foreword

THEOLOGY FOR A GENUINELY World Christianity cannot be simply European or North American ways of doing theology writ on a larger scale. It will have to take a number of things into consideration. First of all, it must deal with issues and challenges that span the interest of more than one region of the world, and allow multiple voices to be heard and understood. Secularization, for example, may be a pressing issue in the Global North, but is not likely to engage a world where most people are still deeply religious. Second, within those issues and challenges a theology for Word Christianity takes up, it must focus first on those issues that are the most pressing and need special attention. Secularization may be high on the agenda for churches in Europe or North America, but poverty is the central experience for a majority of the world's Christians. Third, the distinctive resources of these multiple regions have to be brought into engagement with one another, so that the outcome can illuminate each of the regions—and their issues—in a new kind of way. Thus, climate change affects all parts of the world, but its immediate impact is different for rich and for poor countries.

The book you have before you does a masterful job of dealing with all three of these considerations for a theology for World Christianity. Kevin Considine takes up a question that, while ancient, has gained a new urgency as the voices of the poor cry out in their suffering. The poor now constitute the majority of the worldwide Christian Church, and the various theologies of liberation that have developed over the last five decades have brought this to the attention of the wealthier parts of the world in a manner that cannot be avoided. In a special way, these voices have not only made suffering a central theme for contemporary theology, but have put how suffering is addressed into a new register. Much of traditional theologies of suffering focused upon the question of theodicy, or why does God permit suffering. The voices to which Considine attends here raise quandaries about the sinned-against: those who suffer because of the sins of others. He notes that this is an area to which Roman Catholic official thinking has devoted little reflection. Addressing this issue is one of the central themes of this book.

To do this, he brings into conversation two distinctive voices and approaches that heretofore had not been connected. From European Christianity, he enlists the work of Flemish theologian Edward Schillebeeckx on the question of suffering. Schillebeeckx's notion of the "contrast experience"—that the outrage of "what should not be" as the beginning point for addressing suffering—has attracted the attention of over half a dozen younger theologians from around the world for how it articulates the protests of the sinned-against and points to a possible Christian response. Underlying the contrast experience is an anthropology that offers a kind of normative picture of what the human being "should be"—an anthropology that helps us understand the cry of "This should not be!" Schillebeeckx's "anthropological constants," a series of six guidelines for anthropological discourse, offer a framework for exploring together the meaning of the human. In so doing, they offer a sort of methodological middle ground between a modern essentialist and a postmodern relativist framework for dialogue about the human and what violates fundamentally who the human being is. This too has attracted the attention of the youngest generation of theologians seeking a way between the various polarities that have marked late-twentieth-century theological argumentation.

From the emerging theologies in Korea, Considine brings the work on the concept of *han*, a concept difficult to translate from Korean into other languages. *Han* connotes especially the consequences of suffering in the lives of people long burdened with being sinned-against. In a compelling way, Considine then puts the notion of *han* into dialogue with Schillebeeckx's reflections on suffering to produce new insights that cast a different light on how to understand the consequences of suffering for the sinned-against, as well as illumine the work of Schillebeeckx and the potential of the notion of *han* for World Christianity today.

Considine's work here is not only interconceptual; it is intercultural as well. To that end, he devotes a chapter of this book to intercultural hermeneutics, the frameworks for dealing with the communication of meaning across cultural boundaries. What he presents is not only a state-of-the-question exposition of this emerging field, but also a methodological advancement of the field itself. To be able to bring voices from diverse backgrounds into dialogue on some shared themes is itself a demanding task. To be able to advance the underlying hermeneutical frameworks that make such dialogue possible is a distinctive achievement. In this, Considine has done some of the best work that I have seen.

For readers seeking to see what kind of theological discourse will be necessary to keep different regions of World Christianity in communication with one another in the years to come, this book provides an excellent example. It sets a standard for what kind of theological thinking is needed for a World Christianity to be genuinely "catholic," in the sense of all-embracing and respectful of the myriad voices of Christians today. That it does so around a topic so central to a church of and for the poor makes it even more valuable. It deserves a wide and receptive audience.

Robert J. Schreiter
Catholic Theological Union, Chicago

Acknowledgments

THE NUMBER OF PEOPLE who deserve my gratitude and appreciation for making this work possible are overwhelming. I have been blessed by you, am greatly indebted to all of you, but unfortunately cannot name all of you in the space provided. My apologies. But there are several people who deserve special mention.

First and foremost, I want to express my gratitude, appreciation, and love to my wife, Kiae. She has stood with me, through years of graduate school, job searching, and the composition of this work, despite an overabundance of adversity, obstacles, and loss. This took great courage, love, and perseverance and for this I will always be grateful. Words fail to describe all that you have been to me as a spouse, partner, and true friend.

I would also like to thank my "church family." Among others, I am especially indebted to Josh and Quinetta Bellows-Miller, Jonathan and Sarah Dickson, Tim Fister and Andrea Lee, David and Jessica Kiragu, Daniel and Edith Michmerhuizen, Paul and Emily Moore, and David and Yeena Yoon-Yoo. All of you have shown me the meaning and healing power of a true community and without your love and support, this work would not exist. And I want to thank all of our children, most of who were but a "twinkle in their parents' eyes" when I began this journey, for the inspiration, challenges, joy, and meaning they bring into community life: Madeleine, Mario, Julian, Liam Hoon, Jude, Theo, Genevieve, Elias Chul, Mateo, Eve, Alex, and Juniper. Also, I wish to extend my gratitude and appreciation to Tharu, Kay, and Anya Linek-Rajapaksha. Your friendship has been an anchor and a cause for joy.

I also must express my appreciation and gratitude to my parents, James and Ann Considine. The fact that I am where I am is in no small part a testament to the foundation that you have laid for your two sons. Thank you to my brother, Brian, his wife Brittiny, and little Clare for offering support, encouragement, and good conversation from the Pacific

Northwest. I also wish to extend my thanks to *Halabeoji* in California and Kisu, Dorothy, Ellie, Erin, and Eoin in Singapore. And thank you to our dearly departed *Halmeoni*, Park Sun-Cha. You were Liam's first roommate and you embodied God's love to all of us.

I also must express my deep gratitude to Robert Schreiter for many things, most of which I do not have space to mention adequately. He has been a kind, reliable, and supportive guide and mentor throughout my entire education and my development into (hopefully) an effective teacher and scholar of Roman Catholic theology in higher education. Moreover, his groundbreaking work on intercultural hermeneutics and the importance of culture for envisioning theology is at the heart of this work and is at the center of my argument. Thank you to Andrew Sung Park for graciously agreeing to be a reader on my dissertation, without whom this present work would not exist. Since much of it is based upon his groundbreaking work, this too is an honor. Thank you to Stephen Bevans for encouraging me to submit to this series, to Paul Chung for his valuable feedback, and to Craig Nessan and Veli-Matti Kärkkäinen for seeing enough value in this work to accept it for publication. Thank you to Matthew Wimer for his guidance and patience as I negotiated the process of preparing this manuscript for publication.

Finally, thank you to Joan Crist, Joi Patterson, Daniel Lowery, and the entire college family at Calumet College of St. Joseph. You took a chance and hired me. Without this opportunity to be a faculty member at such a unique institution, this work would never have developed.

Short Glossary of Korean and Chinese Terms

Character	Transliteration	Rough Meaning
한	*han / haan*	"wounded heart" "frustrated hope" "black hole in the soul" "non-orientability" "Southern people of China (i.e., *Han* dynasty)"
恨	*han / haan*	"wounded heart" "frustrated hope" "black hole in the soul"
韓	*han*	"non-orientability"
漢	*Han*	"Southern people of China" (i.e., *Han* dynasty)
정	*jeong*	"relational 'stickiness'" "confluence of *eros, philia, agapē*"
情	*jeong*	"relational 'stickiness'" "confluence of *eros, philia, agapē*"
민중	*minjung*	"'Politically oppressed, economically exploited and culturally alienated'" peoples
民衆	*minjung*	"'Politically oppressed, economically exploited and culturally alienated'" peoples
기	*ki*	"breath" "energy of life"
氣	*ki / ch'i*	"breath" "energy of life"

Introduction

Re-envisioning Roman Catholic Soteriology

THE PURPOSE OF THIS study is to *point toward* a Roman Catholic soteriology for the sinned-against creature. This study is an investigation, and an experiment, in beginning to envision an intercultural soteriology that uses *han* as a fundamental theological source. In this study, I do not intend to fully articulate the content of an intercultural Roman Catholic soteriology for the sinned-against creature to a degree of relative adequacy that is based upon *han*. Rather, my intention is to lay a foundation upon which it is possible, subsequently, to more adequately envision and articulate an intercultural soteriology of this kind. This current work represents a skeleton upon which to flesh out the fullness of such a soteriology. In this way, this study is preliminary and cautious in nature.

This study is concerned with two main areas: Roman Catholic soteriology and intercultural theological dialogue. I have decided to focus upon these two areas due to their growing importance in the twenty-first century in which globalization continues to be the driving force that organizes the economic, social, cultural, and political structures of the world, for the benefit of some and the dehumanization and detriment of many others. In light of a "barbarous excess" of human suffering, degradation, and violence, not to mention reckless ecological stewardship, Edward Schillebeeckx argues that "one can no longer theologize and make church pronouncements in the same old way."[1]

I have chosen to focus upon soteriology for two reasons. First, a renewed investigation into Roman Catholic soteriology is needed not because the doctrines are incorrect. Rather, Catholic soteriology needs to be further developed in order to provide a greater focus upon God's work of healing, liberation, and salvation for those men and women who are the *sinned-against*.[2] In light of the intercultural context and often

---

1. Schillebeeckx, *On Christian Faith*, 83.

2. The term *sinned-against* originates from the work of Raymond Fung. See

destructive results of globalization upon humankind and its ecological context, such a supplemented soteriology must not only focus upon the wounds of sin but also be articulated in a way that is more intelligible to this context. Thus, I intend to assist in envisioning a soteriology that is better equipped to account for the breadth and depth of the wounds of sin carried by countless men and women, as well as the parallel wounds carried by the sinners and perpetrators.

Furthermore, I am in agreement with Schillebeeckx that soteriology is the entryway to Christology, and thus to the praxis of Christian life and discipleship. As Schillebeeckx observes, "Christianity is thus essentially concerned with human integrity: with being whole or 'salvation.'"[3] This means that we theologians must strive continually to make the message and experience of salvation from God, through Jesus the Christ, intelligible to the contemporary context. To this end, Schillebeeckx observes:

> Christians may have the searchlight of faith, but they often do not realize that a new object is presenting itself in our human experiences and that this new object is in special need of theological interpretation. Anyone who arrives at the phenomenon too late is also too late to throw Christian light on them with a view to a better Christian praxis.[4]

Schillebeeckx further elucidates the problem of timely and intelligible engagement with and interpretation of the "signs of the times":

> Without constantly renewed experience a gulf develops between the content of the experience in on-going life and the expression in words of earlier experiences, a gulf between experience and doctrine and between people and the church. This already means that Christianity is not a message to be believed, but an experience of faith that becomes a message, and as an explicit message seeks to offer a new possibility of life-experience to others who hear it from within their own experience.[5]

Second, soteriology is the axis upon which Christian praxis rotates. It is where mysticism and politics, contemplation and action, theory and practice, ethics and doctrine converge and converse. The topic of soteriology is not only one in which we formally envision what God's

"Compassion for the Sinned Against," 162–69.
   3. Schillebeeckx, *God Among Us*, 157.
   4. Ibid.
   5. Schillebeeckx, *Interim Report*, 50.

salvation, through Jesus the Christ and for humankind, looks like and what it means. It also has a spiritual and ethical call for us to participate in God's ongoing work of salvation within history, society, and the cosmos.[6] As Schillebeeckx points out, "God wants to make secular history in this world a salvation history through human mediation."[7]

I have decided to focus simultaneously upon intercultural theological dialogue for two reasons. First, there is great need for development within this field at the level of academic discourse. There is a need for theological experiments that seek to rearticulate soteriology (and other aspects of Christian theology and praxis) through asymmetrical encounters among the signs, codes, and messages embedded within disparate global cultures.

Second, I think that much of academic theology—the pursuit "to give the most exacting account possible of Christian faith as it relates to reality"[8]—such as the tradition to which this present work is beholden and in which it is written, has not fully engaged with the category of *culture* to a degree of relative adequacy. More often than not, academic theological discourse engages culture in a way that neither provides a *thick description* nor takes into account asymmetries in power among cultures manifest in such problems such as orientalism, white supremacy, male dominance, and static, ontologized understandings of racialization and human culture.

Although highly commendable for its rigor, achievements, furthering of knowledge, and theological understanding this type of theological work can result in an unfortunate and unintended dominating discourse. As Robert Schreiter points out, calling this "theology as sure knowledge," "[T]here needs to be greater awareness that theology as sure knowledge is

---

6. Regarding a renewed interpretation of the cosmos, see Garcia-Rivera, *The Garden of God*.

7. Schillebeeckx, *On Christian Faith*, 32. In a similar vein, elsewhere he writes that "the question for the theologian is therefore whether a coming, and approach (not *the* coming) of the kingdom of God can be seen in this particular human action." See Schillebeeckx, *God Among Us*, 157.

8. Schreiter, *Constructing Local Theologies*, 88. Schreiter goes on to point out several distinct attributes of this kind of necessary, although imperfect, theological discourse, two of which are concerns for: a) "The quality of theological knowledge and how it measures up to other forms of knowledge"; b) "giving a rigorous internal account of the experience of faith and sets for itself the task of studying exhaustively different aspects of faith and the sacred texts. Analysis is the key word here: the ever more subtle distinction, the ever-better defined relation, which allows the fullness of the faith- experience to unfold and so be extended."

but one form of theology, alongside wisdom theology, theology as praxis, and theology as more occasional variations on sacred texts."[9] Rather than the construction of a truly intercultural theology, from an outer hearer's perspective, that accepts the risks of hybridity, syncretism, miscommunication, and critical assessment and rejection from the inner speakers, oftentimes an intercultural dialogue can lead to non-Western, non-white, cultural philosophies, anthropologies, and cosmologies becoming little more than multicultural accessories to theology that, at its core, is "business as usual." This study is but one small, tentative step in the direction of an intercultural soteriology that goes beyond making theological assertions and church statements in the "same old way."

Overview of Argument

In this short study, I argue that Korean-American theologies and anthropologies of *han* provide one important resource for developing a more relatively adequate Roman Catholic soteriology that explicitly focuses upon God's work of healing the wounds of sin inflicted upon countless men and women, living and dead. I contend that *han* provides a "thick description" of the breadth and depth of human woundedness and in this way acts as a fundamental cultural anthropology upon which to articulate this soteriology within a globalizing and intercultural context. My argument proceeds in five chapters.

In chapter 1 I introduce the basic problem with which I am concerned. I argue that the Pastoral Constitution in the Modern World, *Gaudium et spes*, offers a relatively inadequate soteriology for the sinned-against human being. The document provides an authoritative articulation of soteriology and outlines the central problem of human beings as the sinners and God as the Sinned-against. But, it fails to offer a sufficient understanding of salvation for the sinned-against creature to supplement this central soteriological paradigm. I argue that the foundation of this relative inadequacy is the lack of a thick description of the wounds of sin inflicted upon human beings by one another. In other words, the problem of a relatively inadequate soteriology has its roots in a relatively inadequate anthropology.

Chapter 2 offers a theological bridge to span the gap between *Gaudium et spes* and Korean-American theologies of *han*. As chapter 1 shows,

9. Ibid., 91.

there is great debate over the meaning of the Second Vatican Council, let alone *Gaudium et spes,* and thus it is not self-evident how to adequately bring its soteriology into dialogue with *han.* This bridge is the work of Flemish-Dominican theologian Edward Schillebeeckx, whose soteriology can be loosely defined as *extra mundum nulla salus* ("no salvation outside the world") and as such, is in continuity with the soteriology of *Gaudium et spes.* I will discuss Schillebeeckx's soteriology and offer four elements as points of dialogue with *han*: definition, location, foundation, and encounter. These four elements follow the general trajectory set by *Gaudium et spes* and are relevant for a dialogue with *han.*

Chapter 3 offers a method for undertaking this study: intercultural hermeneutics and a semiotic understanding of culture. This is the apparatus through which I attempt to make the intercultural dialogue possible. In this chapter, I discuss three understandings of the ambiguous term *culture*, introduce the basics of a semiotic approach to studying and interpreting culture, provide an overview of the field of intercultural hermeneutics, and finally discuss the problem of communication distortion. In short, I demonstrate that I am approaching the intercultural dialogue between Schillebeeckx and *han* from the perspective of an outer-hearer, I interpret culture as a semiotic text that can be read, and I do this through using a particularist intercultural hermeneutic and a globalized understanding of culture. I conclude that, through employing this method, although I cannot offer a definitive understanding or translation of *han*, I can approach a measure of *relative adequacy* and *intercultural communication competence* in my reception and interpretation of *han* through a thick description.

Chapter 4, the lengthiest chapter, offers a thick description and interpretation of *han* from a cultural outsider's location. Here, I discuss the understanding and use of *han* in the theologies of Andrew Sung Park and Wonhee Anne Joh and do so while contextualizing their theologies within the long history of meanings that are associated with *han*. In order to do this, I engage Korean linguistic philosophy, political, religious, and social history, the traditional religion of Shamanism, its gender dynamics, as well as *han's* contemporary development by Korean *minjung* theologians, poets, and other thinkers. This chapter concludes by offering three shared characteristics of the *han* theologies, so to speak, of Park and Joh that provide points of dialogue with Schillebeeckx's soteriology. These three characteristics include: an anthropology of woundedness, a preference for narrative and praxis, and a focus upon the crucifixion as the site for reinterpreting God's salvation for humankind.

Chapter 5 concludes my argument by commencing an intercultural dialogue between Schillebeeckx, Park, and Joh—within a third or interstitial space—and arrives at four fundamental guidelines that must undergird the outer-hearer's reception and interpretation of *han* as it moves from the Korean-American Protestant theological-semiotic domain to the domain of Roman Catholic soteriology as illustrated by *Gaudium et spes* and Edward Schillebeeckx. These include:

1. A necessity for the cross to be the primary (but not the only) Christian symbol for understanding and articulating *han*.

2. A possibility of interpreting *han* as a resource for rearticulating human experiences of God's salvation despite a barbarous excess of human suffering within a twenty-first-century globalizing context of ongoing intercultural encounters and greater cultural hybridity.

3. A necessity for imbuing *han* with a robust understanding of sacramentality and creation, as well as the perspective of an *analogical imagination*, in order to function more adequately among the signs, codes, and messages of Roman Catholicism.

4. A possibility for articulating a *han*-mysticism to complement and critique the concrete political and social action for justice, healing, and *han-pu-ri* in this world.

I contend that these four guidelines constitute a foundation for a subsequent articulation and vision of a Roman Catholic soteriology for the sinned-against creature. They provide a skeleton to be fleshed out by the subsequent work of articulating the content of this intercultural soteriology and how it supplements the relatively inadequate soteriology illustrated by *Gaudium et spes*.

In light of the narrow focus of this study, there are three contributions toward academic scholarship that I am offering. First, I demonstrate that an intercultural theological dialogue that is mutually-critical and mutually-informing is possible and necessary. Moreover, I show that such dialogue is not limited to the realm of what are often pejoratively termed "identity," "hyphenated," or "adjectival" theologies—for example, Black and Womanist theologies, U.S. Hispanic and Latino/a theologies, and Asian and Asian-American theologies, to name but a few. Rather, I contend that the work of intercultural theological dialogue as attempted here, with all of its uncertainty and ambiguity, is imperative for the basic future articulations of Roman Catholic soteriology that is appropriate to the tradition and intelligible to the contemporary context.

Second, I am offering an interpretation of *han* from my own social location that takes seriously the *relative incommensurability of cultures,* as well as the legacy of colonization and orientalism, in attempting to unlock some of the meanings associated with this rich anthropology. To the best of my knowledge, little, if any, Roman Catholic theological work has been attempted to receive and interpret *han* to a degree of relative adequacy and intercultural communication competence into soteriology. In short, *han* remains a mostly untapped theological source that carries an excess of meaning and can be carefully received to assist in developing a Roman Catholic soteriology for the sinned-against creature.

Third, I am offering a vision for how academic theologians can assist in articulating soteriology within a globalizing, intercultural context, and one that continues to be good news to those most wounded—the *han*-ridden *minjung*. In other words, if we better understand the breadth, depth, and nature of the wounds of sin, in all of their messiness and complexity within our bodies, minds, souls, and in all of creation, we may be better equipped for discerning the ways in which we can participate in God's ongoing work of forgiveness, liberation, healing, and salvation among us. Here lies the importance of developing and articulating this soteriology: Christian praxis. Much of the hope carried by Christians is that, through Christ, wounds indeed can be healed, the oppressed liberated, sinners forgiven, enemies reconciled, and men and women able to find peace with God. This hope is connected to a particular understanding of God to whom we bear witness. To again quote Schillebeeckx:

> [M]y hope is based on my faith that God is a God of pure positivity. He is the promoter of all that is good and he opposes all that is evil . . . Everywhere where people promote what is good and human, moreover, and combat evil, whether they are believers or not, they are affirming God's being. In their praxis, that is, making the world a more human place to live in, they are confirming God is love. That is for me the most convincing proof of God's existence—the praxis of good and the fight against every kind of evil.[10]

---

10. Schillebeeckx, *God Is New Each Moment,* 113. Dorothy Day also describes this praxis in an insightful manner. She writes, "What we would like to do is change the world—make it a little simpler for people to feed, clothe, and shelter themselves as

Obviously, this work is but one small attempt at such difficult and important work. To borrow a metaphor from Alejandro Garcia-Rivera, although out of context, perhaps this study can be one small tile in the creation of the larger mosaic of intercultural soteriologies. The wounds of human beings, and all of creation, are deep, diverse, and complicated. If not sufficiently addressed and cared for, such wounds (*han*) engender a vicious cycle of violence in which wounds fester, enhance one's proclivity for sinning and participating in structural sin, and enable one to choose to inflict more wounds upon others. As Park points out, this is the intertwining of sin and *han* that leads to the spread and intensification of sin and *han*, and the perpetuation of a darker state of affairs called evil. A mosaic of intercultural soteriologies, when articulated to a degree of relative adequacy, can assist us in discerning how to participate in God's relentless work of salvation in this world.

God intended them to do." She expands upon this, when she writes, "Yes, he poor are always going to be with us . . . But I am sure that God did not intend that there be so many poor." See *Selected Writings*, 98, 111.

1

Gaudium et spes: A Relatively Inadequate Soteriology for the Sinned-Against Creature

IN THIS CHAPTER, I will briefly discuss the anthropology and soteriology in the document Pastoral Constitution on the Church in the Modern World, *Gaudium et spes*, solemnly promulgated by Pope Paul VI and the Second Vatican Council in 1965.[1] The purpose of this chapter is to outline the anthropology and soteriology of this document and then offer a critique that demonstrates its relative inadequacy: a lack of a thick description of the effects of sin upon the sinned-against creature as a supplement to its anthropological focus upon the sinning creature and the Sinned-Against Creator. This underdevelopment in anthropology leads to a relatively inadequate soteriology.

The Pastoral Constitution's Christian anthropology rightfully focuses upon the sinning creature's alienation from the Sinned-Against Creator, as well as the modern questions of meaning, existence, and atheism to which this is connected. But this Christian fundamental anthropology and soteriology needs to be supplemented, at the foundational level, by an accounting of a Christian anthropology of woundedness of the sinned-against creature and the work of the Living God of Jesus Christ in

---

1. During the Council, there was heated debate over the idea and practice of *conciliarism*. That is, the relationship between the primacy of the pope and the authority of the bishops dispersed throughout the globe. Therefore, it was initially unclear how the pope would promulgate the documents approved by the council fathers. In the end, Pope Paul VI decided on a kind of conciliarism in which he promulgated the documents that were already ratified by the Council as his own laws, particularly through the phrase *sacro approbante concilio* ("with the sacred council approving"). See Alberigo, *A Brief History of Vatican II*, 59.

healing the victims' wounds and calling the violators to repent. In other words, the Pastoral Constitution offers a vision of Christian salvation that primarily focuses upon the sinner with reference to the problems of meaning and atheism while failing also to focus sufficiently upon the sinned-against creature with reference to the problems of innocent suffering and non-persons.[2]

This chapter will proceed in three sections. First, I will briefly introduce the Second Vatican Council (1962–1965), its purpose, and accomplishments. I will discuss Pope John XXIII's underlying theme of *aggiornamento* in convening the Council, the global reach in the preparation for and execution of the Council, and the diversity of the documents promulgated over its four sessions. I will also discuss the genre of a *Pastoral Constitution* that is unprecedented in the history of documents solemnly promulgated by the Roman Catholic Church.

Second, I will discuss the basic anthropology and soteriology expressed in the document and in particular in chapter 1. I will outline the Pastoral Constitution's understandings of original human dignity, the violation of human dignity through sinning against God the Creator, the connection between this sinning and the problem of modern atheism, and a focus upon eschatological salvation over moments of fragmentary salvation. I will also show that this Christian anthropology and soteriology is connected to the priority that the Council Fathers give to the problems of human meaning and modern atheism—the non–believer—over the problems of oppression and innocent human suffering—non–persons.[3]

Third, I will offer a critique of the basic Christian anthropology of *Gaudium et spes* and make an argument as to why this anthropology and

---

2. It is important to point out, as Andrew Sung Park often does, that all human beings always exist simultaneously as sinners and sinned-against. Nevertheless, it is helpful to make a distinction between the two positions in order to account for the particular wounds that have been inflicted upon an individual, community, or people group by another individual, community, or people group. In other words, within *this* world there are clear situations in which there is violator and victim, oppressed and oppressor. All human beings are an amalgamation of both, but one facet often manifests within a specific situation and becomes a site for Christian soteriological reflection.

3. This language and critique of a European-Catholic theological focus on meaning and atheism as opposed to suffering and non-persons is not original to me. It has been voiced by many theologians of liberation, two of whom will be referenced below: Virgilio Elizondo and Gustavo Gutiérrez. From a European perspective and in a similar vein, J. B. Metz has critiqued Vatican II as the bourgeois revolution in the Church. See Metz, *The Emergent Church*.

soteriology are relatively inadequate: the document does not provide a sufficient description or understanding of the effects of sin upon the human person in this world. In other words, *Gaudium et spes* concerns itself with the "joys and hopes, griefs and anxieties" of modern women and men but it does not provide a thick description of the woundedness inflicted upon the sinned-against creature, by sinners, in the presence of the Living God. I will discuss the roots of my critique in Latin American theologies of liberation and in particular observations by Virgilio Elizondo and Gustavo Gutiérrez. I will then examine the evidence in the text of *Gaudium et spes* that would seem to contradict my critique and argument through its discussion of the sinned-against creature and the work for healing, liberation, and reconciliation in this world. Nevertheless, I will show how my critique and argument dispels these counterpoints and then I will reiterate that much of the Pastoral Constitution's relative inadequacy is linked to its primary concern with non-believers and its secondary concern with non-persons. This is a shortcoming in the anthropology that is at the foundation of its soteriology. I will conclude with an observation about the dual concern of Edward Schillebeeckx with non-persons and human suffering as well as non-believers and human meaning.

At the outset, it is important to point out that the purpose of this chapter is neither to engage nor to evaluate the ongoing hermeneutical debates concerning the most faithful way to interpret Vatican II. Much of this debate revolves around questions of continuity or discontinuity with the other ecumenical councils as well as the question whether or not anything happened at all. These questions continue to be explored in depth by other scholars (although no broad consensus has been reached).[4] The purpose of this chapter is quite narrow. I will examine the document itself, and in particular Part One, in order to describe and critique the anthropology and soteriology that it articulates. I choose *Gaudium et spes* because it is an authoritative articulation of Roman Catholic anthropology and soteriology. Although I will not ignore the context in which it

---

4. An exemplary, but not exhaustive list of the literature includes: Alberigo and Komanchak, *History of Vatican II*; Schultenover, *Vatican II: Did Anything Happen?*; Marchetto, *The Second Vatican Council;* Dwyer, "*Questions of Special Urgency*,"; Alberigo, *A Brief History of Vatican II*; O'Malley, *What Happened at Vatican II*; Rynne, *Vatican Council II*; Ratzinger, *Theological Highlights of Vatican II*; Gaillardetz and Clifford, *Keys to the Council*; Faggioli, *Vatican II: The Battle for Meaning*; Ormerod, "Vatican II: Continuity or Discontinuity?," 606–39; as well as Colberg's "The Hermeneutics of Vatican II," 230–52.

was written nor the history of its development, I will focus my analysis upon the text of *Gaudium et spes* in its final form.

Section One: The Second Vatican Council: A Brief Introduction[5]

It is not an exaggeration to describe the Second Vatican Council as the most important event for Roman Catholicism since the Council of Trent. Stephen Schloesser observes that the Council had a broad vision and intended to address the pressing issues of the day. Schloesser writes that, in light of the monumental changes in the world at the time, "the council needed to go back to the big issues and revisit fundamental questions. In such a world as this, What or who is God? What or who is the human person? What is the point of human existence? What is salvation? If salvation is available to those outside the Church, what is the Church? What is its role in history?"[6]

The Second Vatican Council, as envisioned by Pope John XXIII, found its theme in *aggiornamento*.[7] In Italian, this term refers to the work of "bringing up to date" or "modernizing." This is the term used by Pope John XXIII as he announced his intention to convoke an ecumenical council in 1959. The Pope's announcement occurred just a few months after the conclave that elected him and caught most of the Church (and the world) by surprise.[8]

---

5. One important aspect of the document that I am unable to engage, due to the limited nature of this chapter, is its development through drafts, revisions, commissions, and debates. In a more lengthy analysis of the anthropology of *Gaudium et spes*, this would be a necessary analysis to undertake. For the purposes of this chapter, however, the anthropology within the finalized text is sufficient.

6. Schloesser, "Against Forgetting: Memory, History, Vatican II," 96.

7. O'Malley argues that *aggiornamento* is merely one of three themes of the Council, the other two being *ressourcement* and *development*. In O'Malley's estimation, *aggiornamento* refers to the present, *ressourcement* to the past, and *development* to the future of the Church. See O'Malley, "Vatican II: Did Anything Happen?," 63–83.

8. Alberigo observes that evidence of the surprise within the Roman Curia can be found in the fact that some Cardinals didn't even attend the speech that Pope John XXIII gave in 1959 at St. Paul's Outside the Walls at the concluding liturgy for the week of prayer for Christian Unity. In his remarks, the Pope announced three endeavors: a synod for the Diocese of Rome, an ecumenical Council, and a call to update the Code of Canon Law. When elected, Cardinal Angelo Roncalli, Bishop of Venice, was seen to be a "transitional figure" or interim pope. At eighty years old when elected, the Cardinals expected tranquility and relative stability and quiet during Roncalli's papacy. See

The Pope made it clear that this was to be a pastoral council. The Council was neither to be fully confrontational with the world nor to be solely concerned with condemning its errors. Rather, Pope John XXIII hoped to address the problems arising in the global church as it found itself in a rapidly changing world. Pope John XXIII hoped that the Council would enable the Church to begin to dialogue with the modern world and not merely condemn it through canons and anathemas. Pope John XXIII's theme of *aggiornamento* was embraced by a majority of participants in the Council. As John Langan has observed:

> The Fathers of the Council give up the defensive, admonitory, regretful, alienated tone that has so often shown up in church pronouncements about the state of the modern world. They show more readiness to learn and less to condemn, more inclination to respect the complexity and worth of the world on its own terms, and less inclination to treat it as simply the object of religious imperialism.[9]

In Pope John XXIII's 1959 speech, in which he expressed his intent to convoke an ecumenical council, the Pope provided some comments as to what the Council would entail.[10] His comments, however, were ambiguous and led to great speculation as to what the nature and purpose of the council would be. Giuseppe Alberigo argues that the pope did indeed have a clear intent in convoking the council:

> The pope wanted a council that would mark the end of an era; a council, that is, that would usher the Church out of the post-Tridentine era, and to a certain extent out of the centuries-old

---

Alberigo, *A Brief History of Vatican II*, 1–7.

9. Langan, "Political Hopes and Political Tasks," 113–14. For a concise overview of the Council's reassessment of the Church's past condemnation of the modern world and its transition to engaging with it, see Wright's "The Thrust of the Council," 1–7.

10. O'Malley observes that the Pope's remarks in 1959, as was expected, called for the reaffirmation of doctrine and discipline. In addition, however, O'Malley quotes Pope John XXIII's speech to illustrate two more innovative motivations for the Council: "The first was to promote 'the enlightenment, edification, and joy of the entire Christian people' and the second was to extend 'a renewed cordial invitation to the faithful of the separated communities to participate with us in this quest for unity and grace, for which so many souls long in all parts of the world.'" See O'Malley, *What Happened at Vatican II*, 17. O'Malley also points out that an additional interesting characteristic of these two motivations was their positive and optimistic rhetoric. In that, the pope seemed to envision the Council as an invitation to dialogue and renewal (17–18).

Constantinian phase, and into a new phase of witness and proclamation. The major permanent element of tradition judged most suitable would be enlisted to nourish and guarantee the fidelity to the gospel during such an arduous transition.[11]

Moreover, Alberigo argues that the intention of Vatican II was not strictly doctrinal. "The Council did not intend to produce a new doctrinal *summa* (as John XXIII said, 'a council was not necessary for this') or to respond to all problems. What characterized Vatican II was a sense of the duty of renewal, a thirst for understanding, a willingness to confront history, and a concern for all people as brothers and sisters."[12]

To ensure a truly ecumenical and global council, Pope John XXIII asked that the Pre-preparatory commissions in the Roman Curia send out a letter to every bishop and superior-general of men's religious orders in the world asking them to respond freely with the problems that they considered the most pressing for the Church. The letter was distributed to 2,598 recipients, of which, 1,998 responded—a 77 percent response rate.[13] After the work of the Pre-Preparatory and the Preparatory Commissions was completed—a time period lasting from 1959–1962—the formal invitations were sent out calling cardinals, patriarchs, bishops, archbishops, abbots, and superior-generals to participate. This was a group totaling 2,850 men, most of who attended. Moreover, the bishops who attended came from 116 different countries and brought with them advisors and colleagues. The majority of participants were from Europe and North America but a great number of bishops and representatives from Latin America, Asia, the Pacific, and Africa also played a role in the Council.[14] The center of theological and ecclesiastical power remained in the hands of the European bishops and theologians but the entirety of the global church was brought into the conversation for the first time.[15]

11. Alberigo, *A Brief History of Vatican II*, 10.

12. Alberigo, "Preface," ibid., xiii. The quote continues and culminates in Alberigo's own method for interpreting the council. He writes, "This is why priority should be given to the phenomenon of the Council itself as an event that assembled a deliberating body of more than two thousand bishops. The same is true of its decisions, which are to be interpreted not as cold, abstract norms but as an expression and continuation of the event itself."

13. O'Malley, *What Happened at Vatican II*, 19.

14. Ibid., 22–23. See also Alberigo, *A Brief History of Vatican II*, 77–82, 87.

15. The Council's work on collegiality and the establishment of regional conferences of bishops laid the groundwork for the important statements by the Latin American Bishops' Conference—CELAM—at Medellín (1968) and Puebla (1972). As

Virgilio Elizondo argues that, although far from perfect in its attempt to truly represent the various peoples of the globe, Pope John XXIII's convening of the Council "was the beginning of the breakthrough from a European-North American church to a pluri-cultural and pluri-centric world church."[16] Karl Rahner had a similar observation when he argued that Vatican II was the first truly global ecumenical council.[17]

The Council itself met in four sessions, from 1962–1965. At any given time there were around 2,500 participants—bishops, theologians, observers, etc. The work of the Council was prolific. Although the preparatory commissions drafted a total of seventy documents for consideration, the Council ultimately promulgated a total of sixteen documents. These documents dealt with issues, among others, that ranged from the reform of the liturgy to the nature of social communication, from the self-understanding of the Church to a declaration of religious freedom, and from the nature of divine revelation to the relationship between Roman Catholicism, other Christian churches, and non-Christian religions. These documents remain authoritative articulations of theology, faith, and doctrine in the spirit of *aggiornamento*. John O'Malley indicates that the sixteen documents of the Council "cover an extraordinarily wide range of subjects and do so at considerable length. They are the council's most authoritative and accessible legacy, and it is around them that the study of the council must obviously turn."[18]

Elizondo argues, "I dare say that the transformative impact of the Medellín Conference on the church's pastoral practice and theology was far greater than any other council of the church." He continues, "In fidelity to the spirit of Vatican II, the church of Latin America challenged itself and the entire church. For the first time, the poor became the central focus and primary subject of theological reflection." See Elizondo's "Emergence of a World Church and the Irruption of the Poor," 108. For one of the definitive articulations of what became the Latin American theologies of liberation, see Gutiérrez, *A Theology of Liberation*. In addition, Elizondo points out that there were other regional councils that had the same global importance and impact of Medellín, namely, the 1969 "All India Seminar" and the 1974 "African Synod on Evangelization." See Elizondo, "Emergence of a World Church and the Irruption of the Poor," 111. One of the later fruits of this global movement was Pieris's groundbreaking work, *An Asian Theology of Liberation*.

16. Elizondo, "Emergence of a World Church and the Irruption of the Poor," 104–5.

17. See Rahner's essays, "Basic Theological Interpretation of Vatican II"; "The Abiding Significance of Vatican II"; and "The Future of the Church and the Church of the Future."

18. O'Malley, "Introduction," in *Vatican II: Did Anything Happen?*, 5. To be clear, this does not mean that O'Malley advocates for propositional or uncontextual interpretations of the documents. Such a contextual interpretation is, in fact, his own

In his 1962 opening address, *Gaudet Mater Ecclesia*, Pope John XXIII reiterated that the underlying purpose of the council was *aggiornamento*. The windows of the Church were to be open to mutually informing and mutually critical dialogue with the modern world. Similar to Pope John XXIII's intention, as was argued by Alberigo, many bishops also interpreted the Council as an end to the theology and ecclesiology of the Counter-Reformation that were part and parcel with the normative interpretations of the documents of the Council of Trent. For many (often known as "the majority" at the Council), *aggiornamento* signaled the end of this era, and even of the Christendom of the Constantinian Church. This is best exemplified by the famous critique by Bishop Emile de Smedt of Bruges of the first draft of the Dogmatic Constitution on the Church (*De Ecclesia*, which later became *Lumen Gentium*), for its "triumphalism, clericalism, and juridicism." De Smedt's critique crystallized the sentiments of the majority of the bishops and gave voice to the reason for sending the document back to committee for a thorough reworking to reflect *aggiornamento*.[19]

Purpose and Genre of *Gaudium et spes*

The documents produced and promulgated by the Council are the work of an overwhelming variety of hands, committees, and theological and political interests.[20] As John O'Malley observes, "The documents of the council are not literary masterpieces. They are committee documents forged in the heat of debate and disagreement, filled with compromises, misleading euphemisms, and stylistic inconsistencies. Yet, despite their many and obvious weaknesses, they in their most characteristic expressions pertain to a literary genre, and, as such evince a literary unity."[21] The documents are indeed authoritative. But they also reflect the contentious atmosphere of the Council and the heated debates and negotiations in drafting and ratifying the sixteen documents.

---

position. This quote merely points out the authoritative nature of the text of the documents as it stands.

19. See Alberigo, *A Brief History of Vatican II*, 155–56.

20. For one insider account of the process of drafting documents and seeking consensus, see Congar, *My Journal of the Council*.

21. O'Malley, *Vatican II: Did Anything Happen?*, 81.

In order to place *Gaudium et spes* in context, it is important to briefly touch upon the authoritative nature of the various documents, or their genres. The promulgated documents were of three kinds: Constitutions, Declarations, and Decrees.[22] *Constitutions* had the highest authority, followed by the lower authorities of the *Declarations* and *Decrees* (although the exact relationship of these two genres to one another remains ambiguous).

The Pastoral Constitution on the Church in the Modern World, *Gaudium et spes*, however, was a unique document. A document with the genre of Pastoral Constitution did not have any precedent among the authoritative documents of the Roman Catholic Church. John O'Malley has shed some light on the genre of *Gaudium et spes* by highlighting the Council's desire to discuss the Church *ad intra* and *ad extra*. That is, the Council Fathers wanted to provide two, interconnected understandings of the Church: an authoritative self-understanding (*ad intra*); and an authoritative account of the Church's relationship to the modern world (*ad extra*). O'Malley argues that the Dogmatic Constitution on the Church, *Lumen gentium* represented that *ad intra* purpose and theological perspective whereas the subsequent Pastoral Constitution on the Church in the Modern World, *Gaudium et spes* represented the *ad extra* purpose and theological perspective.[23]

In other words, the Pastoral Constitution was addressed to all persons of good will throughout the world. The Church, *ad extra*, clearly articulated that its goal was not to retain a bunker mentality that had characterized the negative relationship between the Roman Catholic Church and the world in which the Church is manifest and functions.[24]

---

22 The sixteen documents promulgated by the Council have different levels of authority. A *constitution* has the greatest authority of all the documents. At the Council, four constitutions were promulgated: The Constitution on the Sacred Liturgy, *Sacrosanctum concilium*, The Dogmatic Constitution on the Church, *Lumen Gentium*, The Dogmatic Constitution on Divine Revelation, *Dei verbum*, and The Pastoral Constitution on the Church in the Modern World, *Gaudium et spes*. The other kinds of authoritative documents that were promulgated were *declarations* and *decrees*. The exact authority of these two kinds of documents remains somewhat unclear. See O'Malley, "Introduction," in *Vatican II: Did Anything Happen?*, 6–7. For an overview of the historical genres of the documents that the various ecumenical councils have promulgated, see O'Malley, *Vatican II: Did Anything Happen?*, 67–83.

23. O'Malley, *What Happened at Vatican II?*, 156–59. See also Kaspar, "The Theological Anthropology of *Gaudium et spes*," 132.

24. See Baum, *The Twentieth Century*, 14–26. This "bunker mentality" is illustrated by papal encyclicals such as *Quanta cura* and its *Syllabus of Errors* (Pius IX, 1864),

Instead, the Council Fathers declared that at a fundamental level of existing as Church, they must read the "signs of the times" and enter into mutually critical and mutually beneficial dialogue with the modern world. The Church was an institution within the world and not floating above it. As such, its *ad extra* purpose was to make permeable the boundary between the Roman Church and the modern world.

The Council declared that a Christian could learn from the world as well as instruct the world regarding all matters not essential to the Christian faith. This means that humans innately could claim freedom of inquiry, thought and expression that no religious authority had the right to suppress.[25] In addition, John Langan points out that *Gaudium et Spes* offered a vision of the human community that did not place barriers between Catholics and those of other Christian and non-Christian faiths.[26] Instead, the Council's vision entailed a mandate for Catholics to be actively involved with the secular world, Protestant and non-Christian religions in order to jointly solve the many problems plaguing contemporary society.

Finally, George Higgins points out that *Gaudium et Spes* was not meant to be exhaustive with regard to the Church's relationship with the modern world but rather to articulate the Church's re-envisioning of its basic orientation to the world as one of dialogue. Higgins points out that the Council declared that this document was intended for all humankind and as such should remind the world and Christians that the Church's purpose was to serve and accompany humankind as all women and men search for answers to the difficult and complicated problems of modern life.[27] Although the genre of a Pastoral Constitution was without prece-

---

Lamentabili sane exitu (Pius X, 1907), and *Pascendi dominici gregis* (Pius X, 1907). The Catholic Church's hostile posture led to a mandate that all seminaries study only scholastic philosophy and theology and the subsequent Vatican antagonism toward the various theological faculties in France and Germany.

25. Higgins, "The Church in the Modern World," 16–18. This line of thinking can be seen more concretely in the document, Declaration on Religious Freedom, *Dignitatis humanae*.

26. Even though the two primary documents of Vatican II that lay out the relationship between the Catholic Church, non-Catholic Christians, and non-Christian religions are Decree on Ecumenism, *Unitatis redintegratio,* and Declaration on the Relationship of the Church to Non-Christian Religions, *Nostra Aetate*, Langan is pointing out the ecumenical and interreligious goodwill that underlies *Gaudium et Spes*'s view of the human community that calls for service to the world, including the political arena.

27. Higgins, "The Church in the Modern World," 11–12.

dent and was an innovation, O'Malley, Higgins, and Langan have clarified the purpose of the genre of *Gaudium et spes*: to provide an *ad extra* account of the fundamental orientation of the Roman Catholic Church to the modern world. Instead of condemnation of and withdrawal from the modern world, the Church intended to engage in mutually-critical and mutually-beneficial dialogue with all "men of goodwill."[28]

Section Two: A Brief Analysis of the Theological Anthropology and Soteriology of Gaudium et spes

Having provided a brief introduction to the Second Vatican Council and the genre and purpose of The Pastoral Constitution on the Church and the Modern World, *Gaudium et spes*, I now move to the document itself in its finished form. In short, this document places the human person, as created in the image of God and as the pinnacle of creation, as the fundamental question for understanding the Church *ad extra*. The Pastoral Constitution shows that mutually-critical and mutually-constructive dialogue with the modern world uses the human person as its point of departure. As the document states:

> Though mankind is stricken with wonder at its own discoveries and its power, it often raises anxious questions about the current trend of the world, about the place and role of man in the universe, about the meaning of its individual and collective strivings, and about the ultimate destiny of reality and of humanity. Hence, giving witness and voice to the faith of the whole people of God gathered together by Christ, this council can provide no more eloquent proof of its solidarity with, as well as its respect and love for the entire human family with which it is bound up, than by engaging with it in conversation about these various problems. The council brings to mankind light kindled from the Gospel, and puts at its disposal those saving resources which the Church herself, under the guidance of the Holy Spirit, receives from her Founder. *For the human person deserves to be preserved; human society deserves to be renewed. Hence, the focal*

---

28. I am aware of the problem of not using non-sexist, gender-inclusive language. This problem is particularly acute because often the Latin from which it is translated does not use sexist and gender-exclusive language. Nevertheless, I have decided to retain the language used by the official translations from the Vatican for the sake of consistency.

point of our entire presentation will be man himself, whole and entire, body and soul, heart and conscience, mind and will.[29]

Similarly, Walter Kaspar also has highlighted the uniqueness of the focus on the human person in the Pastoral Constitution. He observes,

> *Gaudium et spes* signals the first time a council has consciously endeavored to set forth a systematic account of Christian anthropology in an independent thematic context. There are, of course, statements concerning anthropology in earlier conciliar texts. Nevertheless, such statements are always made in connection with the treatment of individual questions relative to Christology, the theology of creation, or grace. Prior to Vatican II no council had produced a 'general outline' of Christian anthropology. The Pastoral Constitution was the first to attempt to do so.[30]

Kaspar's observation is illustrated by many passages throughout Part One of the Pastoral Constitution. For example, the Council Fathers state:

> Nevertheless, in the face of the modern development of the world, the number constantly swells of people who raise the most basic questions or recognize them with a new sharpness: what is man? What is this sense of sorrow, of evil, or death, which continues to exist despite so much progress? What purpose have these victories purchased at so high a cost? What can man offer to society, what can he expect from it? What follows this earthly life?[31]

It is clear that anthropology is the foundation of this document and this is the point of departure for my examination of its relatively inadequate soteriology.

---

29. *Gaudium et spes*, no. 3; my italics. Similarly, Langan writes, "[T]heological anthropology enjoys pride of place in *Gaudium et spes* and provides a basis for the treatment of specific issues." See Langan, "Political Hopes and Political Tasks," 108.

30. Kasper, "The Theological Anthropology of *Gaudium et spes*," 129.

31. *Gaudium et spes*, no. 10. The passage goes on to relate these questions to the Church's profession of Jesus Christ as the Son of God "and the light and strength to measure up to his supreme destiny . . . [and] can be found the key, the focal point and the goal of man, as well as of all human history. The Church also maintains that beneath all changes there are many realities which do not change and which have their ultimate foundation in Christ, Who is the same yesterday, and today, yes and forever. Hence under the light of Christ, the image of the unseen God, the firstborn of every creature, the council wishes to speak to all men in order to shed light on the mystery of man and to cooperate in finding the solution to the outstanding problems of our time."

This section will proceed in three parts. First, I will discuss the heart of the Pastoral Constitution's Christian anthropology and soteriology: the dignity of the human person. Second, I will discuss the Council Fathers' foundational articulation of Christian anthropology and, subsequently, Christian soteriology through their understanding of the sinning creature and the Sinned-Against Creator. Third, I will discuss the connection that the Pastoral Constitution draws between these doctrines and the modern phenomenon of atheism.

Human Dignity: The Heart of Gaudium et spes[32]

The dignity of the human person is at the heart of the Pastoral Constitution on the Church in the Modern World, *Gaudium et spes*. The focus of the Pastoral Constitution's Christian anthropology is the human person, who is created good and in the image of God. As Pope John Paul II observes, the Pastoral Constitution is "a sort of 'Magna Charta' of *human dignity* to be safeguarded and promoted."[33] Similarly, Joseph Gremillion indicates that the Constitution's articulation of human dignity remains one of its two most significant ongoing contributions to both Church and world.[34] He writes that its basic statement of human dignity ". . . is a bold and heroic affirmation, standing in contradiction to the litany of atrocities, economic theories, scientific and technological advances proposed as the reality of the modern world."[35]

The Pastoral Constitution locates the roots of human dignity in the relationship between Creator and creature:

> [T]he root reason for human dignity lies in man's call to communion with God. From the very circumstances of his origin man is already invited to converse with God. For man would not exist were he not created by God's love and constantly preserved by it; and he cannot live fully according to truth unless he freely acknowledges that love and devotes himself to his Creator.[36]

---

32. It is not possible to provide a comprehensive account of human dignity within Catholic Social Teaching, or within *Gaudium et spes* and the trajectory in which it can be interpreted, in this chapter. For a more comprehensive account, see *Compendium of the Social Doctrine of the Church*, nos. 105–59.

33. Pope John Paul II, "Only Christ Can Fulfill Man's Hopes," 127; italics original.

34. Gremillion, "Pastoral Constitution on the Church in the Modern World," 227.

35. Ibid.

36. *Gaudium et spes*, no. 19.

In addition, *Gaudium et spes* connects human dignity to God's creation of the human person as pure gift and as originally good. As such, the human person is a unique creature within the fabric of the cosmos. As the opening of chapter 1 of the Pastoral Constitution states, the human person is the pinnacle of creation and thus ". . . all things on earth should be related to man as their center and crown."[37]

The human person is broken and sinful, yet he or she retains original dignity by virtue of carrying the *imago dei*, the image of God. The loving Creator has endowed human beings with an original goodness that is part and parcel of being a creature, and especially the privileged creature made in God's image. Although sinful and finite, men and women remain intrinsically connected to the infinite God, their Creator.

The Pastoral Constitution makes the claim that through carrying the *imago dei*, and always existing in relationship with the Creator, the human person is intrinsically given a dignity that surpasses what he or she can imagine and that is impossible for others to fully take away. As the Pastoral Constitution declares, the dignity of the human person is intrinsic within the Creator/creature relationship. God guarantees the dignity of the human person, providing him or her depth that is beyond what can be understood and beyond what can be taken away through violence.

The Violation of Human Dignity: Sinning Humanity and Sinned-Against God

I have briefly shown that the heart of this document is a Christian anthropology that is rooted in the intrinsic dignity of the human person as created good in God's own image. The Pastoral Constitution goes on to address the origin of the violation of the human being's God-given dignity. It discusses this in the traditional framework of the human person sinning against God. As the Council Fathers state:

> Although he was made by God in a state of holiness, from the very onset of his history man abused his liberty, at the urging of the Evil One. Man set himself against God and sought to attain his goal apart from God. Although they knew God, they did not glorify Him as God, but their senseless minds were darkened and they served the creature rather than the Creator . . . Often refusing to acknowledge God as his beginning, man has

---

37. Ibid., no. 12.

disrupted also his proper relationship to his own ultimate goal as well as his whole relationship toward himself and others and all created things.[38]

This passage indicates a basic Christian anthropology of the human person as sinner and God as Sinned-Against. Human dignity remains part and parcel of being human, however, it has been violated by the human person sinning against God. He or she has refused to acknowledge the Creator as the source and sustenance of his or her life and well-being. Not only does this alienate men and women from God but also from their true and authentic selves and their right relationships with each other and all of creation.

In order to better articulate this focus on the Sinned-Against God and the sinning human being, the Council Fathers connect this theological focus to the traditional understanding of the misuse of human freedom.

> For its part, authentic freedom is an exceptional sign of the divine image within man. For God has willed that man remain "under the control of his own decisions," so that he can seek his Creator spontaneously, and come freely to utter and blissful perfection through loyalty to Him. Hence, man's dignity demands that he act according to a knowing and free choice that is personally motivated and prompted from within, not under blind internal impulse nor by mere external pressure . . . [but] since man's freedom has been damaged by sin, only by the aid of God's grace can he bring such a relationship with God into full flower. Before the judgment seat of God each man must render an account of his whole life, whether he has done good or evil.[39]

Human beings have misused their free will, the exceptional sign of the divine image within men and women. To more fully regain human dignity, a person must approach God, repent of sinning against God, and accept God's healing grace in order to accept God's free and open invitation to enter into communion. From this quote, it becomes clear that the Pastoral Constitution's primary vision of salvation is from sinning against God with the hope of being resurrected to full communion with God through the life, death, and resurrection of Jesus Christ. Through grace, God empowers the sinful human person to repent from sinning and to seek communion with the Creator.

38. Ibid., no. 13.
39. Ibid., no. 17.

Gaudium et spes's Primary Concern: Modern Atheism

The Pastoral Constitution connects its Christian anthropology of the violated dignity of the sinning-creature who is estranged from the Sinned-Against Creator to the problem of modern atheism. Joseph Gremellion provides a clear description of this connection. He writes, ". . . we are created in God's image but also caught in the web of sin. The noble realities of human freedom and intelligence, the beauty of moral sensibility, are set over against the mystery of death. The tension between these two aspects is viewed as a source for a particularly modern issue: atheism."[40]

The Pastoral Constitution depicts the modern belief system of atheism as the greatest threat to human dignity in the twentieth century. "The root reason for human dignity lies in man's call to communion with God . . . Still, many of our contemporaries have never recognized this intimate and vital link with God, or have explicitly rejected it. Thus atheism must be accounted among the most serious problems of this age, and is deserving of closer examination."[41]

Gaudium et spes offers a broad understanding of modern atheism. Atheism is not merely an individual belief against the existence of God and it is not an agnostic perspective. Rather, the document discusses modern atheism as an entire systematic ideology and dogma that offers an insufficient and hazardous understanding of the human person. Although sympathetic to its roots and cognizant of the role that the Church occasionally has played in unintentionally giving credence to an atheistic philosophy, the Council Fathers argue that atheism is a fundamental scourge to be combated.

In numbers 19–22 the Council Fathers provide a nuanced description and understanding of the roots, reality, and manifestations of the modern phenomenon of atheism. They make an important connection between systematic atheism, as the root of an anthropology, and the dehumanization and loss of human dignity that is all too prevalent in the world. They argue that one of the deep-seated problems is that atheism cannot offer a basis for ultimate hope in the salvation of humankind along with action to better humanity and all of creation. As they write:

> [The Church] further teaches that a hope related to the end of time does not diminish the importance of intervening duties

---

40. Gremellion, "Pastoral Constitution on the Church in the Modern World," 217–18.

41. *Gaudium et spes*, no. 19.

but rather undergirds the acquittal of them with fresh incentives. By contrast, when a divine instruction and the hope of life eternal are wanting, man's dignity is most grievously lacerated, as current events often attest; riddles of life and death, of guilt and of grief go unsolved with the frequent result that men succumb to despair.[42]

The Pastoral Constitution then argues that atheism has an intrinsic inability to provide hope for human salvation, a hope at the heart of the Gospel, and in this way is an impediment to realizing human dignity and flourishing. Combating atheism is not the exclusive purpose of Christian life and salvation. As the Council Fathers write, "While rejecting atheism, root and branch, the Church professes that all men, believers and unbelievers alike, ought to work for the rightful betterment of this world in which all alike live ... The Church calls for the active liberty of believers to build up in this world God's temple too."[43] But atheism is presented as the fundamental problem for the Church to address theologically in order to safeguard human dignity in the modern world in which it finds itself. For the Council Fathers, atheism is of utmost importance.

Summary—Eschatological Salvation from Sinning through Christ's Death and Resurrection

Having discussed the original dignity of the human person, the violation of this dignity through sinning against God, the possibility of redemption through an engraced exercise of free choice for relationship with God, and the problem of modern atheism, I move on to the Pastoral Constitution's discussion of the ultimate soteriological implications of its basic anthropology of a sinning human creature and the Sinned-Against Creator. In short, its vision of salvation for the sinning human person, through Christ, is fundamentally eschatological. The Council Fathers describe salvation in this way:

> [T]hat bodily death from which man would have been immune had he not sinned will be vanquished according to the Christian faith, when man who was ruined by his own doing is restored to wholeness by an almighty and merciful Saviour. For God has called man and still calls him so that with his entire being he

---

42. Ibid., no. 21.
43. Ibid.

might be joined to Him in an endless sharing of a divine life beyond all corruption. Christ won this victory when He rose to life, for by His death He freed man from death.[44]

The Council Fathers pick up the importance of hope again at the end of chapter 1, as they more clearly articulate a primarily eschatological Christian soteriology. This entails creation, incarnation, death, and resurrection. They write:

> [L]inked with the paschal mystery and patterned on the dying Christ, he will hasten forward to resurrection in the strength which comes from hope. All this holds true not just for Christians, but for all men of good will in whose hearts grace works in an unforeseen way. For, since Christ died for all men, and since the ultimate vocation of man is in fact one, and divine, we ought to believe that the Holy Spirit in a manner known only to God offers to every man the possibility of being associated with the paschal mystery . . . through Christ and in Christ, the riddles of sorrow and death grow meaningful. Apart from His Gospel, they overwhelm us. Christ has risen, destroying death by His death; He has lavished life upon us so that, as sons in the Son, we can cry out in the Spirit; Abba, Father.[45]

The document's anthropology and soteriology are connected also to the Incarnation, and the Incarnation is what initiates the restoration of human dignity and a reconciled relationship with God. To this end, the Council Fathers point out that the human being only makes sense in light of the Incarnation. They write:

> The truth is that only in the mystery of the incarnate Word does the mystery of man take on light . . . He Who is 'the image of the invisible God' (Col. 1:15), is Himself the perfect man. To the sons of Adam he restores the divine likeness which had been disfigured from the first sin onward. Since human nature as He assumed it was not annulled, by that very fact it has been raised up to a divine dignity in our respect too. For by His incarnation the Son of God has united Himself in some fashion with every man.[46]

The document then proceeds from the Incarnation of the Son to the Passion and Death of Jesus. The Fathers state:

---

44. Ibid., no. 18.
45. Ibid., no. 22.
46. Ibid.

As an innocent lamb He merited for us life by the free shedding of His own blood. In Him God reconciled us to Himself and among ourselves; from bondage to the devil and sin he delivered us, so that each one of us can say with the Apostle: The Son of God 'loved me and gave Himself up for me' (Gal 2:20). By suffering for us He not only provided us with an example for our imitation, He blazed a trail, and if we follow it, life and death are made holy and take on a new meaning.[47]

In short, *Gaudium et spes* provides a fundamental Christian anthropology upon which a soteriological vision is constructed in the following manner. The human person, who is originally good and created in God's image, possesses an innate dignity by virtue of being a daughter or son of God and always existing in God's presence. This original dignity and goodness, however, has been disfigured and marred through the human person's sinning against God the Creator. Through free choice, men and women decided to reject God's free gift of self and became alienated from their Creator and their true selves. Through Christ's Incarnation, Passion, Death, and Resurrection, the possibility of reconciliation with God, and everlasting life, has been made available as well as the healing of the wounds that have perverted free will.

This salvation and reconciliation with God, however, is primarily eschatological and connected to the mystery of death. The central problems of death and non-existence, as consequences of sinning against the Creator, have been overcome through Christ's incarnation, passion, and resurrection. The human person is understood primarily as a sinner whose intrinsic dignity in this world and eternal salvation in the next are at stake in his or her choice of repentance (or lack thereof). Within the modern world, the Council Fathers connect this anthropology and soteriology to the problem of modern atheism. As a belief system and ideology, they argue that modern atheism has an intrinsic inability to offer ultimate hope and salvation to the sinning and suffering human being. Thus, the Council Fathers state that modern atheism is a grave threat to human dignity, salvation, and belief in the Christian God whose forgiveness and reconciliation has been offered in Jesus Christ.

Pope John Paul II provides a succinct expression of the foundation of the Pastoral Constitution, as articulated in chapter 1. He argues, ". . . *Gaudium et spes* shed light on the *perennial human quest for meaning*: our origin, the purpose of life, the presence of sin and suffering, the

47. Ibid.

inevitability of death, the mystery of life after death are all unavoidable questions."[48] The Pope invokes the "perennial quest for human meaning" as the center around which the other questions revolve. The human quest for meaning, then, provides the central framework for the Christian anthropology and soteriology of the document.

Section Three: The Need to Envision a Roman Catholic Soteriology for the Sinned-Against Creature

Having outlined the general anthropology and soteriology of the document, as well as its contextual focus on modern atheism, I now move to my critique of the Pastoral Constitution. I contend that its anthropology and soteriology are relatively inadequate because its Christian anthropology does not offer a thick description of the effects of sin upon the sinned-against in *this* world at a fundamental theological level as a supplement to the Christian anthropology of sinning creature and Sinned-Against Creator.[49]

The primary framework in *Gaudium et spes* for understanding the human person is sinning against God. This is not a problem in itself. It becomes a problem, however, when it is almost the exclusive focus of theological anthropology and soteriology. All human beings indeed are sinners and have sinned against the Living God of Jesus Christ. Nevertheless, there needs to be a supplemental account of the effects of sin upon the human person in *this* world; that is, an account of the physical, psychological, and spiritual wounds carried by the sinned-against, inflicted by the sinners, and how the God of Jesus Christ works for the healing of these wounds and the realization of fragments of salvation for both sinners and sinned-against.

---

48. Pope John Paul II, "Only Christ Can Fulfill Man's Hopes," 124; italics original. It is important to point out that the pope's observations are made within the context of a christological or, perhaps even christocentric understanding of the document's anthropology. To this end, he quotes *Gaudium et spes* no. 10, where the document declares that Christ is "the key, the center and the purpose of the whole of man's history."

49. To be fair, the council fathers most likely did not have salvation for the "sinned-against" creature in the forefront of their minds as they drafted the anthropology and soteriology of *Gaudium et spes*. This concern would come to the fore at CELAM's Conference at Medellín in 1968. CELAM intended that its focus on the poor and the sinned-against be in continuity with the Second Vatican Council, and *Gaudium et spes*. For the proceedings, see *The Church in the Present-day Transformation of Latin America in the Light of the Council*.

Through placing the sinning creature and the Sinned-Against God at the foundation of its anthropology and through a lack of supplementing this foundation with a fundamental accounting of the effects of sin upon the sinned-against creature, the Pastoral Constitution gives greatest importance to the problem of non-believers and human meaning in the modern world as distinct from the problem of non-persons and innocent suffering in the modern world.

I am not suggesting that the Pastoral Constitution is unconcerned with non-persons and innocent suffering. As the opening lines indicate, this very question hangs heavy upon the hearts of the Council Fathers and is part of the foundational purpose of this document. Nevertheless, the Christian anthropology and soteriology of chapter 1 of the Pastoral Constitution gives precedence to the human person's existential alienation from the Sinned-Against God and the subsequent problems of the meaning of human life and the mystery of death, rather than robustly supplementing this theology with a thick description of the effects of sin upon the sinned-against creature. This supplement would provide the foundation for a vision of the fragments of salvation that can be realized in *this* world through participating in God's ongoing work of creation and salvation.

Roots of My Critique: Latin American Theologies of Liberation[50]

I am not the originator of this critique of the Roman Catholic Church's giving theological precedence to atheism and non-believers over innocent suffering and non-persons. Much of this criticism arose from the *irruption of the poor* that was part of the inspiration for the various Latin American liberation theologians in the decades after the Council. Although their critiques are not directed at the Pastoral Constitution as such, and in fact are much inspired by the underlying vision of the document, I am adopting them as the clearest and most relevant critiques of the theological priorities and trajectory outlined in this document. I adopt this critique at the level of fundamental Christian anthropology

---

50. One other important source for my critique of this document is the work of Andrew Sung Park. In particular, Park has expounded upon this in *The Wounded Heart of God*. Because I will be engaging with Park's theology thoroughly in chapter 4, I refrain from invoking it here. But his critique shows great similarity, from a Protestant perspective, to those of the Roman Catholics Elizondo and Gutiérrez who will be discussed below.

and soteriology as discussed in chapter 1 of the document. In particular, the document's focus upon the ideology and belief system of modern atheism as the most pressing problem that is at the core of the violation of human dignity poses a problem.

Among many others, Mexican-American theologian Virgilio Elizondo and Peruvian theologian Gustavo Gutiérrez have criticized the different theological priorities between wealthy North Atlantic countries and more impoverished countries in the Global South.[51] As Elizondo writes:

> While the Churches of Europe and North America anguish about secularism, modernity, and the relation between faith and reason, the Churches of Latin America anguish about the dehumanization of the masses. How can anyone talk about God when millions of human beings are treated as non-persons by economic exploitation, political repression, and exclusion from full participation in the church's life?[52]

Gutiérrez offers a more nuanced view of the differing theological priorities between the wealthy countries of North America and Europe and the impoverished nations of the Global South. He writes:

> In the development of liberation theology our awareness of this new presence has made us aware that our partners in dialogue are the poor, those who are 'non-persons'—that is, those who are not considered to be human beings with full rights, beginning with the right to life and to freedom in various spheres. Elsewhere, on the other hand, the best modern theology has been sensitive rather to the challenge posed by the mentality that asserted itself at the European Enlightenment; it is therefore responsive to the challenges posed by the nonbeliever or by Christians under the sway of modernity.
>
> The distinction between these two approaches is not an attempt to juxtapose two theological perspectives. It tries only to be clear on their respective starting points, to see their differences, and then correctly to define relationships between the

---

51. It is important to reiterate that neither Elizondo nor Gutiérrez are specifically critiquing the Pastoral Constitution. Rather, they are pointing out and critiquing the divergent trajectories in Christian anthropology and soteriology that have arisen in the later twentieth century. Somewhat anachronistically, I am reading their critique backwards into the Pastoral Constitution. Although they are not concerned with the document as such, I think that their critique highlights the relative inadequacy in the Pastoral Constitution's fundamental Christian anthropology and soteriology.

52. Elizondo, "Emergence of a World Church and the Irruption of the Poor," 108.

two . . . [it is] both possible and necessary to be clear on the perduring basis and inspiration of our theological thinking.[53]

Elizondo and Gutiérrez respect the trajectory set by the Pastoral Constitution's focus upon atheism while also critiquing it. In fact, they are inspired by its vision of mutually-critical and mutually-informing dialogue with the world. But they contrast the theological priorities within Christian anthropology and soteriology among the contexts of non-believers and non-persons. As I have shown above, the Pastoral Constitution does highlight the problem of the non-believer more so than the non-person. The Pastoral Constitution prioritizes professed religious belief systems of the sinner over the reality of innocent suffering and destruction of life that goes part and parcel with situations of violence.

Edward Schillebeeckx, who will be discussed in the next chapter, poses a similar challenge as Elizondo and Gutiérrez, (again, with reference to a later theological trajectory, although one that I think already is present within *Gaudium et spes*) when he states unequivocally that "God does not want humankind to suffer." Schillebeeckx argues neither that God does not want Christians to suffer nor that God condones atheists suffering. Schillebeeckx argues that God does not want any human being to suffer unjustly. Atheism and secularity are important problems, as are religious confession, identity, and affiliation. But, I defer to Elizondo, Gutiérrez, and finally Schillebeeckx in their arguments that the problems of non-persons and innocent human suffering comprise at least an equally important fundamental theological problem to human dignity as non-believers and atheism. This is the root of the Pastoral Constitution's relatively inadequate Christian anthropology and soteriology.

Counterpoint: The Pastoral Constitution's Concern with Suffering

Although its soteriological vision is primarily eschatological, the Pastoral Constitution does affirm the need for healing in this world and this life throughout much of its later chapters. Its famous opening paragraph also

---

53. Gutiérrez, "Introduction: Expanding the View," in *A Theology of Liberation*, xxix. For similar critiques, see Sobrino, *Jesus the Liberator*, 180–92; and Protestant James Cone's discussions of heresy and the different questions asked and priorities of "White" and "Black" theologies. *God of the Oppressed*, 33–35, 42–56.

attests to this concern,[54] as well as its purpose of being an *ad extra* account of the Church in dialogue with the modern world. The Pastoral Constitution indeed does assign great importance to the work of tending to the brokenness in the temporal world. The Council Fathers state:

> This faith [of Christians] needs to prove its fruitfulness by penetrating a believer's entire life, including its worldly dimensions, and by activating him toward justice and love, especially regarding the needy. What does most reveal God's presence, however, is the brotherly charity of the faithful who are united in spirit as they work together for the faith of the Gospel and who prove themselves a sign of unity.[55]

This affirmation of worldly *fragments of salvation* (to borrow a phrase from Schillebeeckx), however, is secondary to the eschatological vision of salvation. Although eschatological salvation may be the source for fragments of salvation in this world, the document seems to downplay its importance through its greater focus upon the eschatological at its fundamental theological level.

It is important to point out that the Pastoral Constitution is indebted to *aggiornamento* and reading the "signs of the times." This means that the problems of human suffering and oppression—that of nonpersons—are extremely important to the Council Fathers. For example, the Pastoral Constitution declares, "The Christian who neglects his temporal duties, neglects his duties toward his neighbor and even God, jeopardizes his eternal salvation."[56] One's actions and lifestyle within this world do indeed have far reaching consequences and even eschatological consequences. The way in which a Christian attends to the wounds and sufferings of others is of great import for following Jesus and living an authentically Christian life. "He taught us by example that we too must

---

54. "The joys and the hopes, the griefs and the anxieties of the men of this age, especially those who are poor or in any way afflicted, these are the joys and hopes, the griefs and anxieties of the followers of Christ. Indeed, nothing genuinely human fails to raise an echo in their hearts. For theirs is a community composed of men. United in Christ, they are led by the Holy Spirit in their journey to the Kingdom of their Father and they have welcomed the news of salvation which is meant for every man. That is why this community realizes that it is truly linked with mankind and its history by the deepest of bonds" *Gaudium et spes*, no. 1.

55. *Gaudium et spes*, no. 21.

56. Ibid., no. 43.

shoulder the cross which the world and the flesh inflict upon those who search after peace and justice."[57]

For example, the Pastoral Constitution's deep concern for human suffering in the modern world is crystallized in No. 27. The Council Fathers write:

> [W]hatever is opposed to life itself, such as any type of murder, genocide, abortion, euthanasia, or willful self-destruction, whatever violates the integrity of the human person, such as mutilation, torments inflicted on the body or mind, attempts to coerce the will itself; whatever insults human dignity, such as subhuman living conditions, arbitrary imprisonment, deportation, slavery, prostitution, the selling of women and children; as well as disgraceful working conditions, where men are treated as mere tools for profit, rather than as free and responsible persons; all these things and others of their like are infamies indeed. They poison human society, *but they do more harm to those who practice them than those who suffer from the injury.* Moreover, they are a supreme dishonor to the Creator.[58]

This representative statement demonstrates that the authentic concern of the Council Fathers for innocent suffering and the violation of human dignity in this world cannot be contested. *Gaudium et spes* unequivocally declares the Church's solidarity with the triumphs and travails, joys and sufferings, of men and women in the modern world.

Nevertheless, and as the italicized portion of this passage demonstrates, the basic Christian anthropology and soteriology of *Gaudium et spes* needs to be supplemented by a robust anthropology and soteriology accounting for the effects of sin—the wounds of the sinned-against creature, inflicted by the sinner, in the presence of the Living God. For example, this passage argues that the sinners are harmed more greatly by their actions than the sinned-against. This claim is to be commended for its intent to highlight the concurrent wound carried by the sinner, who must repent. But this claim must be critiqued for focusing more greatly upon the wound of the sinner as opposed to the suffering of the sinned-against. By emphasizing the wound of the sinner rather than the sinned-against, its Christian anthropology again falls short in adequately accounting for the effects of sin upon God's creatures in this world. Although this passage opens up the possibility of accounting for the nature of the wounds of sin in this world

---

57. Ibid., no. 38.
58. Ibid., no. 27; italics added.

and God's work of fragmentary salvation on behalf of the victims here and now, the Council Fathers give soteriological precedence to the sinner. In their fundamental Christian anthropology, they do not assign as much importance to the effects of sin upon the sinned-against that would assist in envisioning their healing and salvation.

Furthermore, the Council Fathers state that "... if anyone wants to know how this unhappy situation can be overcome, Christians will tell him that all human activity, constantly imperiled by man's pride and deranged self-love, must be purified and perfected by the power of Christ's cross and resurrection."[59] As theologically true as this statement is, how does this soteriology apply to the sinned-against creature? How does he or she experience "the power of Christ's cross and resurrection" in his or her wounds that have been the effects of being sinned-against?[60]

God is working continually in this world and *Gaudium et spes* does not neglect the need for ministry and action—for the realization of fragments of salvation from God in this world. Its intention is quite the opposite. But in its formulation of a Christian anthropology and soteriology, the work of participating in God's ongoing soteriological work on behalf of human dignity primarily is eschatological and focused upon meaning and atheism, as opposed to focusing simultaneously upon this world's innocent suffering and non-persons at a fundamental level of Christian anthropology and soteriology.[61]

---

59. Ibid., no. 37.

60. This is a question that I will address through an intercultural dialogue and reception of *han* in chapter 5.

61. My rhetoric here would seem to be contradicted by No. 28, in which the council fathers argue that "it is necessary to distinguish between error, which always merits repudiation, and the person in error, who never loses the dignity of being a person even when he is flawed by false or inadequate religious notions. God alone is the judge and searcher of hearts, for that reason He forbids us to make judgments about the internal guilt of anyone. The teaching of Christ even requires that we forgive injuries, and extends the law of love to include every enemy." My contention is not that the Pastoral Constitution makes a qualitative distinction between the religious affiliation (or lack thereof) of the sinner or the sinned-against. My contention is that the Pastoral Constitution needs to offer an equal treatment of the sinned-against. Even in this excerpt, the council fathers are focused upon the sinner and not on the sinned-against. In addition, the call to forgiveness of the sinner by the sinned-against does not offer a description of the wounds that are the effects of sin. There is neither a description nor a thick description of such woundedness. This, again, suggests a relative inadequacy in the document's theological anthropology and soteriology.

From Status Quaestionis to the Bridge: Rationale for Edward Schillebeeckx's Soteriology

In this chapter, I have discussed the basic anthropology and soteriology of the Pastoral Constitution on the Church in the Modern World, *Gaudium et spes*. The foundation of its anthropology is the sinning creature and the Sinned-Against Creator. Hence, its soteriology is primarily concerned with human repentance and reconciliation with the Living God through Jesus Christ. In dialogue with the modern world, this anthropology and soteriology are connected to the problems of modern atheism and the question of meaning.

I have suggested that *Gaudium et spes's* anthropology and soteriology are relatively inadequate. This is because, at the foundational level, the Pastoral Constitution does not offer a supplementary emphasis upon the effects of sin upon the sinned-against creature in *this* world. The Pastoral Constitution's foundational anthropology does not offer a "thick description" of the wounds caused by sin, nor an adequate focus upon the problems of innocent suffering and non-persons. Instead, the Pastoral Constitution provides a foundational anthropology and soteriology that focuses primarily upon human alienation from God through sinning and its connection to modern atheism and the question of meaning.

When the Council fathers focus upon the plight and suffering of the victims, which occurs quite often as the document proceeds, the wounds of the sinned-against creatures are not given their full importance as a supplement to the human being sinning against God. In short, the experience of the sinned-against creature is not adequately accounted for nor is it treated as a fundamental *locus theologicus* from which its anthropology and soteriology must be constructed. My critique is with the fundamental anthropology and soteriology of Part One of the document and not with the subsequent articulations of the care and ministry needed for participating in God's work of fragmentary salvation here and now.

My critique has been, to some extent, a retroactive reiteration of the critiques of Latin American liberation theologians such as Gustavo Gutiérrez and Virgilio Elizondo. Their concern for supplementing the Western theological emphasis upon non-believers with a global theological emphasis upon non-persons is relevant to the fundamental Christian anthropology and soteriology of *Gaudium et spes*. They argue for making the poor, oppressed, and suffering human being and human communities—the sinned against—also a privileged subject of theological reflection. Flemish-Dominican theologian Edward Schillebeeckx shares their critiques and concerns. The problems of innocent suffering and non-persons are at the heart of Schillebeeckx's later work, particularly as he engaged with Critical Theory and Latin American theologies of liberation. As he has written:

> [T]here is an evident difference of approach between bourgeois middle-class Christians—which is what all of us in the West have become—and Christians in the Third World. Here in the West we seek as Christians, theologians, to address modern secularized men and women in order to make this faith in Jesus Christ acceptable; theologians in the Third World, on the other hand, address dehumanized people, non-persons, who ask, rather how one can believe in a good and liberating God in a world of suffering and oppression. I think that this last approach is closer to Jesus' concern than the first. I think that our Western theology will have to combine both forms of concern if we are not ultimately to land up with a Western theology of emancipation which by-passes Christian belief and Christology.[62]

With this in mind, it is to Schillebeeckx's soteriology I now turn.

---

62. Schillebeeckx, *On Christian Faith*, 29.

2

The Bridge: The Soteriology of Edward Schillebeeckx

IN THE PREVIOUS CHAPTER, I discussed the relatively inadequate anthropology and soteriology of the Second Vatican Council, as exemplified in *Gaudium et spes*. The Pastoral Constitution's foundational anthropology does not offer a sufficient thick description of the wounds caused by sin, nor an adequate focus upon the problems of innocent suffering and non-persons. Instead, the Pastoral Constitution provides a foundational anthropology and soteriology that focuses primarily upon human alienation from God through sinning and its connection to modern atheism and the question of meaning. I then suggested that the root of its relatively inadequate soteriology was its lack of offering a thick description of the effects of sin upon the sinned-against creature—human beings. That is, in articulating salvation through Christ it neither adequately describes nor accounts for the wounds inflicted upon the sinned-against, by the sinner, in the presence of the Living God. This is an underdevelopment in theological anthropology that leads to a lack of clarity regarding how to envision fragments of salvation in this world.

In addition, chapter 1 briefly showed that the meaning and implications of the Second Vatican Council and the document *Gaudium et spes* remain contentious. I showed how the legacy of the Second Vatican Council is a point of heated debate within the Roman Catholic theological world. Moreover, I briefly discussed how *Gaudium et spes* was a committee document that was forged in the heat of theological debate. Much of this debate hinged upon the question of the church and salvation. As Erik Borgman points out, the fault line revealed in the wake of the Second Vatican Council was "in what form do faith, the church, and theology bring salvation in the present situation?"⁶³ In my larger argument, I will be contending that Korean-American theologies of *han* can be a reference point for addressing this relative inadequacy in the anthropology and soteriology of *Gaudium et spes*; that is, in envisioning salvation from the effects of sin in this world. *Han* can be a foundation upon which to further develop the anthropology and soteriology described in *Gaudium et spes*.

In this chapter, I will offer a theological bridge to span the gap between *Gaudium et spes* and Korean-American theologies of *han*. This bridge is the work of Flemish-Dominican theologian Edward Schillebeeckx, whose soteriology can be loosely defined as *extra mundum nulla salus*, and as such, is in continuity with the soteriology of *Gaudium et spes*. This chapter will proceed in three sections. In Section One, I will introduce the broad trajectory of Schillebeeckx's life, work, and theological concerns. After describing Schillebeeckx's intellectual formation, I will discuss his theological connection to and influence upon the Second Vatican Council. I will also briefly mention Schillebeeckx's role in co-founding the international journal, *Concilium*, after the Second Vatican Council.

In Section Two, I will provide a brief overview of Schillebeeckx's soteriology—*extra mundum nulla salus*. I will examine his soteriology in four steps. First, I will outline Schillebeeckx's general definition of *salvation*. Second, I will discuss the location at the heart of Schillebeeckx's soteriology, namely, human experience. I will elaborate upon Schillebeeckx's conception of human experience through discussing its interpretive, surprising, and narrative character; the experience of unjust suffering and negative contrast; and the concepts of the *humanum* and seven *anthropological constants*. Third, I will examine the foundation of Schillebeeckx's understanding of salvation: his correlation of human experience with the God revealed in Jesus Christ. This is a God whom Schillebeeckx characterizes as a God of pure positivity and creativity. There are two aspects of Schillebeeckx's theology of God that are most pertinent to my discussion: God the Creator and God revealed in Jesus Christ as salvation for humankind through the entirety of his life, death, and resurrection. That is, a God who is new each moment and is akin to what Gustavo Gutiérrez has termed the *God of Life*.⁶⁴ Fourth, I will discuss the means by which human beings encounter and envision salvation from God: the related concepts of *mediated immediacy* and moments of

---

63. Borgman, *Edward Schillebeeckx: A Theologian in His History*, 370.
64. Gutiérrez, *The God of Life*.

fragmentary salvation. These two concepts are the glue that adhere human experience to God's offer of salvation in Schillebeeckx's soteriology.

In Section Three, I will summarize my discussion of Schillebeeckx's soteriology and offer four elements as points of dialogue with *han*: definition, location, foundation, and encounter. These four elements follow the general trajectory set by *Gaudium et spes* and are relevant for a dialogue with *han*. A further exploration and dialogue with *han* will occur in chapter 5. For the purposes of this chapter, I will provide a brief elucidation of how these contours emerge from Schillebeeckx's soteriology.

Section One: An Introduction to Edward Schillebeeckx's Theology

Edward Schillebeeckx was one of the most influential of the Vatican II generation of European-Catholic theologians, along with others such as Karl Rahner, Yves Congar, Henri de Lubac, and Joseph Ratzinger. Schillebeeckx was a prolific thinker whose writings were not systematic in the traditional sense. Instead, he attempted to make Christian faith intelligible to modern women and men through in-depth studies of a timely and topical nature, often focusing on Soteriology, Christology, the Sacraments, and Ministry. It is for this reason that he argued "I am not writing for posterity."[65] His work often attended to the social context in which he lived.

In light of the narrow focus of this chapter, it is not possible to do full justice to the biographical details that underpin the life and work of Edward Schillebeeckx. This is true with regard to his earliest experiences of family, education and spiritual formation, as well as with regard to his intellectual formation. For the purposes of this chapter, it must suffice to briefly discuss his life and intellectual formation.[66]

---

65. Schillebeeckx, *God is New Each Moment*, 123.

66. For more detailed information on Schillebeeckx's life, see Borgman, *Edward Schillebeeckx: A Theologian in his History*; Schreiter, "An Orientation to his Thought", 1–24; as well as the Schillebeeckx's own recollections in the book-length interviews *I Am a Happy Theologian:* and *God is New Each Moment*. See also McManus, *Unbroken Communion: The Place and Meaning of Suffering in the Theology of Edward Schillebeeckx*, 8–16; Schreiter, "Edward Schillebeeckx,"152–55; and Hilkert and Schreiter, *The Praxis of the Reign of God*, 1–18. Finally, see Schreiter's "The Relevance of Professor Edward Schillebeeckx, O.P. for the 21st Century."

Edward Cornelius Florentius Alfons Schillebeeckx (1914–2009) was born into a middle-class, Flemish family (with thirteen brothers and sisters) in Belgium and was raised in Kortenberg, outside of Antwerp.[67] He received his secondary education at the Jesuit School at Tournhout, where he demonstrated his exceptional academic ability and discerned his calling to the religious priesthood. He decided to join the Dominican Order and in 1934 journeyed to the novitiate house of formation in Ghent. After his novitiate, he was sent to continue his studies at the Dominican House of Studies connected with the Catholic University in Louvain. He was ordained a priest in 1941.[68]

While studying at Louvain, Schillebeeckx became a pupil of philosopher/ theologian Dominicus De Petter. Despite the Catholic Church's official exclusive adoption of neo-Scholastic philosophy and theology and its later condemnation of modernism and modern philosophy,[69] De Petter introduced Schillebeeckx to modern forms of philosophy such as existentialism and phenomenology. De Petter advocated for a phenomenological approach to reading and interpreting Thomas Aquinas, particularly through the category of *implicit intuition*. In Schillebeeckx's interpretation, De Petter's category of implicit intuition is a

---

67. Regarding Schillebeeckx's cultural background, Hill locates two cultural strands that have influenced Schillebeeckx's theological orientation from an early age: Dutch practicality and French spirituality. Hill speculates that these two currents that were interwoven into the culture of his native Belgium may shed light upon Schillebeeckx's continuing interest in this intersection between the mystical and the political in theology. In Hill's own words, "At the risk of a vast oversimplification, the Flemish ingredient explains the social and political orientation in Schillebeeckx's Christian thought, while the French explains the leaning toward personal communion with God." See, Hilkert and Schreiter, *The Praxis of the Reign of God*, 8.

68. Schillebeeckx observes that his decision to enter the Dominicans was, in part, connected to his disenchantment with his education and experience at Turnhout, a Jesuit College. He writes that originally he wanted to become a Jesuit missionary like his eldest brother, but that an incident in which he was disciplined for breaking the rule of silence by attempting to help a fellow student with his studies helped to change his mind. He wrote, "Enough with the Jesuits, they were ruining my life." He eventually decided to become a Dominican after reading the lives of Saints Dominic, Francis, Ignatius, and Benedict. He was most taken with Dominic and his "healthy balance, the joy, the openness to the world, the study, the research, the theology centered on preaching." See *I Am a Happy Theologian*, 4–5. This ambivalence toward the Jesuits would occasionally resurface throughout his career. For example, this can be seen in his distinction between an "esoteric" Jesuit mysticism and an "ordinary" Dominican mysticism. See *Church*, 68–70. See also *On Christian Faith*.

69. See, for example, Pope Leo XIII's *Aeterni Patris* (1879); Pope Pius X's *Lamentabili Sane Exitu* (1907); and Pius X's *Pascendi Dominici Gregis* (1907).

non-conceptual aspect of reason. In other words, De Petter thought that human beings have an initial orientation towards and direct experience of the totality of the world around them and its full meaning. This was the beginning of all knowledge and of knowledge of God.[70] Schillebeeckx later claimed to have abandoned this philosophical foundation for theology—particularly that of implicit intuition—as taught by De Petter.[71] But Schillebeeckx's concerns for human experience as a *locus theologicus*, for salvation within the world, for the importance of *encounter*, and the *turn to the subject* can be traced, in part, to his early studies with De Petter.[72]

In 1945, Schillebeeckx was sent to Paris for post-graduate studies with the Dominican faculty at Le Saulchoir, the center of the theological *ressourcement* that had become pejoratively known as *nouvelle theologie*. Schillebeeckx undertook his advanced theological and historical studies under the influence of Yves Congar and Marie-Dominic Chenu.[73] As Schillebeeckx recalled, "under the guidance of Chenu I read St. Thomas from a historical perspective and not just literally, in the context of the philosophy of his time."[74] Chenu and Congar provided Schillebeeckx with a contextual theological sensibility and orientation that had great

---

70. Schillebeeckx, *God is New Each Moment*, 14–15.

71. Schillebeeckx's claim, however, is disputed in a recent essay by Stephan van Erp who also offers a clear and precise understanding of De Petter's concept of *implicit intuition*, particularly in contrast to the work of Joseph Marechal. See Boeve et al., *Edward Schillebeeckx and Contemporary Theology*, 209–24.

72. De Petter's influence in these areas can be seen, for example, in Part 6, in Schillebeeckx's *Christ: The Sacrament of the Encounter with God*, 197–216.

73. Schillebeeckx observes that, although Chenu had been removed from the faculty of theology at Le Saulchoir in 1942, he remained a professor at the École des Hautes Études, where Schillebeeckx encountered him. Chenu was perhaps the most important influence upon Schillebeeckx's formation as a theologian. Much of this was due to Chenu's personality, his approach to theology, his concern with the world, and his practice of *presence a Dieu* and *presence au monde*. See *God is New Each Moment*, 16–19. Describing Chenu on this idea, Schillebeeckx wrote: "Well before 'theology of hope,' 'political theology,' 'economic theology,' and the various branches of liberation theology, Chenu had initiated theological renewal." Schillebeeckx goes on to point out that, despite the fact that Chenu was a man of scholarly genius, "we must not forget that Chenu was anything but a student living outside the world. He was also the great inspiration behind the French worker priests. Because of this, in 1954, he was exiled from Paris on the intervention of the Vatican." See the entire eulogy, "In Memory of Marie Dominique (Marcel) Chenu OP."

74. Schillebeeckx, *I Am a Happy Theologian*, 8.

appreciation for the tradition and for human experience as exemplified in history, sociology, and philosophy.[75]

Schillebeeckx returned to Louvain and from 1947 to 1957 he resided in a twofold position: as lecturer in dogmatic theology and as *magister spiritualis*, the director of spiritual formation for students in the Dominican House of Studies.[76] In 1952, he successfully defended his doctoral dissertation on sacramental theology, entitled *De Sacramentele Heilseconomie*. In 1957, Schillebeeckx accepted the position of Professor of Dogmatic and Historical Theology at the University of Nijmegen (now known as Radboud University) in the Netherlands, which was the primary academic institution to which he remained connected until his death in 2009.

William Portier provides a concise overview of Schillebeeckx's philosophical dialogue partners[77] as his career progressed upon leaving

---

75. It is also important to point out that during this time Schillebeeckx attended lectures given by the French existentialist Jean-Paul Sartre and French phenomenologist Maurice Merleau-Ponty.

76. For more on this time period, see *God is New Each Moment*, 15–19.

77 Along with his studies with de Petter, Chenu, and Congar, one other aspect of Schillebeeckx's early intellectual formation deserves attention, but cannot be discussed here. This is Schillebeeckx's encounter with the Catholic intellectual current of Neo-Scholasticism. When he entered the Dominican Order in 1934 and began his theological studies, Schillebeeckx encountered this neuralgic point for many of the twentieth-century modern theologians.

Even though Schillebeeckx's earliest formation occurred within a neo-scholastic intellectual environment, he did not embrace the manual theology of the time. It seems that his philosophical studies with De Petter at Louvain, as well as his historical and critical studies of the sources with Congar and Chenu in Paris, provided Schillebeeckx with a different theological orientation. Through these teachers, among others, Schillebeeckx found an alternative foundation for articulating Roman Catholic theology.

Schillebeeckx's derision for the neo-Scholastic manual theology of the pre-Vatican II era is shown by his passing remark that he was much more interested in philosophy than theology during his novitiate and early years with the Dominicans. See *I Am a Happy Theologian*, 7–8. See also Schreiter's "Introduction" in *The Language of Faith*, vii–xiii. Schillebeeckx's disdain for neo-scholasticism was shared by many of his contemporaries. For example, Swiss theologian Hans Urs von Balthasar called it "sawdust Thomism" and remarked, with characteristic flair, that it was "a grim struggle with the dreariness of theology, with what men had made out of the glory of revelation. I could not endure this presentation of the Word of God and wanted to lash out with the fury of a Samson: I felt like tearing down, with Samson's own strength, the whole temple and burying myself beneath the rubble." See Moss and Oakes, "Introduction," 3. As Oakes and Moss point out, this quote's origin is in the Introduction to von Speyr's published journals, in particular *Erde und Himmel*. See Moss and Oakes, "Introduction," 7n6.

Louvain.[78] After obtaining his first professorship in 1957,[79] Schillebeeckx engaged with phenomenology (1957–1966), hermeneutics (1966–1971), and finally critical theory (1971–2009), the latter being the area for which he is most well-known in contemporary theological discourse.[80] To this developmental trajectory, Robert Schreiter adds that while Schillebeeckx was engaging with hermeneutics in the middle part of his journey he also was engaging with Anglo-American linguistic philosophy.[81] Schillebeeckx published many monographs and countless essays during his career,[82] and representative works from each of these periods of his intellectual development include *Christ: The Sacrament of the Encounter with God* (1963), *God: The Future of Man* (1968), and his trilogy *Jesus: An Experiment in Christology* (1979), *Christ: The Experience of Jesus as Lord* (1980), and *Church: The Human Story of God* (1990).[83]

78. There is an aspect of his intellectual formation that is underdeveloped in the secondary literature on Schillebeeckx: his spiritual formation as a Dominican and his subsequent understandings of spirituality and the *theologal life* that are threads running through his large corpus of writings. For example, Schillebeeckx founded and wrote for *Tijdschrift voor Geestelijk Leven* (loose translation: "Journal of the Spiritual Life"). For an introduction to Schillebeeckx on this understudied aspect of his thought, see Hilkert and Schreiter, *The Praxis of the Reign of God*, 117–31; Dolphin, "Spirituality and Practical Theology"; Hilkert, "Grace-Optimism," 220–39; as well as portions of Schillebeeckx, *I Am a Happy Theologian; God is New Each Moment; God among Us; Christ: The Experience of Jesus as Lord; On Christian Faith;* and *Church: The Human Story of God*. See also Cooper, *Humanity in the Mystery of God*, 12–34, who offers a particularly good overview of the influence of de Petter and Chenu on Schillebeeckx in this section, particularly pages 29–34.

79. A more detailed account can be found in Borgman's *Edward Schillebeeckx: A Theologian in His History*.

80. Hilkert and Schreiter, *The Praxis of the Reign of God*, 26.

81. Schreiter, "Edward Schillebeeckx," 154.

82. For an extensive list of Schillebeeckx's publications, see Schoof and van de Westlaken, *Bibliography*. See also "Bibliography" in *Edward Schillebeeckx and Contemporary Theology*, 273–92. Currently, a project has been completed that compiles and edits his works into one set of eleven volumes to be published in English by Continuum.

83. See Hilkert, "Edward Schillebeeckx: Encountering God in a Secular and Suffering World," 376–87, for an additional discussion of the intellectual development of Schillebeeckx. Hilkert's essay is particularly helpful with regard to Schillebeeckx's continued concern with articulating God's salvation for human suffering.

The Second Vatican Council[84]

As Professor at Nijmegen, Schillebeeckx quickly gained a reputation for his intellectual abilities and his theological and philosophical knowledge.[85] Consequently, when the Dutch Council of Bishops published a pastoral letter in 1961 in which they offered their progressive vision for the Second Vatican Council, Schillebeeckx had a great influence upon it and drafted much of the letter himself.[86] The letter was not well-received by the Roman Curia, however, and as Schillebeeckx recalls, "From then on the Holy Office began to take an interest in me."[87]

Consequently, Schillebeeckx was denied the position of *peritus*[88] by the Roman Curia for the Second Vatican Council. Schillebeeckx, however, did attend the Council although he never participated in the formal sessions. Instead of a *peritus* to the Council, he attended as theological advisor to the Dutch Bishops and in particular, he was an advisor to Bernard Jan Cardinal Alfrink, Archbishop of Utrecht. Moreover, he was a "behind the scenes" teacher who gave lectures to gatherings of other bishops outside of the official sessions in order to bring them up to date on current theological developments and perspectives, and provided critiques of the draft documents to many bishops. Schillebeeckx's direct involvement in drafting and envisioning the Council documents was minimal. He worked directly only on the marriage section of *Schema XIII*, the document that became the Pastoral Constitution on the Church

---

84. Schillebeeckx provides his own brief recollections of the time of the Council in *I Am a Happy Theologian*, 13–31; and *God is New Each Moment*, 125–29. See also Schillebeeckx's notes from the first two sessions of the Council, edited and published by Karim Schelkens.

85. For example, his work on sacramental theology was becoming well known and well respected in the years leading up to the Council, as exemplified in his now-famous *Christ: The Sacrament of the Encounter with God* (1959 in Dutch, 1963 in English) as well as his work in founding and continuing to publish in the Dutch journals *Tijdschrift voor Theologie* and *Tijdschrift voor Geestelijk Leven*.

86. Schillebeeckx, *I Am a Happy Theologian*, 17.

87. Ibid.

88. A *peritus* is an official theological consultant to the Council as ratified by the Roman Curia. They not only act as advisors but also attend and participate in the formal sessions of the Council. Figures such as Karl Rahner, Yves Congar, Marie-Dominique Chenu, Henri de Lubac, and Joseph Ratzinger, were all named *periti* for Vatican II.

and the Modern World, *Gaudium et spes*. But that was the extent of his direct involvement in drafting the Council's documents.[89]

Before concluding this introduction to Schillebeeckx and the Second Vatican Council, it is important to point out that he positioned his lifelong theological work to be in continuity with the work of *aggiornamento* initiated by Pope John XXIII and the Second Vatican Council. Schillebeeckx dedicated much of his career to reading the signs of the times and engaging in a mutually-critical and mutually-informing dialogue with the modern world as inspired by *Gaudium et spes*. One way in which he succeeded in this endeavor was through forming constructive relationships with theologians at the Council from other countries. These relationships culminated in Schillebeeckx's role in co-founding the international journal *Concilium* in 1965, along with others such as Karl Rahner, Hans Küng, Yves Congar, and Johannes Baptist Metz. The purpose of *Concilium* was to create a theological journal that would continue the debates and dialogues begun by the Second Vatican Council and allow new ideas to develop. It was a journal particularly indebted to the vision of *Gaudium et spes*.[90] In addition, *Concilium* was to be published in several languages so as to create permanent connections between the various Catholic theological faculties in and around Europe. Its scope was multilingual and international in order to continue the work begun by the Council for the benefit of the global Church.[91]

89. Schillebeeckx, *God is New Each Moment*, 125-26.

90 As the participants in the Council continued to reflect upon the course of the Church in the years after its closing and as the modern world underwent a time of revolution, a split developed among various groups of prominent theologians. One outcome of this split was the 1972 founding of a rival journal to *Concilium* entitled *Communio*, which was cofounded by, among others, theologians Hans Urs von Balthasar, Joseph Ratzinger, and Henri de Lubac. For more on this fault line within the European post-Vatican II theological world, see Tracy, "The Uneasy Alliance Reconsidered," 548-70. See also Kerr, "Rebels with a Cause," 297-304.

91. There are two important aspects of Schillebeeckx's career that I am unable to examine in this short chapter. The first are the three investigations (1968, 1979, 1984) into his work and orthodoxy conducted by the Congregation for the Doctrine of the Faith. Schillebeeckx was exonerated each time and was not censored or removed from his position as theologian or professor. For Schillebeeckx's own reflections upon these investigations, see *I Am a Happy Theologian*, 32-40. Regarding the second of the investigations (1979), see the documents collected by Schoof, *The Schillebeeckx Case*. The second is Schillebeeckx's reception of the Erasmus Prize in 1982 for his contribution to European culture. He was the first and only theologian to receive the prize. For his reflections upon receiving it, see *God among Us: The Gospel Proclaimed*, 249-53. His reception of this prize was the impetus for the interviews with Schillebeeckx

Dialogue with Critical Theory

Having provided a brief overview of Schillebeeckx's intellectual influences and role in the Second Vatican Council, I now turn to his most important philosophical dialogue partner for the purposes of this chapter—Schillebeeckx's engagement with the Frankfurt School of Critical Theory. As William Portier describes it, the Frankfurt School of Critical Theory was a product of the German-Jewish intellectuals who witnessed Germany's development from the weak Weimar Republic to the horrific governance of National Socialism. Portier argues that their experiences of the barbarism of the Nazi regime led them—figures such as Theodor Adorno and Max Horkheimer—to strongly critique Western rationality on two fronts: *the dialectic of Enlightenment* and *the critical negativity of the negative dialectic*.[92] Both were to have an influence on Schillebeeckx's theological trajectory.[93]

Regarding the dialectic of Enlightenment, Portier points out that Max Horkheimer and Theodor Adorno coined the term with reference to the paradox in which the very same scientific-technological forces of the Enlightenment that were supposed to be liberating humankind had in fact become the most dire threats to humankind's survival. Regarding the critical negativity of the negative dialectic, Portier defines this term as a call to protest in the face of the supposed rationality of a system that in effect produces an excess of human misery and destruction. In short, this two-pole dialectic provides a radical skepticism of any total or final socio-political solution to the on-going problems and suffering of humankind.[94] This critical stance of the Frankfurt School toward modernity was meant to uncover the barbarous human cost that has accompanied the progress of the modern project and to theorize that the only

---

conducted by Huub Oosterhuis and Piet Hoogeveen that resulted in the *God is New Each Moment*.

92. Hilkert and Schreiter, *The Praxis of the Reign of God*, 30–31.

93. One other important influence who must be mentioned is German Marxist Ernst Bloch. For a brief reference regarding the influence of Bloch upon Schillebeeckx, see Hilkert and Schreiter, *The Praxis of the Reign of God*, 56.

94. Hilkert and Schreiter, *The Praxis of the Reign of God*, 31. As Portier articulates on the same page, these dialectics provide a challenge to "any theoretician from any discipline, including theology, who dares to give an account of the necessary rationality and meaning of the present order makes a mockery of all those voiceless ones on the margins, all those who have suffered and died needlessly or what passes in traditional theory for the rationality of the present order."

reaction to such horror is protest and concrete action for change. This encounter with the Frankfurt school challenged Schillebeeckx to articulate a Christian theology that is directly concerned with the problem of unwarranted human suffering.

For all of the insight gained through the Frankfurt School's dialectics, Portier points out that their theorizing lacked an ability to articulate a positive vision of hope for human salvation. This is a weakness that Schillebeeckx realized and in response he was to draw upon the Christian faith tradition and in particular the story of Jesus Christ, as his foundation for this hope.[95] In other words, Critical Theory challenged him to envision a renewed soteriology that addressed the "signs of the times" and that was intelligible to modern Western women and men.

Section Two: The Soteriology of Edward Schillebeeckx: Extra Mundum Nulla Salus[96]

In Section One, I introduced the life and intellectual formation of Edward Schillebeeckx. I now move on to his understanding of salvation for human beings from the Living God of Jesus Christ that crystallized in his later work: *extra mundum nulla salus*. As Erik Borgman observes, "In his theological project Schillebeeckx is ultimately engaged in finding the God of salvation in the midst of the complexity in which human beings lead their lives, in a world that it is impossible to comprehend completely."[97] This is what Schillebeeckx references as *extra mundum nulla salus*—no salvation outside the world. There are four points upon which I will focus in order to provide a broad overview of Schillebeeckx's soteriology: its definition, location, foundation, and the way in which human beings encounter and envision it.

---

95. Ibid., 32.

96. This phrase, which is expanded upon in *Church: The Human Story of God*, is a phrase that accurately characterizes Schillebeeckx's later soteriology (although Jennifer Cooper might add that it is already present in his early theological anthropology. See Cooper, *The Humanity in God*). This is suggested in one of Schillebeeckx's last writings. "Letter from Edward Schillebeeckx," xiv–xv. Although one cannot push this too far, it is an adequate general characterization of his theology, along with other phrases such as *Gloria dei, vivens homo* and that the "human is the royal road to God."

97. Borgman, *Edward Schillebeeckx: A Theologian and His History*, 6.

Definition: Schillebeeckx's Understanding of Human Salvation from God

The salvation that we experience from God within the world—and Schillebeeckx explicitly points out that there is no salvation outside the world (*extra mundum nulla salus*)—is true salvation.[98] For Schillebeeckx, salvation is indeed human wholeness through "the conquest of all human, personal and social alienations; salvation is man's wholeness, his world and his history."[99] In other words, Schillebeeckx thinks that "salvation" is the full re-creation of humankind and a broken world. It is the multifaceted experience of wholeness that is a gift from God. As he writes:

> Salvation cannot be identified exclusively with political liberation; exclusively with 'being nice to one another'; exclusively with ecological efforts; exclusively with identifying oneself either with micro-ethics or macro-ethics or with mysticism, liturgy and prayer; exclusively with concerning oneself with education or geriatric techniques, and so on. *All this* is part of the concept of *salvation* or *wholeness* of mankind, and is therefore also essentially concerned with salvation from God, which may be experienced as grace.[100]

Schillebeeckx thinks that salvation from God for humankind occurs in this world and is intrinsically connected to human wholeness. This is a mode of existence that Kathleen McManus calls "Unbroken communion."[101] Phrased differently, Schillebeeckx argues, "Christianity is above all the praxis of the reign of God, an entryway or pathway to the eschatological revelation of God's own name."[102] It is God's salvation for humankind that bears upon the whole of human history and the entirety of humankind and all of creation.[103]

---

98. Schillebeeckx, *Church: The Human Story of God*, 5–13. Schillebeeckx's main reference points for envisioning human salvation are the seven *anthropological constants* and the *humanum*, both of which will be discussed below.

99. *Christ: The Experience of Jesus as Lord*, 814. Again, I am acutely aware of the problem of sexist and gender exclusivist language. I am also aware that the original Dutch may not employ sexist language. However, I again opt for readability by retaining the masculine language of the original translation.

100. Ibid., 779.

101. McManus, *Unbroken Communion*.

102. Schillebeeckx, "Prologue: Human God-Talk and God's Silence," xvii.

103. Schillebeeckx, *Christ: The Experience of Jesus as Lord*, 800–801.

Schillebeeckx argues that God's salvation is something that is primarily a worldly experience that only secondarily is interpreted in religious language. Salvation from God through Christ is experienced in the secular world and subsequently thematized and articulated in the churches that are the sacrament of God's salvation.[104] As Schillebeeckx observes, "Salvation from God comes about first of all in our worldly reality of history, and not primarily in the consciousness of believers who are aware of it."[105] Schillebeeckx clarifies this claim, however, in light of the Christian understanding of God. He argues, ". . . God and his initiative of salvation are a reality independent of human consciousness, and independent of our expression of God in experience. But our experience of God and his saving initiative is dependent both on the divine initiative and on the historical context in which human beings express him."[106] Salvation may be experienced within the world, but it remains God's own free-initiative that is mediated within human history. It is a divine gift and not the fruit of solitary human achievement. This gift, however, is not merely manifest in this world. Schillebeeckx also affirms the importance and ultimacy of God's eschatological salvation for humankind. Earthly salvation is indeed salvation but it is incomplete. It is a realized fragment of salvation that points to and makes present, imperfectly, God's full salvation for humankind.

Schillebeeckx points out that human salvation from God is fragmentary in this finite life and finite world. Schillebeeckx observes, ". . . human salvation is only salvation, being whole, when it is universal and complete. There cannot really be talk of salvation as long as there is still suffering, oppression, and unhappiness that we experience, in our immediate vicinity or further afield."[107] This means that although salvation from God for humankind in this world is true salvation, it remains fragmentary. As Schillebeeckx writes, "[I]n the context of fragmentary experiences of salvation we may rightly—metaphorically and with real depth—speak the word of God and his promise of eschatological salvation which transcends all expectations of experience and is yet recognized as what is familiar and evident."[108] These are moments of *fragmentary*

---

104. Schillebeeckx, *Church: The Human Story of God*, 11–15.
105. Ibid., 12.
106. Ibid., 13.
107 Schillebeeckx, *Christ: The Experience of Jesus as Lord*, 727.
108. Ibid., 643.

salvation and as such are a foretaste and a glimpse of God's final salvation for humankind that will arrive with the fullness of the *basileia tou theou*, God's final reign here on earth.

In other words, salvation, for Schillebeeckx, is the confluence of redemption and liberation that occurs fragmentarily within human history.[109] In the work of human salvation, God redeems sinners and liberates the sinned-against. God's salvation for humankind is related to humankind's liberation from all the personal and social structures that oppress and alienate. There cannot be salvation without liberation and there cannot be liberation without God's saving action.[110] This is the theological warrant that motivates him to make the perhaps controversial claim that God's saving action can be discerned "wherever good is done and injustice is challenged, through a praxis based on love of the fellow human being."[111]

In this way, Schillebeeckx places any discussion of soteriology firmly within the concrete reality of human history. He argues that God's salvation for humankind will not arrive from outside of human history but through human history. In Elizabeth Tillar's words, "God in his eschatological freedom is the universal subject and meaning of history."[112] This is the God revealed through Jesus Christ who through Creation and the Incarnation enacts human salvation and liberation. Schillebeeckx asserts that how we live our lives, address structures of injustice in society and treat our neighbors do indeed have consequences. Human history, with its joys and horrors, has intrinsic and lasting value in Schillebeeckx's theology. Exactly what those consequences entail and precisely how human history is imbued with ultimate worth, however, remains a mystery.[113] Humankind remains anchored to an unpredictable God in an enigmatic world. Nevertheless, this is a God mindful of humanity who seeks the salvation of all humankind and creation. To quote Schillebeeckx at length in a broad definition of God's salvation for humankind:

> What, then, is salvation in Jesus from God? I would want to say: being at the disposal of others, losing oneself to others (each in

---

109. For a more detailed discussion of the problem of the connection between redemption, salvation, and liberation in Schillebeeckx's thought, Simon, "Salvation and Liberation in the Practical-Critical Soteriology of Edward Schillebeeckx," 496–99.

110. See Schillebeeckx, *Jesus*, 624–25.

111. Schillebeeckx, *On Christian Faith*, 74–75.

112. Tillar, "Critical Remembrance and Eschatological Hope," 18.

113. Schillebeeckx, *Christ: The Experience of Jesus as Lord*, 792.

his own limited situation) and within this "conversion" (which is also made possible by structural changes) also working through anonymous structures for the happiness, the goodness, and the truth of mankind. This way of life, born of grace, provides a real possibility for a very personal encounter with God, who is then experienced as the source of all happiness and salvation, the source of joy. It is a communicative freedom which is actively reconciled with our own finitude, our death, our transgression and our failure. It sounds almost inauthentic: reconciliation with oneself as a useless servant, although we know that God says to us 'You may exist.' It is being justified freely through faith by grace. Even if there is not human love in return, sometimes if there is even misunderstanding, the believer knows in his sovereign freedom, which is at the same time grateful humility, that there is love in return: God first loved us. Real redemption or salvation always passes over into mysticism: only here can the tension between action and contemplation be sustained. This is existing for others and thus for *the* Other, the wholly intimate and near yet 'transcendent God', with whom Jesus has made us familiar.[114]

Location: Human Experience in the World[115]

Essential for understanding Schillebeeckx's soteriology is his theological starting point: human experience.[116] This is one of two fundamental

114. Ibid., 838. In addition to this quote, Simon offers another quote from *Christ* that offers a similar understanding. In Simon's words, "[Schillebeeckx] defines soteriology as 'the teaching of redemption: views and expectations which humans have in respect of their salvation, well-being and wholeness, redemption and liberation.'" See Simon, "Salvation and Liberation in the Practical-Critical Soteriology of Edward Schillebeeckx," 496. Simon's quote from Schillebeeckx comes from *Christ*, 906.

115. One important aspect of human experience of salvation that I do not treat at length in this section is the human experience of God's salvation from sinning and being sinned-against within this world and its subsequent articulation within the religious language offered in the sacrament of God's salvation through Christ—the churches. As Schillebeeckx writes, "We cannot suddenly experience God in the church's liturgy if we can no longer see him outside the church," *Christ: The Experience of Jesus as Lord*, 811. See also *Church*, 12–28; and *On Christian Faith*, 2–14.

116. This problem of human experience is discussed by Schreiter and also by McManus. Schreiter asserts that Schillebeeckx wishes to prioritize the soteriological over the christological when talking about Jesus because this is more intelligible and relevant to modern women and men. See Hilkert and Schreiter, *The Praxis of the Reign of God*, 192. McManus provides a detailed discussion of this problem of the connection between the actuality of salvation and one's knowledge of it. She asserts that

theological sources in his method of mutually critical correlation (the other being the confluence of Christian Scripture and Tradition). Schillebeeckx's understanding of human experience, however, is multifaceted. Human experience is interpreted, new, and narrative; it is grounded in human suffering and negative experiences of contrast; and it points to the eschatological reality of the seven *anthropological constants* and the *humanum*.[117]

Schillebeeckx argues that human experience is always interpreted experience. There is no unmediated experience. There is only human experience that is interpreted through an already-given framework or mindset. The concrete structures of human history affect, although do not fully determine, these interpretive frameworks within a human being's cognitive process. That is, human experience is comprised of both the context in which a person lives and the internal cognitive structures that mediate the person's interaction with this context.[118] As Schillebeeckx remarks, "Experience means learning through 'direct' contact with people and things."[119] Humans experience the world and themselves through direct interaction with people and things within a specific context and this interaction is interpreted through the concepts in which a person understands the world around them.[120]

Human experience is interpreted and is always open to the authority and critical force of new and surprising experiences. This means that

---

Schillebeeckx holds two simultaneous truths in tension as christology becomes soteriology and vice versa: the "cognitive order" and the "order of reality." In the "cognitive order," that is the order of knowing and epistemology, soteriology precedes Christology. Humankind is saved through Jesus of Nazareth *a priori* to a woman or man knowingly encountering the resurrected Jesus through the power of the Holy Spirit. In other words, "Christians come to know who God is in Christ in and through their human experience" (McManus, *Unbroken Communion*, 76). In the "order of reality," however, the person of Jesus must precede and be the foundation for soteriology. This is a more ontological assertion in which God's existence and immanent perfection must precede the creation of human beings in order for any guarantee that the promise of salvation can be fulfilled. In other words, "Christ, through whom God created all that exists, precedes all being and knowing." McManus, *Unbroken Communion*, 76; for the entirety of her discussion, see pp. 75–122.

117. For a study of greater depth into Schillebeeckx's earlier writings (from the 1940s to the Second Vatican Council) on theological anthropology and understanding of human experience, see Cooper, *Humanity in the Mystery of God*. For a compelling, if unpersuasive, critique of Schillebeeckx's understanding of human experience see Rochford "The Theological Hermeneutics of Edward Schillebeeckx," 251–67.

118. Hilkert and Schreiter, *The Praxis of the Reign of God*, 63.

119. Schillebeeckx, *Christ: The Experience of Jesus as Lord*, 31.

120. Ibid.

human experience can always develop as its interpretive framework also develops. Since all human experience is mediated through models and human constructs and since there is always a given in a particular experience that is independent of the human being, there is no neutrality in an experience.[121] Schillebeeckx asserts that new experiences possess unforeseen content that compels a human being to rethink the way he or she understands a person or thing in the world. Moreover, for Schillebeeckx, reality is disclosed in experience through the scandal, the surprising, and the stumbling block rather than the self-evident.[122] Mary Catherine Hilkert points out that for Schillebeeckx these surprising and unexpected experiences have a certain authority in their ability to challenge and unsettle previous convictions.[123] In short, this surprising character to human experience sets up a dialectic between human thought and experience, meaning that thought makes experience possible and at the same time experience makes new thinking necessary.[124] This means that there is a dialectical structure between perception and thought.[125]

Schillebeeckx's understanding of human experience is not only interpreted and open to development through the critical force of new experiences. In addition, Schillebeeckx argues that human experience finds its most adequate articulation not in abstract theory but through narrative. In short, our human stories are the most powerful forms for expressing our experiential dialectic between perception and critical reflection and are the form through which our human experiences are most intelligible. As Robert Schreiter points out, for Schillebeeckx, "experience can be organized conceptually, but it functions for us most powerfully when threaded together narratively. Concepts focus our experience, but it takes narrative to allow them to express their full range of meaning."[126]

---

121. Hilkert and Schreiter, *The Praxis of the Reign of God*, 63–65. As Schillebeeckx points out, due to the dialectic between perception and thought, there is a difference in perception between human beings with very different experiences. This means that identical facts and reality can indeed be experienced quite differently by a religious and a non-religious person. See Schillebeeckx, *Christ: The Experience of Jesus as Lord*, 50–52.

122. Schillebeeckx, *Christ*, 35.

123. Hilkert and Schreiter, *The Praxis of the Reign of God*, 64.

124. Schillebeeckx, *Christ: The Experience of Jesus as Lord*, 32.

125. Ibid.

126. Hilkert and Schreiter, *The Praxis of the Reign of God*, 188.

Mary Catherine Hilkert elaborates upon Schillebeeckx's preference for a narrative structure to human experience when she points out that a dialectic between perception and critical reflection coalesces into a narrative structure for explaining human experience. She points out that human experiences, and in particular surprising and new experiences, are best communicated through a narrative. These narratives, however, must be tested by critical reflection and through this critical reflection are vetted to bring out the truth therein.[127]

Schillebeeckx points out that we no longer have the narrative innocence of the ancient world. Our contemporary culture is shaped by historical sciences and historical-critical narratives that focus on factualness as opposed to a deeper truth. This leads Schillebeeckx to point out a two-step process in our contemporary understanding of narrative. On the one hand, without narrative innocence we need a critical acceptance of narratives that is facilitated by the historical sciences. This is because stories can veil real suffering and injustice that must be unveiled. On the other hand, human reason and our historical sciences do not have the ability to embrace the whole truth embodied by these stories. Thus, we must turn to the deeper truth within stories and parables that is captured through our narrative understandings.[128]

When Schillebeeckx applies the narrative structure of human experience to his understanding of Jesus the Christ, he comes to the conclusion that christology must come to fruition in a story or narrative rather than a universal christological system—he prefers narrative over abstract theory.[129] As John Galvin points out with regard to Schillebeeckx's option for narrative, a story is preferable to theory because theories domesticate and perpetuate suffering whereas stories preserve *dangerous memories*[130] and lead to a hope-filled consciousness and concrete action for a better world. This is why Galvin argues that for Schillebeeckx stories are "the only suitable vehicles of communication in a world where evil still

---

127. Ibid., 66.
128. Schillebeeckx, *Jesus*, 79.
129. Ibid.
130. This term comes from the work of Metz. A "dangerous memory" is one that remembers the atrocity of innocent suffering, interrupts the normal course of life, and thus makes demands upon the living to question any and all political structures, systems, and persons who have inflicted suffering upon others. See Metz, *Faith in History and Society,* 109–10. To illustrate, Metz writes, "every rebellion against suffering is fed by the subversive power of remembered suffering" (109).

abounds."[131] To this end Schillebeeckx observes that people tell stories about Jesus the Christ because they have really found some form of salvation from suffering and evil in him. If there were no salvation found in Jesus, there would not be any stories passed on about him.[132]

Suffering and Negative Experiences of Contrast

I have shown that Schillebeeckx understands human experience as interpreted, new and developing, and most adequately organized through narrative. I now turn to the center of Schillebeeckx's understanding of human experience, namely the experiences of human suffering—and in particular unjust suffering—and negative contrast experiences. For Schillebeeckx, the importance of the narrative structure of human experience is directly connected to the experiences of suffering. As he writes:

> People do not *argue* against suffering, but tell a *story* and make statements on the basis of experience without giving an 'explanation': simply because as Christians they look to the suffering and death of *Jesus*. It must have meaning, even if no one knows how or why; the essential presupposition is that suffering should not be made light of. Faith in Jesus as Christ is an 'answer' without arguments: a 'nevertheless'. Christianity does not give any explanation for suffering, but demonstrates a way of life. Suffering is destructively *real*, but it does not have the last word.[133]

Schillebeeckx, however, does not think that all experiences of human suffering are identical. Aloysius Rego highlights a distinction in Schillebeeckx's thought between meaningful and meaningless suffering.[134] For Schillebeeckx, not every form of human suffering is negative and destructive. On the one hand, Schillebeeckx thinks that suffering due to sinfulness, the experience of finitude, or suffering for a greater cause, are all forms of suffering that can be meaningful and constructive.[135] On the other hand,

---

131. See Hilkert and Schreiter, *The Praxis of the Reign of God*, 81.

132. Schillebeeckx, *Jesus*, 82–83. See also, Schillebeeckx, *On Christian Faith*.

133 Schillebeeckx, *Christ: The Experience of Jesus as Lord*, 698–99; italics original.

134 See Rego, *Suffering and Salvation*, 156–66. For a concise and illuminating treatment of Schillebeeckx's theology of human suffering, see McManus, "Suffering in the Theology of Edward Schillebeeckx," 476–91. McManus greatly expands upon this essay in her monograph, *Unbroken Communion*.

135. See, for example, Schillebeeckx, *Christ: The Experience of Jesus as Lord*, 724–25.

Schillebeeckx finds full negativity and no salvific value in experiences of unwarranted and radical suffering—meaningless suffering. "Experiences of meaningless suffering have a critical force because of the disturbing possibility that they may be repeated in the future; experiences of meaning, of love and joy, are meaningful only because they may be possibly established in the future, which is not automatically a given."[136]

In particular, this is the kind of human suffering that has its roots in oppressive and violent social and political systems. This is what Schillebeeckx calls a barbarous "excess of suffering and evil in our history."[137] Schillebeeckx describes this barbarous excess of suffering as that which is meaningless, beyond explanation, and nihilistic. It has no redemptive value and is fully destructive of the human person. To illustrate this point, he references horrors such as Auschwitz and Buchenwald. This senseless, nihilistic, and meaningless suffering is the focus of his theology of suffering. Schillebeeckx calls this kind of senseless suffering a mystery because its existence, prevalence, and persistence go beyond human ability to comprehend.[138]

One conceptual term that Schillebeeckx borrows from the Frankfurt School of Critical Theory and employs to expand upon these experiences of radical, innocent, and meaningless suffering, is *negative experiences of contrast*. These experiences possess a revelatory value because they unveil the inherent injustice in the world within the structures of human experience. Through this unveiling, a demand is brought to the fore that men and women must take action to resist the causes of this suffering and to work for human flourishing and liberation.[139]

Schillebeeckx adopts this concept because it embraces the full horror of innocent human suffering but does not seek to explain it away. It is a basic human experience that reveals the fundamental injustice in the world. It also constitutes a human protest against this injustice for

---

136. Ibid., 791–92.

137 Ibid., 725.

138 Ibid.

139 As Schreiter points out, this epistemological edge of the contrast experience critiques not only intellectual and technological prowess but also the social structures and human relationships that are based on these types of knowledge and cause suffering. This theological posture is skeptical of societal, practical, and intellectual paradigms that claim to fully account for the complexities of human experience and existence. Hilkert and Schreiter, *The Praxis of the Reign of God*, 186.

the purpose of realizing moments of fragmentary salvation.[140] These experiences of contrast confront humans with radical suffering and lead to experiences of conversion that Schillebeeckx argues are the deepest experiences humans can encounter. Through their radical negativity, they lead to a breaking down of an already established identity for the purposes of rebuilding and integrating a new and improved identity no longer blind to such injustices.[141]

The theological value of contrast experiences lies in their implication that human suffering remains a mystery. They serve the purpose of calling into question all that which makes humans suffer. In Schillebeeckx's estimation, these experiences are the pre-religious and most basic human experiences that are the closest that we can approach to a universal experience.[142] They reveal that there is something fundamentally wrong with the world due to the experience of radical suffering. Moreover, they constitute a human protest against radical suffering and evil for the purpose of realizing moments of fragmentary salvation.[143]

Schillebeeckx elaborates further upon the nature of contrast experiences with regard to their epistemological value in modern, Western, secularized cultures. He thinks that contrast experiences have an epistemological edge that critiques two types of modern knowledge, namely radically contemplative and technologically utilitarian. With regard to the former—which seeks knowledge as an end in itself—Schillebeeckx argues that innocent suffering defies logic and theory. Theoretical knowledge loses its voice when faced with the harsh reality of evil, sin and suffering because it finds the pure irrationality of evil unintelligible.

---

140. Schillebeeckx, *Church*, 5–6. See also *Christ: The Experience of Jesus as Lord*, 831–38.

141. Schillebeeckx, *On Christian Faith*, 48. This process of having one's identity deconstructed and reconstructed through contrast experience is similar to Schillebeeckx's description of traditional mystical experience. Instead of direct contact with the experience of unjust suffering, however, the mystical experience is a "cognitive union with God" that breaks one's identity so it can be transformed. Obviously, in Schillebeeckx's work experience of God and experience of (suffering) humankind are always connected. See *On Christian Faith*, 65–70; and *Church*, 70–80.

142. This does not mean that negative experiences of contrast are uninterpreted. Like all human experience, for Schillebeeckx, experiences of suffering and negative contrast are also interpreted experiences.

143. Schillebeeckx, *Church*, 5–6. Schillebeeckx also mentions that "For Christians, the experience of contrast, with its inherent opposition to injustice and its perspective on something better, becomes that in which the unity of history comes about as God's gift" (6).

Regarding the latter—the goal-oriented knowledge of science and technology—Schillebeeckx argues that it has no ethical vision because it is only concerned with humankind's ability to master and manipulate its surroundings. Thus, when faced with the reality of evil and suffering it loses its voice. It has no capacity to judge whether or not an action is just or moral.[144] To this end, Schillebeeckx writes:

> As an experience of contrast, the experience of suffering is possible only on the basis of an implicit longing for happiness, an unjust suffering at least presupposes a vague awareness of the possible positive significance of human integrity. As an experience of contrast it indirectly implies an awareness of the positive call of the *humanum* and to the *humanum* . . . In contrast to the *purposive* knowledge of science and technology and the '*aimless*' knowledge of contemplation, the particular experience of contrast in suffering is a knowledge which looks for the *future* and opens it up.[145]

He concludes, "Therefore the experience of contrast in suffering is the negative and dialectical awareness of a longing for and a question of meaning in the future, real freedom and real happiness to come."[146]

The Humanum and the Seven Anthropological Constants

Schillebeeckx's general understanding of human experience, as well as his more concrete foundation of experience in suffering and negative contrast, is not an end in itself. Schillebeeckx's ultimate concern is God's salvation for human beings who suffer, especially those who undergo negative, meaningless, radically destructive experiences of suffering. This means that Schillebeeckx's understanding of human experience points to a vision of human salvation. Two of the tools that he employs to clarify this vision are the *humanum* and the seven *anthropological constants*.[147]

---

144. Schillebeeckx, *Jesus*, 620–21.

145. Schillebeeckx, *Christ: The Experience of Jesus as Lord*, 818.

146. Ibid., 819.

147. Although Schillebeeckx's concepts of the *humanum* and seven *anthropological constants* offer a glimpse and reference point for what God's final salvation for humankind might look like, they remain only informed speculation. Schillebeeckx points out that we do not have precise or definitive information as to what form eschatological salvation will take. He writes, "[T]o give any positive content to what definitive salvation will be is to run the risk of either human megalomania or a trivialization of God's

Schillebeeckx borrows the term *humanum* from the Frankfurt School of Critical Theory. It is a term that points to the fullness of humanity, its wholeness, healing, and reconciliation, that is present in fragments and is always endangered.[148] As Schreiter points out, it evokes the full humanity that we anticipate and act to bring about but that won't be achieved on this side of eternity. This is because the fullness of humanity is achieved only partially and is always threatened.[149] The humanum is the *telos* to which human experience is oriented and also implies a way of describing the relationship between God and human experience. That is, a God who is mindful of humanity and who self-reveals within the structures of human experience for the always endangered humanum. This same God who is revealed in Jesus who we profess as Christ relays that the "cause of Jesus is the cause of man" which is also the cause of God.[150] Eschatologically-oriented but historically-situated, our humanum is a horizon that Schillebeeckx links to the gospel commandments of love of God and love of neighbor. It is a fragmentary realization of human liberation and flourishing in history that includes bringing about right relationships, ending injustice and suffering, and struggling to realize human dignity and liberation.[151]

The humanum and human wholeness, however, are not self-evident and self-explanatory concepts. Nor are they concrete. Thus, Schillebeeckx offers a set of coordinates through which one can glimpse what the humanum, and God's final salvation for humankind, may look like. This is through a matrix of seven *anthropological constants*. It is important to point out that for Schillebeeckx, these are constants and not universals. That is, they seem to be common, observable human characteristics that cross cultures to some extent and that constitute part of a shared human

---

possibilities." See *On Christian Faith*, 64. See also *Christ: The Experience of Jesus as Lord*, 791–92.

148. Schillebeeckx, *On Christian Faith*, 29–30. In *Christ: The Experience of Jesus as Lord*, Schillebeeckx writes, "The *humanum*, threatened and in fact, damaged, leads specifically and historically to ethical demand and the ethical imperative, and thus to confrontation with quite definite, negative experiences of contrast. Therefore, ethical invitation or demand is not an abstract norm but, historically, an event *which presents a challenge*: our concrete history itself, men in need, mankind in need" (659).

149. Schreiter, "Edward Schillebeeckx," 155–57.

150. Schillebeeckx, *Jesus*, 606–7.

151. Ibid., 606–7. For three metaphors that offer signs for what the eschatological *humanum* may look like, see *On Christian Faith*, 29–30. For an expansion of these into four metaphors, see *Church*, 133–34.

experience and life. They are a set of coordinates, or a matrix, that sheds light upon what the humanum may look like. As Schillebeeckx argues, these constants are:

1. Relationship of human beings to their embodied experience and to their ecological context.
2. Relationship of human beings to one another.
3. Relationship of the individual person to social structures.
4. Contextualization of human beings by time and space.
5. Intrinsic relationship between theory and practice in being human.
6. The religious dimension of human consciousness.
7. The synthesis of the previous six constants into human culture that is healing and liberating.[152]

When put into dialogue with the concept of the humanum, these anthropological constants are aspects of the human person that need attention in order to momentarily realize the humanum. This also provides a guide for what the fullness of the humanum will look like in the eschaton.

Foundation: God of Pure Positivity Revealed in Jesus the Christ

The correlate of human experience within Schillebeeckx's soteriology is his distinctive understanding of the Christian God: a God of *pure positivity*. To briefly clarify Schillebeeckx's understanding of the Christian God, there are two aspects that are most pertinent to this chapter on soteriology: God as Creator and God as definitively revealed in the career, death, and resurrection of Jesus of Nazareth as One who is mindful of humanity who does not want humankind to suffer.

The importance of God as Creator cannot be overemphasized in the voluminous writings of Schillebeeckx. Phillip Kennedy has highlighted this fact and terms it a *creation faith* that is the "oxygen and lifeblood" of Schillebeeckx's theology.[153] Kennedy argues, "Edward Schillebeeckx regards

---

152. Schillebeeckx, *Christ: The Experience of Jesus as Lord*, 731–44. For an earlier articulation of the constants, see *The Language of Faith*, 113–22.

153. Hilkert and Schreiter, *The Praxis of the Reign of God*, 37. Although Kennedy treats Schillebeeckx's theology, and in particular his understanding of creation, at greater length in his monograph *Edward Schillebeeckx*, this provides a concise and

belief in creation as the bedrock of Christian theology."[154] Mary Catherine Hilkert agrees when she writes that for Schillebeeckx "The absolute creative and saving presence of God pervades all of creation, holding it in being and empowering it to achieve its destiny."[155] Schillebeeckx's foundation of God as Creator gives his entire theological project a specific orientation, although it often remains implicit. As Schillebeeckx writes, "Creation is ultimately the meaning that God has wanted to give to his divine life. He wanted, freely, also to be God for others, and expected them, with their finite free will, which was also open to other possibilities, to accept his offer. Otherwise, I do not understand at all why he, God, resolved to take the final precarious decision of creating human beings."[156]

Kennedy correctly observes that Schillebeeckx's understanding of God is that of pure positivity: that is, pure, gratuitous, free creation.[157] For example, Schillebeeckx goes so far as to call God the extreme luxury of our lives.[158] In a secularizing, Western culture Schillebeeckx thinks that it is unintelligible to claim that humans need God (or, more specifically,

---

adequate explication of the importance of creation in Schillebeeckx's thought. The foundation for much of this work is his doctoral dissertation *Deus Humanissimus*. For a helpful and more in-depth analysis of the theme of creation in Schillebeeckx's thought, and its connection to salvation, see Steele, "Creation and Cross in the Later Soteriology of Edward Schillebeeckx," 295–348. For example, Steele observes that in Schillebeeckx's understanding that from God's perspective there is no distinction between creation and salvation in that they comprise "one divine activity," whereas from the creature's perspective the two are distinct and separate. See page 335.

154. Hilkert and Schreiter, *The Praxis of the Reign of God*, 57. Kennedy points out four basic contours in Schillebeeckx's understanding of the Christian God, the Creator: God of pure positivity, God as absolute freedom, God's intrinsic connection to the future of humankind and creation, and the humanity of God. I do not have time to explore each of these contours. They are intertwined, however, and greatly influence my discussion of Schillebeeckx's theology of God. Also, Schillebeeckx's understanding of the "humanity of God" should not be confused with Karl Barth's famous, later essay, "The Humanity of God." Barth continued to emphasize God as "Wholly Other," in that God's humanity is revealed through God's divinity. See "The Humanity of God," 46–66.

155. Boeve, *Edward Schillebeeckx and Contemporary Theology*, 135. See also Hilkert's reflections on how this "creation faith" affects Schillebeeckx's spirituality in "'Grace Optimism.'"

156 Schillebeeckx, *Church*, 232.

157. Hilkert and Schreiter, *The Praxis of the Reign of God*, 55.

158. Schillebeeckx, *On Christian Faith*, 5–6. Godzieba provides a constructive appropriation and insightful transcendental critique of Schillebeeckx's claim that God is not "needed" and is a "luxury." See Boeve, *Edward Schillebeeckx and Contemporary Theology*, 25–35.

particular images of God).[159] Rather, he thinks that the Christian God is the One who creates through absolute freedom and love. Schillebeeckx thinks this Creator God is the primary reference point for understanding salvation, as well as our relationship to God. As he writes:

> [T]he Jewish-Christian tradition defines God as pure positivity; in other words, it rejects all names and images of God which injure and enslave human beings instead of liberating them. Precisely in this concept of pure positivity we maintain the transcendence of God, for we do not know what God ultimately is and what the *humanum,* humanity, can ultimately be, and reserve this for God; or rather, that is God's own divine proviso on all our thought, action, and reflection.[160]

Schillebeeckx thinks that one fruit of understanding God as Creator is a human surplus of hope.[161] Christians retain an excess of hope that good will ultimately prevail and evil will be vanquished despite all evidence to the contrary. As he writes, "For the believer, this surplus of hope over against what has already been realized in history is based on what we call God's creation for the purpose of salvation: God's absolute saving presence in what He has called to life."[162] In other words, the Christian God is a God of Life and not death; a God who seeks justice, reconciliation, peace, and ultimate *shalom* for the living and the dead.[163] This means that only goodness has a future. In a concrete way, sin and evil have no eschatological future. Apart from the goodness and life that have a future in God, the only future that sin and evil have, when completely alienated from God is annihilation and nonexistence.[164]

Second, Schillebeeckx thinks this saving, creator God is revealed definitively, but not exhaustively, in the person, career, death, and

---

159. Schillebeeckx, *On Christian Faith,* 4–9. See also *Church:,* 66–68, 99–101.

160. Schillebeeckx, *Church,* 75–76.

161. See, for example, Schillebeeckx, *Church,* 99. See also, Schillebeeckx, *Interim Report,* 121–24.

162. Schillebeeckx, *On Christian Faith,* 64–65.

163. For example, Schillebeeckx writes, "For the Christian experiential tradition, only a 'God of Life', not a God of life and death; only a living God—a God of the living and dead, who still know a future in him—can be worshipped, revered and celebrated by men and women; not a God who diminishes men and women and hurts them or keeps them under and deprives them of their joys" (*Church,* 33). See also, Schillebeeckx, *Interim Report,* 120.

164. Schillebeeckx, *Church,* 134–39. This is what Schillebeeckx calls the "asymmetry" between good and evil, particularly in an eschatological sense.

resurrection of Jesus of Nazareth. To this end, Schillebeeckx often calls Jesus of Nazareth, who Christians confess as Christ, "parable of God" and "paradigm of humanity."[165] The historical person, Jesus of Nazareth, definitively reveals who God is while also revealing what humankind ultimately can be. This flows from Schillebeeckx's theological foundation in creation. As Kennedy points out, for Schillebeeckx Jesus the Christ is "concentrated creation." Kennedy argues, "For Schillebeeckx, Christology is a way of rendering belief in creation more intelligible, by explaining it in relation to human history in general and the story of Jesus' life in particular. If Christian belief regards creation as the beginning of salvation, then to speak of Christology as concentrated creation is to emphasize that redemption offered by God the Creator is manifested, or condensed, in the man Jesus."[166]

Schillebeeckx's firm belief in the creator God of pure positivity leads him to focus upon the experiences of the earliest disciples with the life, death, and resurrection of Jesus of Nazareth. In short, their encounter with Jesus was an experience of salvation and divine life. Schillebeeckx observes:

> [T]hat it began with an encounter between the man Jesus and his fellow men. Salvation from God is revealed in the encounter of Jesus with his fellow men. Encounter, salvation and happiness are experiential concepts. They are not so much argued about, as narrated in a history which summons men to a critical and liberating way of life.[167]

As stated earlier, the location of Schillebeeckx's soteriology is the human experience of God's salvation in the person of Jesus of Nazareth. In a historical context saturated with unjust suffering and violence, the residents of first-century, Roman-occupied, Jewish Palestine truly experienced salvation (i.e., redemption and liberation), through interaction with Jesus of Nazareth. To this end, Schillebeeckx writes,

> this is a distinctive feature of Christianity: the God of all men and women shows in Jesus of Nazareth who he is, namely universal love for men and women. Jesus Christ is the historical, culturally located expression of this universal message of the

---

165. This phrase can be found in several locations in Schillebeeckx's writings. See, for example, *Jesus*, 626; *The Language of Faith*, 106; and In *God among Us*, 18.

166. Hilkert and Schreiter, *The Praxis of the Reign of God*, 53.

167. Schillebeeckx, *Christ: The Experience of Jesus as Lord*, 638.

gospel. Thus Christianity does have the intention of identifying God: that is its distinctiveness. For Christians, Jesus is the definition of God; otherwise, their Christology makes no sense.[168]

It is within this context that Schillebeeckx makes the claim that humankind is saved not because of the cross but despite the cross.[169] It must be pointed out, however, that this is not a rigid, isolated, claim. It is a nuanced claim in which Schillebeeckx interprets the crucifixion of Jesus of Nazareth as a historical fiasco and the work of an oppressive and violent system claiming another victim. The crucifixion, for Schillebeeckx, was not God's will. Rather, it was a human rejection of God and a thwarting of the fact that God does not want humankind to suffer.

Schillebeeckx carefully nuances his claim of salvation despite the cross by keeping it in context with the career and lifestyle of Jesus of Nazareth, and in particular his Resurrection. He argues that through the resurrection God has corrected and overcome the negativity, injustice, and evil of the crucifixion. Schillebeeckx observes that even though humankind is saved despite the death of Jesus, salvation is related to Jesus' death. This is because God transcends and overcomes the negativity and suffering of Jesus' death through the Resurrection. This is God's demonstration that suffering and evil have ultimately been undone through God's corrective and re-creative action. Through the resurrection, God has demonstrated and promised that suffering, evil, and negativity will not have the final word. Rather, that word will belong to the God of life, goodness, and pure positivity.[170] As he writes, ". . . not only the life, the message and the lifestyle of Jesus, but also his death in the context of his whole life, have a saving significance, a redemptive and reconciling value for Christians."[171]

One the one hand, Schillebeeckx thinks that the cross in itself does not save humankind. God does not will humankind to suffer and God does not send Jesus to the cross to pay for the sins of humankind.

---

168. Schillebeeckx, *Church*, 179.

169. Schillebeeckx, *Christ: The Experience of Jesus as Lord*, 729. See also *Church*, 120–29. For an innovative engagement with Schillebeeckx on this topic, see Mosely, "Salvation despite the Death of Jesus?" Mosely brings Schillebeeckx's soteriology of the cross into dialogue with womanist theologians M. Shawn Copeland and Delores Williams who share theological opinions similar to Schillebeeckx with regard to the salvific value of the cross, although they arrive at different conclusions.

170. Schillebeeckx, *Christ: The Experience of Jesus as Lord*, 729–30.

171. Ibid., 632–33.

Humankind demanded and carried out Jesus' execution, not God. Death, and in particular a violent, unjust, painful death, is destructive, nihilistic, and negative. It has no positivity, no creative power, and no hope. As Derek Simon points out, "Isolating the death of Jesus from his life-praxis results in misrepresenting its redemptive significance in terms of a bloody and even sadistic sacrifice; it renders the interpretation of God's redemptive activity in Jesus liable to mythopoetic distortion."[172]

On the other hand, Schillebeeckx thinks that the crucifixion and death of Jesus retains importance in envisioning human salvation. Jesus' execution is a fact of history and at the foundation of Christian faith and practice that cannot be discarded or ignored. In human terms, Jesus was a failure. His violent death was human judgment upon his message and lifestyle. In his rejection and execution, he was a historical failure.[173] But it is an atrocity that is transcended and overcome by God. God triumphs over suffering and evil despite all evidence to the contrary.

Schillebeeckx gives priority to the Resurrection—God's corrective, life-giving, and re-creative action within human history—because God is a God who wills humankind to life and happiness, or salvation. God seeks the redemption of sinners and the liberation of the sinned-against into a new creation and wholeness of being. As Schillebeeckx writes, "God wants *men's salvation*, and in it victory over their suffering."[174] The cross, on its own, cannot reveal this about the Christian God. The cross is a miscarriage of justice that results in the violent rejection of Jesus of Nazareth and the failure of his ministry. Again, deferring here to Simon, Schillebeeckx thinks, "The death of Jesus on the cross as a criminal signals his definitive rejection of an apocalyptic vengeance on oppressors that would heal human history through a divinely inaugurated or sanctioned violence."[175]

Therefore, the most precise definition that Schillebeeckx allows for how salvation is connected to the crucifixion is: "Jesus belonging to

---

172. Simon, "Salvation and Liberation," 502.

173. For Schillebeeckx's discussion of Jesus as failure, yet still savior, see *Christ: The Experience of Jesus as Lord*, 822–32.

174 Ibid., 730; italics original.

175. Simon, "Salvation and Liberation in the Practical-Critical Soteriology of Edward Schillebeeckx," 502. Simon goes on to point out that, for Schillebeeckx, "Within the death of Jesus, God's solidarity with all the violated and vanquished is disclosed. Schillebeeckx therefore maintains that, in his dying and death, Jesus discloses how the practice of love and justice retain their intrinsic value, even when they end in absurd failure and do not tangibly eliminate or reverse the suffering of others" (503).

God in an anti-godly situation serves to affect our salvation."[176] Schillebeeckx is wary of overly precise soteriological formulations because they reduce the horror of Jesus' death and the mystery of human salvation to a mechanical metaphysics of the crucified. This sort of formulation de-emphasizes Jesus' life and the disciples' Easter experiences. Therefore, Schillebeeckx shifts the emphasis in his soteriology and Christology away from an exclusive focus upon Jesus' crucifixion and asks that we keep the cross in context. Schillebeeckx thinks that the cross does indeed have salvific value. But it is not a good in itself and it has no beauty.[177] It is only a good when understood in the entire life story of Jesus as God's definitive self-revelation and the hope-filled story of God's loving salvation.

This Christian Creator God who is revealed definitively in the life, death, and resurrection of Jesus of Nazareth is, for Schillebeeckx, One who is mindful of humanity and who does not want humankind to suffer. The one and the same God who is the God of creation is in solidarity with those who are poor, oppressed, and who suffer innocently. As he writes, "For the name of God is 'the one who shows solidarity with his people', and this people suffers."[178] In this way, Christians are to follow the example of Jesus in being "aware that [we] act as God would do" and thus "translate God's actions to human beings."[179] As Schillebeeckx observes:

> In this sense, Christianity is a radically committed love which cannot justify itself, which has again and again to transcend its achievement in this world and which has again and again to give itself away in profound darkness in a self-emptying which often seems to be in vain in this world, but which is nonetheless so radical that it is precisely in this giving away of itself for the benefit of others that the very essence of the kingdom of God breaks through into our world.[180]

---

176. Schillebeeckx, *Jesus*, 652.

177. This is true at least in reference to Balthasar's theological aesthetics. See *The Glory of the Lord: A Theological Aesthetics*, vol. 1: *Seeing the Form*. For a reflection on Schillebeeckx and aesthetics, see Schreiter, "Schillebeeckx and Theology in the Twenty-First Century," 262–63.

178. Schillebeeckx, *Christ: The Experience of Jesus as Lord*, 640.

179. Schillebeeckx, *The Church with a Human Face*, 21.

180. *The Schillebeeckx Reader*, 253–54.

Encountering and Envisioning: Mediated Immediacy and Fragments of Salvation

The fourth aspect of Schillebeeckx's soteriology that I will discuss is the way that human beings encounter and envision God's salvation through Jesus: *mediated immediacy* and *fragments of salvation*. Regarding the former, human salvation is from God through Jesus Christ. This means that human beings truly experience salvation in their relationship with God, as did the first disciples with Jesus of Nazareth. Schillebeeckx describes the way in which human beings encounter salvation in relationship to God through mediated immediacy (which he also connects to the *theologal life* or the *mystical-political* dimension of Christianity). Schillebeeckx did not coin this term—others such as Karl Rahner use it—but for Schillebeeckx it most adequately represents the way in which human beings truly encounter salvation from the God of Jesus Christ.

Mediated immediacy is based upon the fact that human beings are contingent, finite creations of the infinite, absolutely free Creator.[181] Schillebeeckx, however, understands contingency and finitude neither as punishment nor as the result of a fallen world. Rather, he thinks that finitude and contingency mean that human beings are not God. As Kennedy observes, "... central to Schillebeeckx's understanding of creation is the conviction that a creature's finitude is neither a flaw nor a mistake. Creaturely contingency simply implies that a creature is not divine ... they are simply not God."[182] Creation is good and this means that the way in which God created humankind and the universe—as finite and contingent—is good. Schillebeeckx writes, "... this belief means that we do not need altogether to transcend our contingent or finite nature and to escape from it or regard it as a flaw. We may and must simply be human beings in a living world which is simply the world: fascinating, but also mortal, failing and suffering. To want to transcend finitude is megalomania or arrogance which alienates people from themselves, from the world, from nature."[183] He continues and argues:

> [B]elief in God the creator does not remove the finitude nor does it distort it into sinfulness or fallenness. It has this finitude taken up into the presence of God, without relieving the world and man of their finitude or regarding these as hostile ... from a

181. See Schillebeeckx, *Church*, 229–34.
182. Hilkert and Schreiter, *The Praxis of the Reign of God*, 49.
183. Schillebeeckx, *God among Us*, 93.

Christian perspective, the world and man are totally other than God, but within the presence of the creator God. Therefore this other-than-God can never emigrate from the divine act of creation; in other words, God remains in and with the contingent, other-than-God—the world in its nature as world, and mankind in its autonomous but finite humanity.[184]

The facts of contingency and finitude are at the foundation of mediated immediacy. This concept implies an ongoing encounter with the Living God revealed in Jesus Christ.[185] In short, Schillebeeckx thinks that our encounters of salvation from God are always mediated through creation. This is because the relationship is asymmetrical: "what we have here is not an inter-subjective relationship between two persons—two mortal men—but a mutual relationship between a finite person and his absolute origin, the infinite God. And that has an effect on our relationship with God."[186] Schillebeeckx points out that the boundary is on the human side, not the divine side. For God, the relationship is fully immediate but for humankind it is always mediated, though remaining immediate.[187] As he writes, "The fact that in this case the unmistakable mediation produces immediacy, instead of destroying it, is connected with the absolute or divine manner of the real presence of God: he makes himself directly and creatively present in the medium, that is, in ourselves, our neighbors, the world and history. This is the deepest immediacy I know."[188]

---

184. Ibid. For example, Schillebeeckx writes, "The basic mistake made by many misconceptions about creation lies in the fact that finitude is regarded as a wound, something which need not really have been and is part of clinging to the things of the world. People then begin to seek a separate cause of this finitude and find it in some dark power of evil or in some kind of primal sin. In other words, finitude is identified with the improper, with an evil, even with a sinfulness or apostasy, a wound in the existence of man and the world . . . Accurate reading will show that the Genesis story represents a protest precisely against ideas of this kind, albeit in mythical terms. If God is creator, then he creates that which is not divine, all that is other than he himself is, in other words, finite things. Creatures are not copies of God," *Interim Report*, 113. For more on Schillebeeckx's understanding of contingency and finitude, see chapter 5, "By Way of an Epilogue," in *Church* and see *Interim Report*, 112–24. Also see page 58 of Hilkert and Schreiter, *The Praxis of the Reign of God*, for a more comprehensive list of sources for Schillebeeckx on creation.

185. Schillebeeckx, *Christ: The Experience of Jesus as Lord*, 815.

186. Ibid., 809.

187. Schillebeeckx, *On Christian Faith*, 66–67.

188. Schillebeeckx, *Christ: The Experience of Jesus as Lord*, 809.

This means that God is immediate to us, but due to human finitude God's presence is always interpreted through the concrete structures of human experience and through the created world. There is no direct experience of God, so to speak. This is because there is a boundary between Creator and creature, from the human side, that cannot be breached. For Schillebeeckx, this mediation of God's presence even includes the recorded experiences of immediate encounters with the divine described by mystics such as Meister Eckhart, John Ruysbroeck, and John of the Cross.[189]

Schillebeeckx connects mediated immediacy to salvation and writes, "'mediated immediacy' seems to me to be the most appropriate way of expressing the mystery of God as the salvation of man."[190] It is an expression of the human encounter with the infinite God who continually offers liberation from being sinned-against and redemption from sinning. Schillebeeckx connects this concept to *extra mundum nulla salus* in that salvation from God for humankind emerges through human mediation in concrete history. This also means that human beings are the source of much of the disastrous suffering in the world through a lack of embracing such a mediating, sacramental, role.[191] Schillebeeckx writes, "There is no encounter with God (whether faith or sin) which is not mediated through an encounter with the world as it is. It is therefore always dangerous to talk of sin in term of a human rejection of God or as sin against God, if we do not at the same time indicate where this rejection also damages our humanity."[192]

Regarding the latter—envisioning salvation as fragmentary—Schillebeeckx argues that even though salvation from God for humankind is truly realized and experienced within history and society, it remains an unfinished work in a finite and contingent world. It is salvation whose incompleteness anticipates the arrival of complete and ultimate salvation with God's full consummation of human history.

Derek Simon offers a helpful description of this through what he calls Schillebeeckx's *practical-critical* soteriology. For Simon, the term

---

189. Schillebeeckx, *Church*, 70–71.

190. Schillebeeckx, *Christ: The Experience of Jesus as Lord*, 809. Schillebeeckx goes on to give an extensive analysis of this concept on the subsequent pages, 810–17. For example, he concludes, "Christianity without God is the end of all Christianity. True, one can neither avoid mediation, but *in* this mediation God himself really comes near to us in salvation. Here, the initiative is utterly his" (814).

191 Schillebeeckx, *Church*, 162.

192. Ibid., 92.

practical-critical is a praxis that connotes a focus on progressive social and political movements for human emancipation within a history saturated with suffering, along with a related task of the interpretation of the promises for fragments of salvation within society here and now.[193] The foundation of this practical-critical soteriology, however, is its fragmentary nature. As Simon points out:

> Historical praxes of emancipation, however fragile or incomplete, are fragments of salvation, the contingent yet real immanence of eschatological salvation in history. Schillebeeckx argues that historical praxes of sociopolitical liberation render the encounter with and response to eschatological salvation from God in Jesus both historically available and intelligible, as well as communicable if not believable.[194]

Simon points out that these fragments of salvation are concrete within history and society. He observes that, for Schillebeeckx, concrete social and political movements can indeed mediate God's saving activity of liberation. This liberation is incomplete, but it is true liberation and also opens up a positive and life-giving future for those who suffer.[195] Any and all movements that seek human healing, liberation, and empowerment in contexts of excessive and unwarranted suffering, in effect, actualize moments of fragmentary salvation from God within the world.[196]

For Schillebeeckx, there is an eschatological proviso and an eschatological surplus connected to the salvific value found in human movements for emancipation and healing. In other words, fragments of salvation remain unfinished due to an eschatological proviso while also holding the possibility of being completely and even excessively fulfilled by God in ways unimaginable to human beings due to an eschatological surplus. They remain fragmentary not only due to the contingency of creation, and the fact that no one political position or movement can be interpreted as fully identical with God's salvation for humankind, but also due to the fact that God's overwhelming and excessive salvation and grace are always more than humankind can ever imagine.[197] Schillebeeckx

---

193. Simon, "Provisional Liberations, Fragments of Salvation," 80.

194. Simon, "Salvation and Liberation," 520. A much more detailed study of Schillebeeckx's understanding of salvation and liberation as "fragmentary" is found in Simon, "Provisional Liberations, Fragments of Salvation."

195. Simon, "Salvation and Liberation," 495–96.

196 Ibid., 514.

197. Ibid., 515, 517. See also Schillebeeckx, *On Christian Faith*.

thinks that even though we have clues and informed speculation, human beings ultimately do not know what full salvation from God through Jesus Christ will look like. We have fragments that make present, point to, and anticipate this full salvation to come. As Simon argues, "Sociopolitical liberations are necessary but transient fragments of salvation."[198] Moreover, the critical power of fragments of salvation resides in the hope that they engender anticipation of the ultimate arrival of God's full salvation for humankind, for both sinners and sinned-against.[199]

To illustrate how salvation is fragmentary, Schillebeeckx argues that God's ultimate offer of salvation to all men and women is universal. God's (and humankind's) goal is the true and concrete manifestation of redemption for sinners and liberation for the sinned-against to redeem all humankind and creation.[200] This universal offer of salvation, however, ". . . is not a purely speculative, theoretical universality, but a universality which can be realized in the fragmentary forms of our history only through the spreading of the story of Jesus confessed by Christians as the Christ, and through Christian praxis . . . But, without fragments there is no total salvation!"[201] Schillebeeckx's understanding of God is of One whose Reign is already breaking into history and society, albeit fragmentarily.

In short, the only experiences human beings have of final salvation are fragmentary and are variously interpreted as meaningful or meaningless. This limit imposed upon life and history by human finitude can be rescued from the abyss of nihilism and meaninglessness by the critical activity of negative experiences of contrast. This same God who is revealed in Jesus whom we profess as Christ relays that the cause of Jesus is the cause of man which is also the cause of God.[202] As Schillebeeckx observes, ". . . the desire for a full and liveable humanity is more alive in humanity as a desire than at any other time, and that in our time the answer to it becomes all the more pressing the more we note on the one hand that people fail, fall short and are above all at a disadvantage, and on the other hand that we are already able to experience fragments of human healing and liberation."[203] He continues, "it is becoming clear more than

---

198. Simon, "Salvation and Liberation," 518.
199. Ibid., 520.
200. Schillebeeckx, *Church*, 176.
201. Ibid.
202. Schillebeeckx, *Jesus*, 606–7.
203. Schillebeeckx, *Christ: The Experience of Jesus as Lord*, 790; italics mine.

ever that human history is the place where the healing or salvation of man will be decided, and people are now explicitly aware of this."[204]

Schillebeeckx links his understanding of a fragmentary, eschatologically-oriented salvation to his Christology. For Schillebeeckx, even Jesus did not have a fully-developed understanding of ultimate human salvation. Instead, Jesus had a fleeting vision of the perfect eschaton and oriented his own life to reflect this vision and thus showed fragmentary actions to reveal this final salvation.[205] Examples of Jesus' fragmentary actions of salvation were his miracles, healings, and exorcisms. As Kathleen McManus observes, Jesus' miracles are experiences of divine grace and a lifting of burdens and the deepening of life's meaning; they are concrete and *metanoia*-oriented signs of God's concern for salvation that showed a true and real possibility for human salvation from sin and suffering.[206] Based on this historical reality, Jesus' example should give us hope. Any and all practices of doing good in society have permanent validity because of Jesus' *a priori* fragmentary actions that were meant to reveal and to bring about good in society.[207] In other words, humans should look to Jesus to understand their fragmentary salvation but they will only be able to understand this in the form of an eschatological mystery.[208]

Four Elements for Intercultural Dialogue from Schillebeeckx's Soteriology

The preceding discussion of Schillebeeckx's soteriology has focused upon four main aspects of Schillebeeckx's soteriology: definition, location, foundation, and encountering/envisioning. I have provided a rough sketch of the broad vision of Schillebeeckx's understanding of salvation from God through Jesus Christ through these guideposts.[209] The four elements that

204. Ibid., 791.
205. Ibid.
206. McManus, *Unbroken Communion*, 91.
207. Schillebeeckx, *Christ: The Experience of Jesus as Lord*, 791.
208. Ibid.

209. These elements are similar to, but not identical with, the four points of continuing significance of Schillebeeckx's work pointed out by Schreiter: an inductive method, the importance of narrative in articulating human experience, a central concern for human suffering and experiences of contrast, and the primacy of soteriology over Christology. See Hilkert and Schreiter, *The Praxis of the Reign of God*, 185–94. For an expansion upon his reflections in this essay almost eight years later, see Boeve, *Edward Schillebeeckx and Contemporary Theology*, 252–64. See also Schreiter, "The Relevance of Professor Edward Schillebeeckx, O.P. for the Twenty-First Century."

I have discussed are not the only possible points of dialogue for Korean-American theologies of *han*. Nevertheless, I think that these elements may be the most fruitful for the intercultural dialogue that will occur in chapter 5, the point of which is to begin to envision a supplementary account of the effects of sin upon the sinned-against creature, to address the relative inadequacy in the anthropology and soteriology of *Gaudium et spes*.

Such an intercultural dialogue with Korean-American theologies of *han*, however, is precarious in many ways. The message of *han* and God's salvation for humankind through Jesus can be distorted, sometimes beyond recognition, in the intercultural encounter. Thus, it is important to carefully lay out a method for responsibly undertaking the task of bringing Schillebeeckx's soteriology into dialogue with the theologies of *han*. The point of such a method is to minimize distortion and maximize the mutually-critical and mutually-informing possibilities of the conversation for each dialogue partner. For this particular study, the point of this method is to responsibly apprehend, engage, and theologically interpret *han* across a cultural-linguistic boundary and into Roman Catholic soteriological discourse as represented by *Gaudium et spes* and the work of Schillebeeckx. It is to a description of this method for envisioning and commencing this intercultural dialogue that I now turn.

3

Theological Method: Intercultural Hermeneutics and the Semiotics of Culture

IN THE PREVIOUS CHAPTER, I discussed the soteriology of Edward Schillebeeckx. After an overview of Schillebeeckx's basic theological concerns and trajectory, I arrived at four elements within his soteriology that may provide fruitful points of dialogue with Korean and Korean-American theologies of *han*: the definition, location, foundation and encountering/envisioning of God's salvation for humankind. Before engaging in an examination of and dialogue with Korean and Korean-American theologies of *han*, however, I must discuss the methodological apparatus that will make this dialogue possible. In this chapter, I will discuss the method to be used in advancing my thesis: intercultural hermeneutics and the semiotics of culture. This method will enable me to bring *han* into constructive, intercultural dialogue with Schillebeeckx's soteriology and the broader trajectory of *Gaudium et spes*'s relatively inadequate anthropology and soteriology.

I will proceed with this chapter in four sections. Section One will discuss the fundamental category that functions at the heart of this method: *culture*. First, I will briefly discuss the way that cultural anthropologist Clifford Geertz envisions culture and the reason for studying it. Then, I will discuss three understandings of culture—classicist, modern, and globalized—and I will make clear which understanding of culture (globalized) I am adopting in my argument.

In Section Two, having clarified my understanding of culture, I will briefly address the semiotics of culture, primarily through the work of Robert Schreiter and Alejandro Garcia-Rivera. This semiotic approach will account for the way in which I am conceiving the cultural boundary between my own context and that in which *han* has been articulated. Second, I will discuss the means by which to listen to culture. I will discuss the three aspects of a culture that must be attended to in a semiotic understanding in its holistic, globalized sense.

In Section Three, I will discuss the field of intercultural hermeneutics. First, I will discuss the terminology describing this field. Second, I will offer three general understandings of intercultural hermeneutics from the work of Robert J. Schreiter—universalist, particularist, and oppositional. I will make clear which understanding of intercultural hermeneutics (particularist) I am adopting in my argument. Third, I will discuss the four possible locations from which one can approach the semiotic boundary for an intercultural communication event—inner-speaker, inner-hearer, outer-speaker, and outer-hearer—through the work of Schreiter and Garcia-Rivera. I will use this fourfold distinction to define my own location and context as the outer-hearer (the one who stands outside the culture of the speaker and who is attempting to receive, interpret, and translate the message) and the articulators of *han* as the inner-speaker (the one who initiates, creates, and sends the message).

In Section Four, I will address the problem of communication distortion. This is because the problem of distortion, misappropriation, or violation of the message as it crosses the cultural boundary is a risk to be acknowledged. To do this, I will discuss the idea of *intercultural communication competence*. Without some measure of intercultural communication competence, the likelihood of a distortion, misinterpretation, or misappropriation of *han* by an outer-hearer like myself becomes highly likely.

I will conclude this chapter with a summary of how I am approaching the intercultural communication event and interpretation of *han* from the perspective of an outer-hearer. That is, using a particularist hermeneutic and a globalized understanding of culture, I will argue that although I cannot offer a definitive understanding or translation of *han*, I can approach a measure of relative adequacy[210] and intercultural commu-

210. Tracy has provided a clear definition of the term "relative adequacy" through his theological engagement with philosophical hermeneutics. Tracy writes: "For relative adequacy is just that: relative, not absolute, adequacy. If one demands certainty, one is assured of failure. We can never possess absolute certainty. But we can achieve a good—that is, relatively adequate—interpretation: relative to the power of disclosure and concealment of the text, relative to the skills and attentiveness of the interpreter, relative to the kind of conversation possible for the interpreter in a particular culture at a particular time." Tracy, *Plurality and Ambiguity*, 22–23.

nication competence in my reception and interpretation of *han* through a thick description.

Section One: Fundamental Understanding of Culture

In order to adequately provide a map for my theological method, I must first provide a working definition for the term at the foundation of my method: *culture*. Culture is a notoriously ambiguous and complicated term to define. As Gerald Arbuckle has pointed out, the term is often used indiscriminately without much thought being given to a coherent definition or understanding. In popular and academic discourse, it has been used to refer to anything from "youth culture" and "pop culture" to "gun culture" and "corporate culture" to "culture of violence" and "culture of poverty."[211] This is in addition to the cultures of social, ethnic, and national groups that are the entirety of their way of life. In response to this ambiguity, I will briefly discuss a few observations of esteemed cultural anthropologist Clifford Geertz in describing the term and the purpose for studying culture and then move on to three general understandings of culture.

As Geertz has observed, culture has accumulated a wide array of meanings and lacks a consensual foundational meaning by having too many definitions and being studied in vague ways.[212] Geertz follows the lead of Max Weber in espousing a semiotic understanding of culture.[213] Like Weber, Geertz holds that the human person is

> an animal suspended in webs of significance he himself has spun, I take culture to be those webs, and the analysis of it to be therefore not an experimental science in search of law but an interpretive one in search of meaning. It is explication I am after, construing social expressions on their surface enigmatical.[214]

---

211. Arbuckle, *Culture, Inculturation, and Theologians*, xx–xxi.

212. Geertz, *The Interpretation of Cultures*, 89. Geertz goes on to argue that "the culture concept to which I adhere has neither multiple referents nor, so far as I can see, any unusual ambiguity: it denotes an historically transmitted pattern of meanings embodied in symbols, a system of inherited conceptions expressed in symbolic forms by means of which men [sic] communicate, perpetuate, and develop their knowledge about and attitudes toward life."

213. My definition and description of semiotics will commence in Section Two.

214. Geertz, *The Interpretation of Cultures*, 5.

For Geertz, the work of studying culture is not analytical, in the strict sense of the term, as much as it is interpretive. It is a hermeneutical enterprise in search of meaning and a measure of understanding.

Geertz argues that the point of studying culture is not to obtain discrete and objective knowledge of the subject.[215] Geertz thinks that definitive, conceptual knowledge about human cultures is not attainable. This is because the more deeply one delves into the anthropological study of another's culture the less sure knowledge one has about the Other's culture. For Geertz, one of the primary purposes of the study of culture, especially through a semiotic approach, is to enable conversation among people of differing cultures. The object is dialogue rather than knowledge per se.[216]

Taking my cue from Geertz, the foundation for using a method of intercultural hermeneutics and the semiotics of culture within my theological investigation is to enable dialogue and mutual understanding rather than probing for verifiable truths and certain knowledge about a given culture. In this study, this intercultural method is intended to facilitate dialogue with Korean and Korean-American theologies of *han* rather than obtain definitive, conceptual knowledge of this cultural theological trajectory.

Three Understandings of Culture—Classicist, Modern, Globalized

Having given a brief summary of the study of culture and its purpose from the work of Geertz, I now move to three generally accepted and broad understandings of culture—classicist, modern, and globalized.[217] In this sec-

---

215. For example, Geertz writes, "Cultural analysis is (or should be) guessing at meanings, assessing the guesses, and drawing explanatory conclusions from the better guesses, not discovering the Continent of Meaning and mapping out its bodiless landscape." See Geertz, *The Interpretation of Cultures*, 20.

216. Ibid., 24–28.

217. One important theoretical issue that is beyond the scope of this study is the connection between race and culture. This is a contested field with a vast amount of literature. For the purposes of this essay, however, I will merely point out that I approach race as a (pseudo) anthropology that is related to, but not identical with culture. This is because the history of the discourse of "race" is an invention of the European Enlightenment that has been projected upon human beings. It is an artificial category that nevertheless has social value and oppressive and destructive consequences. The discourse of race is embedded in the oppressive power dynamics that can distort intercultural communication in that it is connected to culture. But "race" does not have an intrinsic or ontological relationship to culture per se. For various theological perspectives on race and culture, see: Anderson, *Beyond Ontological Blackness*; Carter,

tion, I will discuss each understanding, describe how each might approach the study of Korean culture, and finally opt for the globalized definition of culture as most appropriate for the purposes of my study.[218]

The Classicist understanding of culture

The *classicist* understanding of culture is perhaps the oldest within the Western Intellectual tradition. In the classicist understanding, culture is a normative, universal monoculture that is the pinnacle of human creativity and expression.[219] As Kathryn Tanner points out, the term culture has Latin roots that come from crop and animal cultivation. Just as crops and animals must be tended and nurtured in order to grow properly and reach their maturity, be it bearing fruit, vegetables, milk, or meat, the human person needs to be cultivated or cultured into properly growing into his or her maturity—human civilization and perfection.[220] Thus, the classicist understanding of culture is delineated by the refined aspects of life created by philosophy, art, music, and other pursuits and is meant to

---

Race: A Theological Account; Cone, *Black Theology and Black Power*; Cone, *God of the Oppressed*; Copeland, *Enfleshing Freedom*; Hopkins, *Being Human*; Jennings, *The Christian Imagination*, among many other titles.

218. In my discussion that follows, I am intentionally avoiding the category of *religion*. This may seem strange for a theological study, but the relationship between culture and religion is much debated and has no clear, consensual understanding. As Schreiter points out, the category itself may be a strictly Western understanding that is not applicable to other cultures. For example, it is important that many languages and cultures have no correlative understanding for what Western intellectual discourse terms the discrete realm of religion. See Schreiter, "Possibilities (and Limitations) of an Intercultural Dialogue on God," 19–21. Schreiter also writes, "Is 'religion' ultimately a Western or a Christian category? It cannot be insignificant that so many languages of the world do not even have a word for what we call 'religion.' For many peoples it is a way of being and living so tied up with being part of a particular culture that it is impossible to imagine living that way outside that culture." *Constructing Local Theologies*, 149. Moreover, Schreiter observes "religion is as much a way of life as a view of life" (43). This is not to suggest that the conceptual relationship between religion and culture is unimportant. Rather, it is a complicated, highly contested discussion that is beyond the scope of this chapter. My working assumption is that there is an intrinsic relationship between religion and culture, but religion cannot be fully dissolved into the category of culture.

219. Shorter, *Toward a Theology of Inculturation*, 17–21. Much of his analysis is indebted to the distinction Bernard Lonergan makes between classicist and empiricist cultural understandings.

220. Tanner, *Theories of Culture*, 4.

educate, refine, and edify the human person in morality, thought, and sensibility. It proposes a vision of the ideal, cultured individual.[221]

The roots of the classicist understanding can be found in ancient Greek philosophy[222] but a more recent illustration can be found in Enlightenment Western Europe. Tanner points out that in Enlightenment France and Britain the only referent for culture, per se, was "high brow" culture.[223] It was valued by the upper classes in society as artistic, spiritual, and intellectual pursuits and products that were the pinnacle of human achievement and expression. As such, culture refined the human person into a more civilized, rational, educated, and sensible being.[224] In this classicist understanding, 'culture' included such things such as gastronomy, opera, symphony, poetry, novels, higher education, rhetoric, and philosophy, among others.[225]

This was in opposition to the "low brow" pursuits of the impoverished and working classes that were seen as having little refining value and sometimes being barbaric and uncivilized.[226] Aspects of this low

---

221. Ibid., 4–6.

222. See, for example, Plato, *The Republic*; and *Five Dialogues*.

223. Tanner places this in contrast to Germany in which the cultured person, associated with *Bildung*, was an educated member of the emerging middle class. This man was educated, aesthetically refined, and set upon full participation and leadership in matters of government and state. See *Theories of Culture*, 4.

224. Ibid., 5–6. See also Tanner's discussion of the particular understandings of culture in France, Germany, and Britain. For example, she points out that in France "low brow" pursuits were mere barbaric customs whose adherents needed to be tutored and refined into true "high brow" culture. Britain also espoused a "high brow" view of culture but theorized that it was not class based but a universal expression of the highest aspirations of humankind. See pages 6–16.

225. It is important to point out that the classicist understanding of culture should not be confused with the idea of a cultural *classic*, as discussed by Tracy. For Tracy, the classic is a cultural creation that has a surplus of meaning and that endures throughout time. This may be either "high brow" or "low brow" and refers to an achievement or text within a culture and is not a description of the concept of culture per se. See *The Analogical Imagination*, 99–153. Or, as Tracy writes elsewhere, "classics are those texts that bear an excess and permanence of meaning, yet always resist definitive interpretation," *Plurality and Ambiguity*, 12. There is a difference between highlighting and celebrating the exceptional texts created by a particular culture—that are indeed edifying and formative—and making an identification of culture per se with the closed constellation of such texts from one culture's high points that are then considered the universal norm to which all other cultures must aspire.

226. See Shorter, *Towards a Theology of Inculturation*, 17–22. See also Ormerod and Clifton, "Culture, Mission, and Globalization," 123–45. See also Lonergan, "Transition from a Classicist Worldview to Historical-Mindedness," 1–10.

brow culture could include folk music, folk tales, beer-drinking, excited dancing, superstitious religions, and bawdy plays, among other things. This was the domain of the common people and was not understood as culture, so to speak. The classicist understanding of culture was identified with the so-called high brow and refining aspects of Western European society, as opposed to the so-called banal or non-edifying aspects of a society and people group. In the words of Bernard Lonergan, "on classicist assumptions there is just one culture. That one culture is not attained by the simple faithful, the people, the natives, the barbarians."[227]

Moreover, as Gerald Arbuckle describes the classicist understanding of culture, it is understood as the creation of rational minds and is the summit of human civilization. As such, Arbuckle points out that this understanding is deeply Eurocentric—and even racist—in that European culture and civilization is seen as the pinnacle of human achievement and refinement and all others must be aesthetically measured against this to various degrees of inferiority.[228] Only (Western) Europeans—and particularly the middle and upper classes—have culture and civilization. All others, both European and non-European, to greater or lesser extents, had means for survival and living but were in need of the tutelage of true culture.

To illustrate this classicist view of culture, I turn to the way in which this perspective might have viewed the inhabitants of Korea. First, they would not be seen as having culture, per se. They would have a basic way of life that allowed them to survive. If anything, Korea would be lumped into an imaginary construct of the Orient (along with China, Japan, and perhaps India) that had certain unchanging characteristics. If this "Oriental" way of life was considered a culture at all, it would be greatly inferior to the true culture of Western Civilization that was the universal ideal to which all humankind aspired. Koreans, as part of an imaginary Orient, might have the capability to attain true culture through tutoring and assimilation into European culture. Their own way of life, however, had little intrinsic or transcendent value. At best, it was a natural or even barbaric existence meant for survival and not refinement or even salvation. Obviously, as Arbuckle pointed out, the classicist view can be a rigidly Eurocentric and racist understanding of culture.

---

227. Bernard Lonergan as quoted in Shorter, *Toward a Theology of Inculturation*, 19. Original quote comes from *Method in Theology*, 326.

228. Arbuckle, *Culture, Inculturation, and Theologians*, 2.

The Modern Understanding of Culture

The second understanding of culture to be explored here is the *modern* understanding.[229] In the modern view, which came about in the early twentieth century and which Tanner calls an anthropological view,[230] culture is an empirical reality that encompasses the totality of the life of a social group. Unlike the classicist view, in which culture was confined to European high culture, Tanner's anthropological descriptor suggests that in the modern view culture was part and parcel of being human. Culture was present universally among all humankind but had particular and unique manifestations in various locations and among various social groups. As such, culture was varied, had intrinsic value, and was a static entity with rigid boundaries and essential characteristics. To illustrate, Arbuckle provides a helpful metaphor for the modern understanding of culture—the billiard ball. He writes:

> In brief, modern definitions of culture emphasize a type of "billiard ball" model of cultures as separate, impenetrable units, passing with little or no change from one generation to the next in a quasi-automatic way, self integrating to maintain the status quo, resistant to external influences, homogenous, and devoid of internal dissent.[231]

Tanner offers several basic elements within the modern understanding of culture that are commensurable with Arbuckle's billiard ball

---

229. This is similar to what Schreiter calls an *integrated* understanding of culture. See Schreiter, *The New Catholicity*, 47–53. Although I will draw upon his work to some extent in this understanding, I will employ the generalized term *modern*, because it seems to be the most prevalent and generally accepted within the literature. As shall be discussed below, this will not be the case with the third understanding of culture that is generally called *postmodern*. Instead, I use Schreiter's term *globalized*.

230. This is because culture was interpreted not as the sole possession of Europeans but as part and parcel of being human. If classicist views espoused a dominating universalism, the modern views espoused a universalism connected to a particularism. Culture was universal to humankind, but was particularly manifested throughout the globe. Cultures had their own value and were neither superior nor inferior to any other culture. As Tanner phrases it, this modern understanding was to provide a "nonevaluative alternative to ethnocentrism." See *Theories of Culture*, 36–37.

231. Arbuckle, *Culture, Inculturation, and Theologians*, 4. He goes on to argue that due to such a self-enclosed, static, integrated understanding, this model of culture has been adopted by nationalists who can indicate an essential national or ethnic identity. In chapter 4, this danger within a modern understanding of culture can be suggested, debatably, by the work of Kim Sang-Yil, and perhaps Chang-Hee Son.

metaphor. Tanner points out these elements arose when the study of culture became an academic discipline in the 1920s. These include: all human beings have a culture (but not the same one), culture is connected to particular social groups, culture is the entire way of living, culture is based on social consensus, culture is constitutive of human nature but also created by humans, culture has contingency, and culture definitively forms the members of a society.[232]

In light of these basic elements, the modern understanding envisions a discrete, self-enclosed culture that carries the meaning dimension of social life.[233] Culture is a holistic entity constitutive of social order and communal meaning. As a holistic entity, culture is the product of the totality of its various facets. Tanner offers her own metaphor to describe the modern understanding of culture, that of a machine or an organism. Like an organism, culture, for Tanner, has numerous aspects that work interdependently in order to sustain and better the whole of the organism.[234] It is more than the sum of its parts. As Tanner argues:

> Showing their interrelations establishes that the boundaries that form them all into a discrete cultural unit are not simply artificial ones of geography; those boundaries do not simply reflect the spatial limits of a culture's social group. A culture's own internal order or organization establishes its boundaries as an integral sum total.[235]

Tanner adds that the modern understanding of culture is synchronic, meaning that it is concerned with how the culture exists now as a fact rather than diachronic, that is, how it has developed and changed over time.[236] In sum, the modern view espouses that a given culture has definite boundaries, unchanging, foundational characteristics and creates a singular identity.

This modern understanding would provide a very different view of Korean culture than the classicist understanding. First, Koreans would indeed have a culture of their own that had intrinsic value and that was

---

232. Tanner, *Theories of Culture*, 25–29.

233. Ibid., 31–32.

234. Ibid., 33–34.

235. Ibid., 32. It is important to point out that the cultural importance of geography, space, and landscape in creating identity is being revisited. The modern understanding of culture devalues the connection of the human person to land and some contemporary accounts are addressing this issue.

236. Ibid., 35–36.

the entirety of their way of life. It was neither inferior nor superior to other cultures. It was merely different, particular, and unique. Second, Korean culture would be construed as having definite, and non-porous boundaries that, from time immemorial, rendered it fully distinct from Chinese, Japanese, and other cultures and social groups. In this understanding, there is an essential core of "Korean-ness" that has existed from the earliest founding myth and from the earliest peoples who inhabited this one particular geographical location. Korean culture would have a historical and enduring ethos—for example, *han* philosophy that will be discussed in chapter 4—that is a defining characteristic of the people. When threatened or brought into contact with other external factors (Japan, China, USA, for example), the culture may change or adapt. But it will retain its essential core and will remain a realm of "Korean-ness."

The Globalized Understanding of Culture

The third understanding of culture to be explored here is the *globalized* understanding.[237] Much of this understanding is a correction to the modern understanding under the influence of the phenomena of globalization and the rise of postmodern philosophies. For example, as Arbuckle points out, instead of closed cultural boundaries, there are porous boundaries; instead of an integrated, homogenous culture it is a fragmented, multi-culture (so to speak); instead of being linked definitively to territory, culture is translocal and deterritorialized; instead of cultural identity being essentialist and singular, cultural identity is multiple and plural.[238]

---

237. In referring to the third kind as globalized rather than postmodern, I am following the lead of Robert Schreiter. In addition, Arbuckle offers a helpful, general definition of culture that is akin to Schreiter's globalized understanding, "a pattern of meanings encased in a network of symbols, myths, narratives, and rituals, created by individuals and subdivisions, as they struggle to respond to the competitive pressures of power and limited resources in a rapidly globalizing and fragmenting world, and instructing its adherents about what is considered to be the correct way to feel, think, and behave," *Culture, Inculturation, and Theologians*, 17.

238. Arbuckle, *Culture, Inculturation, and Theologians*, 5. Thangaraj offers a concise understanding of cultural boundaries that seems commensurate with Arbuckle's characteristics and the general globalized understanding of culture discussed here. Thangaraj offers three general understandings of boundaries, from a theological perspective, to allow "God to be God" in theologizing from this location: 1) boundaries are markers of identity; 2) boundaries can be a fence to keep out others and those who are different; 3) boundaries can be conceived as a location of opportunity (and uncharted territory) for expanding knowledge, understanding, and relationships

Robert Schreiter provides a definitive overview of globalized understandings of culture. Schreiter thinks that the two main sources for understanding a globalized culture are postcolonial theory and academic literature on globalization. Regarding the former, Schreiter points out that postcolonial understandings envision culture through the lens of a network of contested relations as opposed to a set of ideas and objects. This means that power dynamics are brought to the fore and culture is something that is constantly being constructed among asymmetries of power.[239] A globalized view accounts for internal protest and resistance by minorities against the power structure and grand narratives of the ruling powers that often are oppressive.[240] As Schreiter observes, "... culture in this sense strives to establish a 'third space' between self and other, beyond colonizer and colonized. Identity too is a concern in globalized concepts of culture, but identity is always viewed as fragmentary or multiple, constructed and imagined."[241]

Regarding the second source, the literature on globalization complicates the modern view of a discrete culture whose essence does not change. In a recent essay, Schreiter points out four primary characteristics of globalized understandings of culture: homogenization, hyperdifferentiation, deterritorialization, and hybridization.[242] *Homogenization* is the destruction of local difference and the extension (or exportation) of modernity by means of a global *hyperculture*. This hyperculture is exemplified by the prevalence and saturation into local cultures of such things as English language, athletic gear as fashion statement, hip-hop and rock music, capitalistic sensibilities, cell phones and smart-phones, internet access, email, social networking internet sites, fast-food chains such as McDonald's, Anglo business models, and many others. This hyperculture is not considered a culture per se, but rather composed of various global *cultural flows*[243]

---

through an intercultural exchange. See Thangaraj, "Let God be God, 99–101.

239. Schreiter, *The New Catholicity*, 54.

240. Ibid., 54.

241. Ibid.

242. Schreiter, "Christian Witness in a New Modernity," 32–34. See also Miller, "Where is the Church?," 412–32. Another helpful discussion of the phenomenon of globalization is Espín, *Grace and Humanness*, 8–25.

243. Schreiter points out that the term *flow* arose from the fields of anthropology, sociology, and communication studies. A flow denotes "cultural and ritual movements, a circulation of information that is patently visible yet hard to define. Flows move across geographic and other cultural boundaries, and, like a river, define a route, change the landscape, and leave behind sediment and silt that enrich the local

in which local cultures participate to greater or lesser degrees. Schreiter points out that this participation creates the phenomenon of the *glocal*, in which the global hyperculture is adapted to local tastes and sensibilities through savvy marketing and product composition.[244] In an integrated global economy, local cultures often do not have a choice whether or not to participate in the hyperculture. This means the glocal is a contested and sometimes violent site of contact between global and local.[245]

Schreiter observes that the expansion of modernity through the world by means of a hyperculture—homogenization— has its roots in the rise and rapid spread of communication technologies and the strengthening of a single, unified, capitalistic global economy.[246] These factors result in an experience of the expansion of the technological hyperculture along with the compression of experiences of time and space.[247] Instead of taking days, weeks, or months to travel to the other side of the world to see a museum piece or historical landmark, one can experience it virtually on the internet. Instead of needing to send letters across the world to keep in touch with friends and family in far flung places, technological advances such as email, video chat, Skype, Twitter, and Facebook enable the users of technology to experience a compressed world. Schreiter also points out that this overwhelming hyperculture and homogenization process tends to spark resistance movements through its elimination of local languages, customs, and ways of life. To greater and lesser degrees of success, minority and indigenous groups robustly claim and espouse their threatened cultures and identities in opposition to the overwhelming forces of the global hyperculture.[248]

The second characteristic, *hyperdifferentiation*, can be understood as a kind of fragmentation. Schreiter writes that hyperdifferentiation is based on the observation that all aspects of culture are becoming commoditized and are for sale. This leads to the wealthy having a greater

---

ecology." See *The New Catholicity*, 15.

244. For example, Coca-Cola has different recipes and McDonald's has special menu items in various parts of the world. Their products are specifically tailored and marketed to local tastes while retaining the distinctiveness of the brand and large menu of products. See, for example, Miller's essay, "Where is the Church? Globalization and Catholicity."

245. Schreiter, *The New Catholicity*, 55.

246. Ibid., 9–12.

247. Ibid., 4–14.

248. Schreiter, "Christian Witness in a New Modernity," 32.

array of choices for life-styles and also leads to their creation of niches isolated from others. These niches are concentrations of those of similar mind, class, and even perhaps ethnicity. As society becomes more plural, the wealthy create more homogenous pockets and become less able to deal with the plurality in culture.[249] In contrast, Schreiter points out that the have-nots experience this hyperdifferentiation as a fragmentation and loss of identity. They grasp tightly to a single identity marker, be it religion or ethnicity, and use this as a means for asserting their power in a context of overwhelming change and fragmentation.[250] Schreiter describes hyperdifferentiation as experienced disparately as an increase of choice and/or a fragmentation of one's identity. Internally, culture becomes greatly polarized and fragmented as true pluralism and integration of difference into a cohesive society is avoided.

Schreiter's third characteristic of globalized understandings of culture is *deterritorialization*. Schreiter defines this as "the disembedding of ideas, customs, and cultural products from their original location."[251] This is the severing of the connection between culture, identity, and land.[252] The roots of deterritorialization are found in the global hyperculture as well as in the massive migrations of peoples. Regarding the former, and as Schreiter points out, useful technology—smart phones and internet—and common cultural currency—styles of dress, music, and websites like Facebook, which boasts more than one billion users worldwide—is part and parcel of the deterritorialized hyperculture. Again, modernity is expanded while time and space are compressed. Culture becomes transportable to some extent from location to location.

Regarding the latter, there has been a massive global migration of peoples from rural to urban settings within one nation-state and transnational migration from less affluent to more affluent nations.[253] For

249. Ibid., 32–33.

250. Ibid.

251. Ibid., 33–34.

252. Schreiter also points out that the importance of place and space for understanding culture and identity is one that has been mostly ignored by Western understandings in lieu of the importance of time. See his "The Possibilities (and Limits) of a Global Dialogue on God," 28–29. For a recent effort that seeks to address this lacuna from a somewhat different perspective, Jennings offers an interesting argument that links colonization and deterritorialization of culture and identity, to the creation of race and racism. See *The Christian Imagination*.

253. For a brief, clear overview of globalization and migration, see Cruz, "Between Identity and Security," 357–75.

these economic migrants, home is no longer the traditional, geographical, home of one's family, community, and ancestors. This home and its cultural significance must be left behind for the purposes of survival. Such deterritorialization threatens identity as traditional boundaries that create identity are broken down and must be recreated.[254] Deterritorialization is one of the causes of the violent encounter between global and local. As Schreiter writes:

> Global-local encounters, then, are experienced by many in the world as uneven, asymmetrical, unequal, and violent. They are experienced as disruptive, as global markets enter local cultures and rearrange their lives. They are disorienting, as people experience what Fernando Calderon has called "tiempos mixtos," a situation in which the premodern, the modern, and the postmodern exist together and in the same place. Or the encounter with the global may mean the destruction of the local altogether, as local communities become migrants and refugees.[255]

Finally, Schreiter's fourth characteristic of a globalized understanding of culture is *hybridity*. This is the historical and ongoing mixing of various characteristics that coalesce to create culture, in its holistic sense, and identity.[256] Or, as Schreiter defines the term, "a hybridity results from an erasure of a boundary between two (cultural or religious) entities and a redrawing of a new boundary."[257] Moreover, "hybridity is part of life in globalized cultures—either as an act of survival among the poor or as an act of choice in fashioning the self among the wealthy."[258]

Schreiter points out that hybridity is a two edged sword. On the one hand, it has positives such as the creation of new peoples and the advancement of technology for survival, health, and flourishing. In addition, a hybrid culture can act as a *third culture* that can mediate between the two cultures from which it was formed.[259] On the other hand, hybridity is often brought about violently, as was the case with colonization

---

254. Schreiter, *The New Catholicity*, 11.

255. Ibid., 55.

256. Schreiter, "Christian Witness in a New Modernity," 34.

257. Schreiter, *The New Catholicity*, 74. For a helpful account of hybridity in Latino/a theological literature, see Elizondo, *The Galilean Journey* and *The Future is Mestizo*.

258. Schreiter, *The New Catholicity*, 76.

259. Ibid., 77.

through the "violent and unequal encounter of cultures."[260] Hybridity carries wounds (*han*) of this violent encounter, as will be discussed in the next chapter.

Moreover, the change that hybridity represents can be seen as a threat by many people. This perceived threat can cause many to claim a kind of cultural or racial purity as a response. As Schreiter writes, "Be it racial purity, theological orthodoxy, or fear of genetically modified plants, a fear of hybridity can evoke profound resistance."[261] In history and reality, however, cultures have constantly borrowed from each other and intermingled with one another. In a sense, all cultures are hybridities to some extent.[262] This does not mean that a particular culture has neither boundaries nor defining characteristics. Rather, this means that the boundaries are permeable and the defining characteristics have a history of development and are constantly being negotiated, because of both internal and external factors.

To again use the example of Korean culture, this globalized vision would offer a revised understanding. First, the culture would have porous boundaries and would have been interacting with other cultures, for example China and Japan, throughout its historical formation. There would not be an unchanging "Korean-ness" that had existed since time immemorial. Rather, there would be an ever changing and ever developing way of life that was shaped by internal and external tensions, conflicts, and dissent. As will become apparent in the following chapter, much of what we Westerners understand as contemporary Korean culture has been deeply shaped by the violent and unequal encounter of cultures—with China, the Mongols, Japan, Russia, the U.S.—as well as its internal oppressive dynamics such as classism and sexism.

This is not to suggest that the globalized view of a Korean culture would argue it had no boundaries or internal characteristics. A globalized understanding would respect that fact that culture is the entirety of a people's way of life that has boundaries and creates identity. What the globalized understanding adds, however, is the claim that the boundaries are porous and contested, identity is multiple within the culture, and the culture is not a discrete, unchanging, monolithic entity. Rather than a billiard ball, it is more like water. Water has definite characteristics, but

---

260. This phrase is found in several locations in Garcia-Rivera, but its source is from Pagden, *Peoples and Empires*.

261. Schreiter, "Christian Witness in a New Modernity," 34.

262. Ibid.

is fluid. Depending on many variables, it can morph into solid, liquid, or gas and can be combined with all kinds of solvents and additives that alter its composition and functioning. It remains water, but in very different forms and compositions.

Second, the globalized understanding of Korean culture would suggest that even though it remains the totality of a way of life and has intrinsic value, it would show signs of homogenization, hyperdifferentiation, deterritorialization, and hybridity. In its participation in the global hyperculture, Korean culture would show signs of the homogenization through the *glocal* such as McDonald's, KFC, hip-hop music, athletic clothing styles, and embrace of advanced technologies. In hyperdifferentiation, the culture of Koreans may perhaps show signs of greater social stratification. Although South Korea remains one of the most ethnically homogenous nations on the globe, it too may show signs of an exacerbation of differences, particularly among class. Through deterritorialization, Korean dramas, food, dress, music, ideas, religion, philosophy, and general sensibility would no longer be anchored to the native soil of the Korean peninsula. Rather, its culture would now be composed of consumable goods to be obtained by other cultures. In addition, Korean culture would be deterritorialized through migration because Korean culture would be carried by migrants to new homes. This leads to the final characteristic, hybridity. Through its encounter with Western, U.S. culture, Korean-Americans (and other migrants) would occupy a precarious, hybrid position. Their culture would inevitably, for better and worse, intermingle with U.S. culture and create a third culture of hybridity. This culture would be their entire way of being in a new country, but would be neither fully Korean nor fully Anglo-American. This would also be true of the historical development of Korean culture, due to its interactions with China, Mongolia, Russia, Japan, and the U.S.

Having discussed three possible conceptions of culture, in this study I opt for the globalized understanding. There are three reasons for this. First, globalization forms the context in which all theology and intercultural communication occurs in the twenty-first century. Although modern, and to a lesser extent classicist, views have their merits, they can account neither for the complexity of technology, communication, and military and economic power dynamics in the world today, nor their effects upon local cultures. Second, a globalized understanding provides a better vision for intercultural communication. The boundaries are porous and allow for communication as well as show a need for it. This can be achieved through the hybridity of a third culture that can be the mediating context in which communication takes place. Third, a globalized understanding of culture accounts for the development and change within culture, both through internal and external negotiation. It also accounts for fragmentation and differentiation within a given culture, despite shared characteristics.

Section Two: The Semiotics of Culture

In this section, I move from a general understanding of culture to a discussion of the semiotic approach to studying culture. As Robert J. Schreiter has described this field, a semiotic approach views culture as a network of communication in which verbal and nonverbal messages circulate along complicated, expansive, interrelated pathways that, as a holistic entity, create a system of meaning.[263] Phrased differently, for Schreiter a semiotic approach to culture is "a method by which culture is studied as a communication structure and process."[264] Signs are the building blocks of meaning, codes are the pathways in which these signs are variously organized, and the confluence of these signs and codes creates a message that is a larger contour within the culture.

One of the primary strengths of a semiotic approach to culture, in which a culture in its entirety is viewed as a system of messages and communications, is its ability to envision a culture as a text.[265] This is similar to Geertz's observation that the purpose of studying culture is not knowl-

---

263. Schreiter, *Constructing Local Theologies*, 49.

264. Schreiter, *The New Catholicity*, 30.

265. Although Schreiter opts for the linguistic metaphor, Garcia-Rivera finds this metaphor of *text* problematic and advocates for a visual or aesthetic metaphor. Garcia-Rivera argues that the linguistic metaphor cannot account for the shading and nuances of the entirety of a culture and its violent and unequal encounters with other cultures. Referencing Schreiter, he remarks that since the semiotic study of culture is more a way of life than a view of life, "A visual metaphor capable of expressing ways of life, rather than views of life, is more appropriate." To this end, Garcia-Rivera offers the metaphor of a cultural mosaic. See Garcia-Rivera, *St. Martin de Porres*, 31–35. Although I think that Garcia-Rivera makes a valid point and a constructive contribution to envisioning the semiotics of culture, I prefer the linguistic metaphor of text. This is because Garcia-Rivera seems to envision the linguistic metaphor as merely a straightforward message, such as a newspaper report or academic discourse, rather than a more artistic creation. A linguistic metaphor can include creations such as poetry, song, myth, narrative, and fiction that are more linguistic (although not necessarily written down) but also polyphonic, just as a cultural mosaic is textured.

edge but meaning and communication. Culture, in this view, is a whole that can be read, so to speak, and interpreted to greater and lesser degrees of relative adequacy. It is comprised of various signs and codes that create larger messages. Schreiter argues that a semiotic approach enables one to engage culture as a text, "that is, to locate its signs, the codes that place the signs in dynamic interaction, and the messages that are conveyed."[266] A text can be on the micro-level—discrete gestures, phrases, daily practices—or a text can be an amalgamation of these smaller units into a large canvass—rituals, celebrations, myths, narratives, ethos. On the macro-level, a system of interrelated texts can be seen as a *semiotic domain*. That is, an entire complex system that has a bewildering network of signs, codes, and messages that creates a larger meaning structure.[267]

There are two helpful analogies for a semiotic analysis of culture. The first is offered by Alejandro Garcia-Rivera in his description of a sentence. Garcia-Rivera argues that a sentence is similar to a message or communication. This sentence is comprised of smaller units called words, which are analogous with *signs*, and function as the building blocks for the cultural message or sentence. This sentence also has a structure and rules called grammar, which is analogous with the cultural *codes*, that govern the structure and meaning of the message. In short, the semiotics of culture is meant to provide the tools through which to receive and interpret the meaning of the sentence—a cultural *message*. In order to do this, it must account for the signs that are the building blocks for the message as well as the codes by which the message is formed and structured.[268]

A second analogy comes from the world of business and marketing (a global hyperculture rather than a globalized culture, per se). The I-pad is a sign/product that signifies technological prowess and class status. Its code is its branding of Apple, which connects it to a complex system of other signs/products, including i-pods, i-phones, computers, and more. These signs/products and code/branding coalesce to create a message of a "cool" and "hip" identity for the consumers of these products. Moreover,

---

266. Schreiter, *Constructing Local Theologies*, 61.

267. Ibid., 62. This semiotic domain Garcia-Rivera prefers to call a *semiosphere*. See Garcia-Rivera, *St. Martin de Porres*, 35–36. This term, however, comes from the work of Juri Lotman. See Lotman's "On the Semiosphere," 205–29. Lotman's original, groundbreaking, essay was published in 1984 in Russian and this is a contemporary English translation of the Russian text.

268. Garcia-Rivera, *St. Martin de Porres*, 31–32.

its consumers can see themselves at the cutting edge of technology and have a privileged place in the global flow of the information economy. The consumers of these products receive and perpetuate this identity, albeit a commoditized identity. In an analogous way, a semiotic approach looks for these signs, codes, and messages that circulate to create identity when engaging a culture.

The point of departure in a semiotic approach, as Schreiter points out, is to listen to culture. Phrased differently, it is to attend closely and in a sensitive and self-aware manner, to a text in order to encounter, read, and perhaps interpret it. In order for this to happen, one must be aware of the cultural and political baggage one brings to the intercultural communication event.[269] In other words, social and cultural locations matter when engaging in intercultural communication.[270] It is difficult to listen to a different culture without first accounting for one's own pre-understandings, biases, religious and cultural values, intention, social identity markers (race/sex/class), etc. These aspects affect the way in which one approaches a cultural boundary and molds the lens through which one tries to interpret a cultural message. In this way, a semiotic approach to culture is helpful when envisioning the cultural locations and boundaries between oneself and the cultural Other.

When listening to culture through a semiotic approach, Schreiter offers three general characteristics of a culture upon which to focus: ideational, performative, and material. The *ideational* refers to the frameworks and complex systems of meaning that coalesce to create a coherent worldview and a way of right living. The *performative* includes "rituals that bind a culture's members together" to coalesce them into one people with a shared history and meaning. The *material* includes things such as food, language, clothing, music, etc.[271] Together, these three characteristics help describe the totality of what is meant by culture, and is applicable, I believe, to both modern and globalized understandings. In the

---

269. Schreiter, *Constructing Local Theologies*, 39–42. In addition, one must use at least three conceptual tools when listening to culture: a holistic understanding, attention to how culture creates identity, and how to account for social change. See *Constructing Local Theologies*, 42–45. These conceptual tools are consonant with the globalized understanding of culture offered above.

270. This accounting for one's social location and the ways in which it has molded oneself is the foundation of contextual theology. For a helpful introduction, see Bevans, *Models of Contextual Theology*, 1–28.

271. Schreiter, *The New Catholicity*, 29.

chapter that follows in which I discuss *han*, I will attend to all three of these aspects of culture even though focusing upon the ideational aspect.

Section Three: Intercultural Hermeneutics

I now turn to the method of *intercultural hermeneutics*. This is a relatively new field, and one that has a very short history in its dialogue with and appropriation by the discipline of theology.[272] Schreiter describes the connection between a semiotic understanding of culture and the work of intercultural hermeneutics. He writes that semiotics:

> focuses on *signs* (Greek: *semeion*) that carry *messages* along the pathways (*codes*) of culture. The purpose of the circulation of those messages within culture is to create *identity*, which involves building group solidarity and incorporating new information as it comes into the culture. The intercultural hermeneutics challenge would be stated thus semiotically: how does the same *message* get communicated via different *codes*, using a mixture of *signs* from two different cultures.[273]

Similar to my discussion of culture above, there is no single, consensual definition of intercultural hermeneutics among scholars. Therefore, I will first offer a brief discussion of terminology and then a more thorough discussion of three modes of intercultural hermeneutics. Regarding the former, there is a distinction between intercultural hermeneutics and intercultural communication, as well as the terms intercultural and cross-cultural. Intercultural communication is more focused upon the communication of the message itself across a cultural boundary. Intercultural hermeneutics, however, is focused upon the conditions for the possibility of communication across cultural boundaries.[274] This means that intercultural hermeneutics is the foundation upon which the work of intercultural communication is constructed.

Furthermore, there is a distinction between cross-cultural and intercultural. In Schreiter's opinion, intercultural denotes communication

---

272. For the sources and development of this emerging discipline, see Schreiter, *The New Catholicity*, 30–32.

273. Ibid., 30.

274. Schreiter, *The New Catholicity*, 28. It is important to point out that my phrase "the conditions for the possibility" in no way signifies a transcendental analysis. Rather, it denotes the necessary apparatus in order to enable a communication event to achieve some measure of adequacy.

across a cultural boundary. The term cross-cultural denotes a generalization that can be abstracted from the intercultural communication across a cultural boundary, based on an analysis of it.[275] Since the intercultural is the foundation for the cross-cultural, I will follow Schreiter's lead in using the term intercultural to refer to both. To quote Schreiter at length:

> Intercultural hermeneutics (narrowly understood) is concerned with cultural distinctiveness or difference, with how meaning will negotiate a cultural boundary. It is wary of homogenization. It resists easy absorption or assimilation. Cross-cultural hermeneutics, on the other hand, seeks those forms of sameness that will allow easier communication in a world with so many cultures. Consequently, it seeks commonalities or at least common categories that will promote communication and understanding.[276]

Three Understandings of Intercultural Hermeneutics

There are three basic understandings of intercultural hermeneutics that I will discuss: universalist, particularist, and oppositionalist.[277] I will briefly sketch the three definitions, that are distinct but not mutually exclusive, and the reason why I choose to embrace a 'particularist' intercultural hermeneutic.

A *universalist* hermeneutic is one that stresses the commonalities among cultures as opposed to the differences. As Schreiter points out, in this view "commonalities are the bases for intercultural communication."[278] This is similar to what Schreiter had earlier termed a cross-cultural hermeneutic as discussed above. In a more recent work, he describes this approach as an objectivist perspective. This perspective is governed by a conviction of the psychic unity of humankind. At the foundation of intercultural hermeneutics, commonality trumps difference. This means that boundaries and cultural difference are marginal, rather than integral, to both one's identity and the message being communicated.[279] To use

---

275. Ibid., 29.

276. Ibid., 42.

277. These positions are proposed in Schreiter, "Christian Witness in a New Modernity," 34–35.

278. Ibid., 35.

279. Schreiter, "Possibilities (and Limitations) of an Intercultural Dialogue on God," 22.

an Aristotelian analogy, in this view of intercultural hermeneutics, the message and the social group are the "substance" and the culture in which they are embedded is the "accident."

A *particularist* hermeneutic takes the opposite perspective. Whereas the universalist stresses the ultimacy of commonality, the particularist stresses the ultimacy of difference.[280] This is what Schreiter also has described as a relativist, or subjectivist hermeneutic. It is also akin to what Schreiter had referred to as the intercultural in his earlier work.[281] In this understanding, there is no easy or final dissolution of cultural difference into human commonality. The differences, rather than the similarities, are integral to one's identity and to the message that is being communicated. This is because this approach tends to be highly sensitive to asymmetries of power and the power dynamics within intercultural communication. As Schreiter writes, "while not disparaging harmony and common understandings among cultures, relativists are acutely sensitive to the misuse of power to homogenize difference or to assimilate one culture into another."[282]

An *oppositionalist* hermeneutic is the one most concerned with the asymmetries of power and the violent and unequal encounter of cultures.[283] Having roots in postcolonial theory and subaltern studies,[284] as well as Latin American theologies and philosophies of liberation, the oppositionalist hermeneutic remembers and highlights the wounds that are carried by a culture due to its violent encounter with another culture.

---

280. Schreiter, "Christian Witness in a New Modernity," 35.

281. See the discussion above from Schreiter's *The New Catholicity*.

282. Schreiter, "Possibilities (and Limitations) of an Intercultural Dialogue on God," 23. On the following page, he observes that there are little, if any, absolute universalists or absolute relativists. Schreiter writes that the former makes difference impertinent and the latter suggests the impossibility of communication. Scholars and practitioners will find themselves somewhere between these two, depending upon 1) the goal of communication; 2) the cultural context from which the interlocutors come and in which the communication occurs.

283. See Premnath, *Border Crossings: Cross-Cultural Hermeneutics*, for representative examples of an oppositionalist hermeneutic.

284. Regarding the field of postcolonial studies, there are three giants whose work is foundational to this field. They are Edward Said, Homi Bhabha, and Gayatri Spivak, who Susan Abraham has called the "trinity of fabulous fame." See Abraham's "What Does Mumbai have to do with Rome? Postcolonial Perspectives on Globalization and Theology," 377. Representative examples include: Bhabha, *The Location of Culture*, Spivak, *The Spivak Reader*, Said, *Orientalism*. For a helpful introduction to its theological appropriations, Keller et al., *Postcolonial Theologies: Divinity and Empire*.

This memory of unwarranted violence and innocent suffering is the starting point for any intercultural exchange, encounter, or communication. An oppositionalist perspective operates with a continual hermeneutic of suspicion towards the asymmetrical and distorted power dynamics in the intercultural encounter.[285]

Even though all three of these perspectives are useful and even necessary, and moreover should work together, it is important that I choose one upon which to focus in my study: the 'particularist' hermeneutic. The primary reason for my choice has to do with what Schreiter defines as the *relative incommensurability of cultures*.[286] In short, relative incommensurability is a stance that respects cultural difference and takes it seriously (which is a weakness of the universalist approach). But it is neither a pure relativist stance nor absolute particularist stance. This is because such a stance would provide an approach to culture in which intercultural communication is impossible. If cultures are fully incommensurate, then there can be no possibility for dialogue and the outlook for mutual understanding and flourishing is dim.

A basic understanding of cultures as relatively incommensurate allows for and promotes intercultural communication. At the same time, it is an understanding that seeks to take difference and power dynamics seriously.[287] Difference and otherness cannot be dissolved. Rather, it is accounted for and respected in intercultural hermeneutics. A culture's boundaries may be porous and its identity multiple, but a particularist approach based on an understanding of the relative incommensurability of cultures enables communication—through taking difference seriously while also allowing, secondarily, for commonality—while also attempting to avoid (or amend for) a violent and unequal encounter of cultures.[288]

---

285. Schreiter, "Christian Witness in a New Modernity," 35.

286. Schreiter, *The New Catholicity*, 45.

287. Ibid., 45.

288. For a historical example of this approach towards difference, and commonality within a violent and unequal encounter of cultures, see Garcia-Rivera's recounting and interpretation of the Valladolid debate. In short, this debate occurred in colonial Spain in 1550 and revolved around the human status (or lack thereof) of the indigenous peoples of the Americas. The three positions on the issue are exemplified by Juan Ines de Sepulveda and Bartolome de Las Casas (with Garcia-Rivera also highlighting the perspective of Francisco de Vitoria). See Garcia-Rivera, *St. Martin de Porres*, 40–57.

Four Locations from Which to Communicate Interculturally

Having discussed intercultural hermeneutics, as well as the relative incommensurability of cultures, I now turn to the four cultural locations from which to engage in a communication event.[289] Schreiter offers two sets of pairings that come together to offer four different locations from which one can locate oneself and one's dialogue partner within the communication event. These are inner/outer and speaker/ hearer. Regarding the former, two locations from which to understand culture are from the inside and from the outside. In other words, is one a cultural insider or cultural outsider? One's cultural location is of great importance in accounting for one's ability to adequately communicate across a semiotic boundary. As Schreiter points out, although both are concerned with narrative, the cultural insider often is more focused on identity formation whereas the cultural outsider is often more focused on explanation of meaning.[290]

In Garcia-Rivera's opinion, as well as that of Schreiter's, both inner and outer descriptions and perspectives are necessary. Garcia-Rivera points out that a problem arises when the cultural locations of each become confused and their perspectives incoherent. He writes:

> This has led some to call for abandonment of any outsider perspectives. Only Hispanics can speak for Hispanics, for example. This is misguided. The outsider perspective is vital to the insider. It protects the cultural insider from the demands and pressures of a more powerful outsider by providing understanding and communicating worth.[291]

In other words, the perspective of the cultural outsider often sees contours and characteristics within a culture that the insider does not. This often focuses upon the unhealthy or sinful aspects of culture that is seen by a cultural insider as merely "the way it is." It is a necessary, although difficult, perspective to articulate.[292]

---

289. Schreiter indicates that the intercultural communication event has three characteristics: interlocutors, context, and message. See *The New Catholicity*, 34. Of these, it is the interlocutors that will be of greatest importance to my purposes here. This is not to suggest that the other two components—context and message—do not warrant an investigation and analysis. They are both very important. I choose to focus on the cultural locations of interlocutors for the sake of brevity. In addition, Schreiter does not treat these other two factors as extensively in his work as he does the first one.

290. Schreiter, *Constructing Local Theologies*, 57–59.

291. Garcia-Rivera, *St. Martin de Porres*, 35.

292. As Ormerod and Clifton point out when referencing Tanner, there must be a

The second pairing that Schreiter offers is speaker/hearer. The speaker intends for the message to cross a cultural boundary with as much integrity as possible and become understandable within the world of the hearer. The hearer is focused upon embracing and bringing that message into his or her own culture to build identity.[293] As Schreiter argues, "intercultural communication is not just about maintaining the integrity of the message; it is also about its impact on the hearing community."[294]

Schreiter points out that the speaker and the hearer have different intentions within the communication event. The speaker's goal is to communicate the message in such a way that the hearer's understanding of it is closely aligned with the speaker's. In short, the speaker is concerned with the integrity of the message. The hearer's goal is somewhat different. The hearer's focus is in receiving and interpreting the message in order for it to make sense within the constellation of knowledge in the hearer's semiotic universe.[295] As Schreiter points out, "The speaker is on the alert for any alteration of the message that might compromise its integrity; the hearer is trying to make the message fit into an identity. The speaker is on the watch for syncretism; the hearer is struggling for synthesis."[296]

These two pairings lead to four possible positions for the interlocutors within an intercultural communication event: *inner-speaker, inner-hearer, outer-speaker, outer-hearer*. To illustrate this paradigm, Garcia-Rivera offers another helpful metaphor: the artist and the art critic. In order for the meaning of the artistic creation to become accessible and intelligible to a larger audience, an artist often needs an interpreter. Garcia-Rivera envisions the artist as the inner-speaker of the message who is not fully concerned with interpreting his or her own work. The art critic, however, as the outer-hearer, is the one who attempts to interpret the work to convey the meaning to a larger audience. The artist is the sender and inner-speaker and the art critic is the receiver and outer-hearer. The artist wants his or her work displayed as it is, without any embellishments or changes. The art critic, however, wants to understand

---

way for a cultural outsider to validly denounce thing such as child labor, slavery, and other violations of human rights. See *Globalization and the Mission of the Church*, 124–25. Another example would be sexism and the disrespectful and harmful treatment of women in many cultures throughout the globe.

293. Schreiter, *The New Catholicity*, 34–35.
294. Ibid., 35.
295. Ibid., 68–69.
296. Ibid., 69.

the work as much as possible and if this means taking it apart or translating it, that is not a serious problem.[297] As Garcia Rivera points out:

> although there is a natural enmity between artists and art critics, they both need each other. The art critic gains wisdom by interpreting the work of the artist and communicates it to others. The artist, on the other hand, depends on the art critic to communicate the value of his or her work, so the work may continue uninterrupted.[298]

Of these four positions, it is the *outer-hearer* position that most accurately defines my location within the intercultural communication event attempted in chapter 4. My own, broad, cultural location is U.S. Euro-American and the broad, cultural locations of the inner-speakers are Korean and U.S. Korean-American. From my own cultural location, I will approach Korean and Korean-American cultural locations, from which *han* is being communicated, through: a globalized perspective, a semiotic approach to culture, and the adoption of a particularist hermeneutic. I hope this approach can account for porous cultural boundaries and messy, hybrid identities, the likelihood of ambiguity in communication, and the power dynamics and cultural difference existing between inner-speaker and outer-hearer. Nevertheless, the possibility of communication distortion is ever present. It is to this problem I now turn.

Section Four: Intercultural Communication Competence

In any communication, and especially in intercultural communication, there is always the danger of a distortion, misunderstanding, or misappropriation of the message. This is true of communication among all four cultural locations discussed above. Without accounting for the possibility of distortion, a misinterpretation or misappropriation of *han* by an outer-hearer becomes highly likely. In the context of this study, a distortion of the message of *han* would negatively affect the relative adequacy of a Christian soteriology that employs *han*. This is because a distortion of *han* would result not only in the loss of *han*'s meaning but, perhaps more importantly, would make a Christian theology based upon it incoherent and unintelligible. In short, work based upon a distortion of *han* would

---

297. Garcia-Rivera, *St. Martin de Porres*, 34.
298. Ibid.

be problematic on many levels and would become a relatively inadequate soteriology.

An exhaustive discussion of intercultural communication competence is beyond the scope of this chapter. Therefore, I will focus upon the outer-hearer's reception of a message created and offered by the inner-speaker. Regarding intercultural communication competence in general, there are two factors that generally need to be met: effectiveness and appropriateness.[299] Again, deferring to Schreiter:

> A communication would be considered *effective* when the speaker feels that it has achieved its goal; namely, that it has become lodged with the hearer on the other side of the cultural boundary in a manner recognizable to the speaker. Thus, the speaker's satisfaction with the conclusion of the communication event is a necessary (but as we shall see, not a sufficient) condition for intercultural communication competence. A communication is *appropriate* when it is achieved without a violation of the hearer's cultural codes.[300]

---

299. In a recent essay in intercultural communication, Chen and Starosta offer seven types of competence: fundamental, social, interpersonal, linguistic, communicative, and relational. They arrive at a synthesis model called *interactive-multiculture building*. They write, "[T]he model aims at promoting interactants' ability to acknowledge, respect, tolerate, and integrate cultural differences, so that they can qualify for enlightened global citizenship. The model represents a transformational process of symmetrical interdependence that can be explained from three perspectives: (a) affective or intercultural sensitivity; (b) cognitive or intercultural awareness; and (c) behavioral or intercultural adroitness." See "Intercultural Communication Competence: A Synthesis," 221. This essay also offers an extensive bibliography documenting the literature surrounding intercultural communication competence. A more extensive investigation as to what comprises intercultural communication competence is beyond the scope of this study. Thus, I will focus upon the two characteristics of effectiveness and appropriateness, as described by Schreiter.

300. Schreiter, *The New Catholicity*, 33; italics are mine. Another criterion may also be in order: an accounting for power-dynamics. This would account for the violent and unequal encounter of cultures that often informs the context for the communication event. It is the oppositionalist hermeneutic that is best-suited for addressing the problem of distortion through power, although my own particularist hermeneutic attempts to account for this as well. An avenue for further investigation, extremely relevant for this study, would be the problem of *orientalism* as distorting the intercultural communication event between my own Western cultural matrix as the outer-hearer and Eastern, or East-West hybrid, cultural matrices of Korean and Korean-Americans respectively as the inner-speaker. That is, a location that is culturally and linguistically different from my own and that has been cast in an "exotic," "spiritual," and even "inferior" light by the colonial Western imagination that is the intellectual and cultural inheritance of my own location. For the classic discussion of *orientalism*, see Said, *Orientalism*.

In other words, *effectiveness* refers to the satisfaction of the inner speaker with regard to the outer hearer's reception and integration of the message as it crosses the cultural boundary. For his or her part, the inner-speaker must recognize the integrity of the message in the outer-hearer's reception, interpretation, and integration of the message. *Appropriateness* refers to the satisfaction of the outer-hearer. In short, the outer-hearer must receive, interpret, and integrate the message into his or her understanding in a way that does not violate his or her own cultural codes. He or she must make the message intelligible within his or her own culture and assimilate the message within this semiotic domain.

Garcia-Rivera's example, noted above, of the artist and the art critic illustrates this dynamic and tension. The artist wants his or her work embraced and received by a larger audience in a way that does justice to the integrity of the artist's vision. The art critic wants to embrace the work and make it intelligible to the larger audience, even if it involves a careful dissection of the artwork to grasp at its meaning. The artist wants an effective reception of his or her work by another and the art critic wishes to understand the work and integrate it into his or her structure of understanding and meaning so that it is appropriate in his or her cultural semiotic domain.

As Schreiter indicates, there is a further problem to be addressed in intercultural communication competence. He points out that the twin criteria of effectiveness and appropriateness, although important, in themselves are insufficient for fully assessing intercultural communication. This is because they do not account for an interlocutor's knowledge (or ignorance) of the culture on the other side of the semiotic boundary, the ambiguity of the communication, the asymmetries of power within the event, nor does it offer a concrete means for evaluating whether or not the speaker's and hearer's understandings of the message are in any way commensurate.[301] It is beyond the scope of this chapter to provide a full set of adequate tools to address this problem. But there is one concept, or tool, that can be of great use as this study proceeds when addressing these serious concerns that come part and parcel with the problem of communication distortion. This concept is what has become known as a "thick description" of culture.

In brief, a thick description of culture can be a response to the problem of knowledge and ignorance of another's culture that can hinder

---

301. Schreiter, *The New Catholicity,* 33–34.

intercultural communication competence. The common understanding of this term comes from the writings of Geertz. As he writes in describing the utility in a semiotic approach to the study of culture:

> As interworked systems of construable signs . . . culture is not a power, something to which social events, behaviors, and institutions, or processes can be causally attributed; it is a context, something within which they can be intelligibly—that is, thickly—described.[302]

In illustrating this concept, which he borrows from Gilbert Ryle, Geertz offers Ryle's distinction between a twitch of the eye and a wink. Although the two gestures are seemingly identical, the origin, context, and reasoning for this gesture are of great importance for interpreting it. One is caused by an involuntary contraction of the eyelids, and the other is a purposeful communication from one person to another. If one does not understand the context in which this occurs, or the cultural code that gives the sign its meaning, one can easily misinterpret this gesture.[303]

A thick description of culture can account for such a distortion in communication. A wink and an involuntary eye movement are almost identical signs, yet they send different messages by being governed and circulated by differing codes within the larger semiotic domain. If an observer did not have foreknowledge of the cultural code along which the sign might circulate to create meaning, such as the possibility that the gesture could be either an involuntary muscle spasm or an intentional communication, a misinterpretation of its meaning would become likely. Moreover, the attempt to engage in intercultural communication from an outside culture to the one in which this gesture occurs, and that incorporates this gesture, would be distorted due to a misinterpretation of the sign, the code that circulates it, and the message it sends.

A thick description would include the three broad characteristics of culture discussed above from the work of Schreiter: ideational, performative, and material. The wink can be interpreted as an intentional communication among "conspirators," as Geertz describes them. It has a shared ideational meaning behind it, performs that meaning, and can be nuanced based on material aspects such as the clothing of the interlocutors

---

302. Geertz, *The Interpretation of Cultures*, 14.

303. Ibid., 6. Geertz also offers a good articulation of the difficulty in assessing the accuracy or a thick description of another's culture: "[W]hat we call our data are really our own constructions of other people's constructions of what they and their compatriots are up to" (9).

or their sharing of a similar language (or dialect). The muscle spasm also can be interpreted medically. It is based upon an understanding of the human nervous system, its performance is a function of this understanding, and the material aspects such as clothing may further indicate its meaning, along with whether the person is in a hospital or on medication. In short, a thick description is not only concerned with the discourse of ideas and philosophy, so to speak, but the rituals, gestures, food, clothing, territory etc. of a culture.

In addition to effectiveness and appropriateness, this thick description could be a further criterion for the possibility of intercultural communication competence. If one does not account for the depth and complexity of the semiotic domain in which a message is born, molded, and transmitted, one is highly unlikely to achieve any measure of intercultural communication competence. Some degree of knowledge and/or experience with the culture of the inner-speaker is necessary. A thick description enables an interlocutor to communicate interculturally to a greater degree of relative adequacy, even if in itself it is not an exhaustive response to this problem.

In this section, I have described the problem of intercultural communication competence, with a particular focus on explaining effectiveness, appropriateness, and a thick description of culture. I have also pointed out the shortcomings in the general understanding of intercultural communication competence that can be addressed through a thick description of culture. This section has not provided an exhaustive discussion of this problem. Its purpose has been much narrower. The purpose has been to highlight the problem of the distortion of a message and briefly summarize a few criteria for addressing, but not solving, this problem.[304]

Conclusion: A Map and Method for Intercultural Communication

In summary, in this chapter I have discussed three broad understandings of culture, the semiotic approach to culture, three broad understandings of intercultural hermeneutics, four cultural locations among which the intercultural message can be transmitted, and the criterion of intercultural communication competence. As I move on to the next chapter, in

---

304. For a good discussion of this problem, and possible responses, see Schreiter, *The New Catholicity*, 33–45.

which I attempt to offer a thick description of *han,* it is important to reiterate the methodological underpinnings I have embraced in this chapter. I am approaching the intercultural investigation as an *outer hearer* and I am receiving the message of *han* from an *inner speaker.* I am employing a *globalized* understanding of culture, a *semiotic* approach to culture, and a *particularist* intercultural hermeneutic. Although I cannot offer a definitive understanding or translation of *han,* through these methodological choices, I can approach a measure of *relative adequacy* and *intercultural communication competence* in my reception and interpretation of *han.* In other words, I can achieve a measure of effectiveness and appropriateness, particularly through a thick description of *han.* It is to a thick description of *han* that I now turn in chapter 4.

4

An Outer-Hearer's Understanding of Korean-American Theologies of *Han*

IN THE PREVIOUS CHAPTER, I laid out the theoretical apparatus for pursuing an intercultural communication event. I described my understanding of culture as *globalized,* my approach to culture as *semiotic,* and my intercultural hermeneutic as *particularist*—one that posits the relative incommensurability of cultures. Furthermore, I located myself as an *outer hearer* and the theologians of *han* as the *inner speakers* and proposed *intercultural communication competence* as one tool for gauging the relative adequacy of the communication of *han* from one location to the other. Chapter 4 will provide my outer-hearer's reception and interpretation of the Korean-American theologies of *han,* particularly through the work of Andrew Sung Park and Wonhee Anne Joh.

This chapter will proceed in three sections. Section One will contextualize Park's and Joh's theologies by discussing the roots of *han* in Korean language, history, and religion. I will do this by first providing a brief etymology of the transliterated word *han* that has more than one meaning. I will delineate the specific understanding of *han* with which I am engaging. Next, I will discuss *han* within several periods of Korean history, as well as Ham Sok-Hon's characterization of Korea as the *Queen of Suffering,* that theologically interprets this history. Then, I will discuss *han* and religion, and in particular, its connection with Korean shamanism. This is because it is in traditional shamanism that *han* has found its most definitive ritual articulation. An outer-hearer cannot approach an adequate understanding of *han* without reference to shamanism.[305]

---

305. I am aware that the traditional way for articulating Korean names is to place the family name first. However, many Korean-American writers, as well as Korean

In Section Two, I will briefly discuss the modern re-embrace and re-articulation of *han* that arose with Christian *minjung* theology in the mid-twentieth century. I will give a brief sketch of those who retrieved *han,* focusing most specifically upon the poet Kim Chi-Ha and first-generation *minjung* theologian Suh Nam-Dong. My purpose here is not to provide an exhaustive survey of their work. Rather, it is to pinpoint the way in which Kim and Suh theologically and culturally re-embraced and re-articulated *han,* a move which enabled Park and Joh to proceed with their later projects. I will conclude this section with a summary of the critiques of the *han* of *minjung* theology by Chung Hyun-Kyung, who employs a critical Korean-feminist hermeneutic to bring to the fore the experience of *minjung* women, as well as the work of Jae-Hoon Lee who offers a psychologically-based critique of the primarily socio-economic interpretations of *han* by *minjung* theologians.

In the third section, I will provide an in-depth discussion of Korean-American Protestant theologians Andrew Sung Park and Wonhee Anne Joh. I will discuss each of their understandings of *han,* their theological reflections upon these understandings, and each theologian's discussion of how Christian salvation from sin and *han* is to be envisioned. I will conclude this section by highlighting three shared contours that arise from Park's and Joh's theologies and that will function as points of dialogue with Schillebeeckx: an anthropology of *han,* a preference for narrative and praxis, and a re-envisioning of a crucifixion soteriology/theology of the cross.

Section One: The Roots of Han in Korean Language, History, and Religion

It is no overstatement to say that *han* is ultimately untranslatable from Korean into English. Therefore, it is important to engage *han* not only from a theological perspective but also from linguistic, historical and religio-cultural perspectives. This pursuit will lay the foundation for a relatively adequate, outer-hearer's reception and interpretation of *han.*

---

writers working in the U.S., use the Anglicized ordering. Therefore, for each thinker I will follow the way in which he or she has presented his or her name as an author.

Han or Haan? The Work of Kim Sang-Yil and Chang-Hee Son

The Korean written language (*hangul*) spells *han* in one way.[306] It is important to point out, however, that this *hangul* spelling can signify three distinct and unequivocal "*hans*." This is a distinction that Chang-Hee Son, whose work is based on the philosophy of Kim Sang-Yil, notes between what he calls *han* of *han* philosophy, *haan* of *minjung* theology, and the Southern *Han* people of China.[307] Son points out that each is based upon a different a Sino-Korean character[308] which emphasizes their unequivocal meanings.[309]

Son's first transliteration, *han*, is similar to a philosophical concept in the Western intellectual sense, although not identical with it. It is associated with the philosophy of *hanism*[310] that was articulated by

---

306. Although I am discussing the distinction that the linguistic-philosophical analyses of Kim Sang-Yil and Chang-Hee Son provide, I am not adopting Son's transliteration "*haan*." This is for the sake of intelligibility and consistency with Park and Joh, both of whom transliterate the term as *han* and which has become standard in the theological literature. Their work will be discussed below.

307. It is important to briefly mention that Ryu's *Pungryu* theology, which Park discusses at length, also makes a distinction between the *han* of Korean thought and the *han* of *minjung* theology. For Ryu (somewhat similar to Kim Sang-Yil and Chang-Hee Son), *han* points to the basic structure and foundation of the Korean culture and mind, and is signified by a constellation of terms such as integrating, synthesizing, inclusive, and unifying, among others. Ryu claims that this retrieval of a cultural-religious *han* is the solution to the problem of Korean "absent-mindedness," or lack of identity, inflicted upon Koreans through colonialism and neo-colonialism. By reconstructing and highlighting an ancient Korean *Pungryudo* religion (synthesis of Shamanism, Daoism, Confucianism, and Buddhism), which Ryu believes is the original religion of Korea and the essence of its mind and culture, Ryu hopes to conceive a *Pungryu* Christianity that emboldens and gives cultural healing, dignity, and life to the Korean people while also enabling them to live out the Gospel. For Ryu, the reintegration of *han*, *mot*, and *sarm* are necessary in order to bring about a true Korean Christianity. These three terms correspond to three basic Korean religious beliefs in a god of heaven, god of earth, and god of divine/human union. See Park's discussion of Ryu in "Minjung and P'ungryu Theologies in Contemporary Korea," 99–148.

308. Following Kim, Son prefers to speak of these characters not as Chinese but as Sino-Korean. This is a question of philosophy, culture, and historiography and the trajectory of the larger philosophical-historical project in which Kim is involved. I need not get into that debate here but will employ Son's terminology to keep this analysis focused upon Korean language. The Korean word for this script is *hanja*.

309. Son, *Haan of Minjung Theology and the Han of Han Philosophy*, 129–30, 135–41.

310. The foundation for *hanism*, or a philosophy of *han*, is found within late twentieth-century Korean studies that worked with a hermeneutic of suspicion toward the

Kim Sang-Yil.[311] Kim argues that the term *han* is at the basis of Korean identity, philosophy and culture. For example, it is found in the words denoting the Korean nation (*hanguk*), the Korean people (*hanminchuk*), Korean spirituality (*hanol*), and the traditional name for God (*Hananim/Hanunim*). Moreover, Kim points out that *han* was a term that the Japanese colonizers attempted to eradicate completely from Korean culture due to its innate connection to Korean identity and self-understanding.[312] As Kim argues, "*Han* is as deeply rooted in the Korean mind as *Yahweh* for the Jewish mind, *Logos* for the Greek mind, *Emptiness* for the Indian mind, and *Tao* for the Chinese mind. But unlike Yahweh, Logos, Emptiness and Tao which are known throughout the whole world, the word Han has been seldom explained and organized ideologically."[313] Son references this aspect of Kim's work, but is quick to point out that it "is not a word which is equivalent to Koreanness. Rather, Koreanness became associated with the term *han*."[314]

Kim's definition of *han* is "non-orientability." Kim describes this concept as connoting "nonsubstantial, nondualistic, neither front nor back, neither left nor right, neither above nor below, neither up nor

---

works on Korean history that had been accepted as authoritative. These had been written primarily by Japanese colonizers who saw little value in traditional Korean culture and a lack of philosophy, as well as Westerners who worked within a Sino-centric paradigm in which Korean culture was little more than a mere derivative of Chinese culture. See Kim Sang-Yil, "What is Hanism?," 10–15. Kim and other scholars used this hermeneutic of suspicion to retrieve the deep roots of Korean culture, particularly through the culture of the earlier Dong-i people who allegedly carried the philosophy of *han* with them. See Son, *Haan of Minjung Theology and the Han of Han Philosophy*, 81–86. See also Yu's *Korean Thought and Culture*.

311. I use Kim as the focus, although he credits Ahn Ho-Sang and Choi Min-Hong as being the true pioneers in the field of *hanism*. See Kim's "What is Hanism?," 20. The majority of Kim's works have not yet been translated into English. So, my primary sources are limited to those few in English translation and the references in Son's work to the untranslated works of Kim. Kim's work is not without its critics and detractors and my purpose here, as a theologian, is merely to flesh out the distinction that he and Son are making within the Korean language among various meanings associated with one *hangul* word.

312. Kim Sang-Yil, "*Hanism*: Korean Concept of Ultimacy," 17.

313. Ibid. It is important to point out that Kim's implied understanding of culture here is not the one with which my own study is working. It seems that Kim is assuming a modern or essentialist view of culture rather than the globalized understanding I have embraced in the previous chapter.

314. Son, *Haan of Minjung Theology and the Han of Han Philosophy*, 69.

down, etc."³¹⁵ Kim goes on to give the example of *Hanbokbajee*, or Korean traditional trousers, that are nonorientable in the sense that they have no delineated front or back. There are no signifying marks for either orientation.³¹⁶ In Son's interpretation, the *han* of philosophy and Korean identity also includes "oneness, sameness, wholeness, totality, extremity, and summit."³¹⁷ In short, this understanding of *han* is an ancient term that historically precedes any community of "Korean" people but has laid its cultural and religious foundation. At the same time, it cannot be dissociated from any accurate description of Korean culture and self-understanding.

Son adopts the distinction between the *han* of *hanism* and the *haan* of *minjung* theology that also is suggested by Kim. The latter is the vein in which Park and Joh are writing. Regarding *haan*, Son traces its origin from two Sino-Korean characters upon which the full character is based. The first, carries the meaning of "heart" or "mind" and the second, caries the meaning "to remain still or calm."³¹⁸ Son describes the fullness of the character as connoting a tree with roots stretching very deeply into the earth. This represents the depth of an individual or group's woundedness that is always there, yet not always apparent.³¹⁹ As Son writes:

> [H]aan is used to describe the heart of a person or people who has/have endured or is/are enduring an affliction but the pains, wounds, and scars are not always apparent and visible because they are the kind that occur deep within the essence, core being, or heart of a person . . . *haan* connotes a mind's or a heart's affliction and struggle with a deep emotional or spiritual pain which

---

315. Kim Sang-Yil, "*Hanism*: Korean Concept of Ultimacy," 18. For a somewhat more detailed description of this "non-orientability," see Kim Sang-Yil, *Hanism as Korean Mind*, 90–96. For Kim Sang-Yil's relation between *hanism* and the *han* of *minjung* theology, see *Hanism as Korean Mind* 103–11. Of particular interest is Kim's claim that the *han* of *hanism* is the cure to the *han* of the people. On page 110, Kim argues that "han is the condition of *orientability* while Han is that of *non-orientability* . . . Han becomes *Han; resentment becomes love*. This kind of transformation is the goal of Korean society at the present time."

316. Kim Sang-Yil, "*Hanism*: Korean Concept of Ultimacy," 18.

317. Son, *Haan of Minjung Theology and the Han of Han Philosophy*, 5. To illustrate Kim Sang-Yil's claim of *non-orientability*, Son describes how in Korean there is very little distinction between "I" and "You." He observes that when a man introduces his wife to someone else, the translation is "this is *our* wife" as opposed to "this is *my* wife" (5).

318. Ibid., 4.

319. Ibid.

either poisons the entire being or even ends up nourishing the person.[320]

Having discussed the linguistic distinction between what Son calls the *han* of philosophy and the *haan* of *minjung* theology, and making it clear that it is the anthropological *han* to which I am referring in this study and not the philosophical "concept," I now turn to the roots of this *han* in Korean history.

The Socio-Political Roots of Han in the History of Korea: A Brief Overview

The purpose of this historical discussion is to highlight the numerous socio-political causes of *han,* both internal and external, throughout Korean history. Although a more thorough investigation of the historical roots of *han* would extend back to the Paleolithic Age, the *T'angun* founding myth, Ancient Joseon, the Three Kingdoms Period, and United Silla (an overarching time period that spans from pre-Bronze age peoples to the fall of Silla in 918 C.E.),[321] I will not discuss these earlier periods.[322] For the sake of brevity, I will begin with the inception of the state of Koryo (918–1388 C.E.), which occurred after the fall of United Silla.

The state of Koryo experienced invasions by the regional great powers on a more extensive scale than earlier in Korean history. For example, from 1231–1279, the Mongols continually invaded Koryo and brought great destruction and loss of life. This eventually led Koryo to become a vassal state of the Mongol Empire for eighty years. It was not external strife, however, but internal strife that ultimately led to the fall of Koryo. After Koryo emerged from Mongolian rule, General Yi Seong-gye was ordered by the king of Koryo to attack China and re-take Manchuria. After departing with his army, General Yi reconsidered and led the army back into Koryo. Once there, he overthrew the rulers, installed himself as king, and thus began the long rule of the Yi (Joseon) Dynasty (1388–1910).

320. Ibid., 14.

321. For a brief history of Korea from the *Joseon* Dynasty until the present, see Kim Sung-Soo's *Ham Sok-Hon,* 27–65. For an extensive overview of Korean History, see Seth, *A History of Korea: From Antiquity to the Present* and also see also Hwang, *A History of Korea: an Episodic Narrative.*

322. For a brief overview of Korean history, from the perspective of the *minjung* that includes the various *minjung* rebellions, see CTC-CCA, *Minjung Theology,* 167–77.

It is during the Yi period that many *minjung* theologians find the more contemporary roots of *han*. In addition to continuous invasions by Japan and other powers, much *han* was fostered due to the kingdom's rigid embrace of neo-Confucianism as a governing and cultural philosophy.[323] This embrace of neo-Confucianism was fostered by the emerging *yangban* class who came to power as part of the ruling class. Neo-Confucianism, as advocated by an emerging scholar-class, provided the philosophical warrant for the *yangban*'s position of power as well as that of the Yi monarchs. This embrace of neo-Confucianism led to a rigidly defined class hierarchy, in which the peasants—the majority of the population—were further impoverished.

In addition, it is during this period that gender oppression intensified as women became officially subordinated to men and confined to the family. As Il-Sun Youn observes regarding neo-Confucianism, "The ethical norms enforced by this social pattern require that women be subjected to three obediences: as a child a girl should be obedient to her father, as a married woman to her husband, and as a widow her son."[324] In addition, Volker Küster points out that in Yi Korea there were only four possible professions open to women who wanted to venture outside of a role as wife: palace woman (who worked in various departments such as the kitchen, clothes-making, and laundry, to name but a few), a female physician—*uinyo*—(who mostly treated women due to gender separation), courtesan (concubine), or shaman. Of these, only the shaman was allowed to marry.[325] This is a further example of the heightened oppression of women during the Yi Dynasty.

If the state of Koryo illustrates the beginnings of external invasions and the Yi Dynasty the intensification of the internal oppression of women and the poor, it was the onset of Japanese Occupation (1905–1945) that collectively deepened the *han* of the entire Korean people. The roots of the occupation are in the late nineteenth century when Korea was

323. Among many other works, see Grace Kim, "Oppression and *Han*: Korean Women's Historical Context," 55–70.

324. Youn, "Toward authentic partnership for mutual ministry in the Korean Catholic Context," 18. For a helpful, extended discussion of Korean Confucianism and neo-Confucianism, see pages 59–74. Youn's summary is particularly illuminating on the ways in which Korean neo-Confucianism was oppressive towards women. For a more concise history, see Grace Kim, "Oppression and *Han*: Korean Women's Historical Context," 58–66. For an extended treatment, see Deuchler's *The Confucian Transformation of Korea: A Study of Society and Ideology*.

325. Küster, *A Protestant Theology of Passion*, 39.

under the influence of China. During the internal Tonghak Rebellion (1894)[326] against the Yi Dynasty, China sent armed forces to Korea to help the Yi rulers put down the Rebellion and Japan followed suit. Since both China and Japan had an interest in possessing Korea, this led to the Sino-Japanese war (1894–1895) in which China was defeated. Korea was scarred but still existed as a somewhat independent nation.

This was to change after the Russo-Japanese War (1904–1905) when Japan warred with Russia over Korea, defeated them, and declared Korea its 'protectorate' in 1905. Then, in 1910, Japan extended its Empire by officially annexing Korea. As a part of the Japanese Empire, the economy, land, people, and resources of Korea had one purpose: to strengthen and glorify the Japanese Empire. This period of Japanese occupation was a time in which Japan attempted to fully assimilate Korea into becoming Japanese, going so far as to outlaw the Korean language and to force Koreans to adopt Japanese names. Everything distinctively Korean was to be annihilated so the Koreans could become "civilized" and "Japanized." In addition to this cultural program, tens of thousands of Korean women were forced into sex slavery during the Second World War. They were forced to be "comfort women" to the Japanese soldiers. That is, they were forced to be prostitutes for the pleasure of hundreds of thousands of Japanese soldiers who were away from their homes and in need of sexual "comfort."[327]

The final period of interest for this study is that of Divided Korea (1945–). Post-WWII, the U.S. and the Soviets divided the Korean

---

326. *Tonghak* (Eastern Learning) religion was a response to the influence of Western (especially Catholic) learning (called *sohak*) and encompassed a fusion of Shamanism, Buddhism, Daoism, and perhaps some elements of Christianity. Its founder, Ch'oe Che-u (1824–1864) proclaimed an enlightenment from heaven and taught that all men bear divinity (*Si Ch'onju*). Later, the third leader of the religion Sohn Pyong-Hui, changed the name to *Cheondogyo* (Religion of Heaven) and proclaimed the unity of God and man. This egalitarian vision was at odds with the hierarchy and class oppression practiced by the Yi Dynasty and attracted both peasants and disenfranchised *yangban*. Thus, this religion was the foundation for the *Tonghak* Rebellions (1894–95) against the Yi Dynasty. These rebellions led to the Sino-Japanese War for cultural and political influence over the Korean peninsula. For a brief overview of *Tonghak*, see Yu, *Korean Thought and Culture: A New Introduction*, 72–75. See also Hwang, *A History of Korea: An Episodic Narrative*, 118–38.

327. See Youn, "Toward Authentic Partnership for Mutual Ministry in the Korean Catholic Context," 25–30, for an overview of Korean comfort women. For a more thorough treatment, see Hicks's *The Comfort Women: Japan's Brutal Regime of Enforced Prostitution during the Second World War*. See also Yoshimi's study, *Comfort Women: Sexual Slavery in the Japanese Military during World War II*; and Keller's novel, *Comfort Woman*.

nation and made it a front in the Cold War. Even before the onset and conclusion of civil war—the Korean War (1950–1953)— the U.S. supported Syngman Rhee —a.k.a., Yi Seung-Man— (1948–1960) as the president of South Korea while Kim Il-Sung became the communist leader of North Korea. A later student protest toppled the oppressive and corrupt Rhee regime (1960) and in its aftermath Gen. Park Chung-Hee overthrew the government and installed himself as dictator (1961–1979). A similar *coup d'état* would occur in the wake of Park's assassination by the KCIA[328] when Gen. Chun Doo-Hwon seized power (1979–1987).[329] Rhee's corrupt regime and Park's and Chun's violent and oppressive dictatorships were the context for the rise of the twentieth-century *minjung* movement and the retrieval and re-articulation of *han* by poets, philosophers, and theologians.[330]

A period of democratization ensued when Chun named Roh Tae-Woo as his successor in 1987 and later Roh was forced to call elections in 1988 and won (Roh's regime lasted from 1988 to 1993). The subsequent history of Korea, that includes the post-Roh presidencies that prosecuted Chun and Roh for their involvement in the Kwangju massacre, the rise and fall of the 'tiger' economy of South Korea, and the continued isolation of North Korea, is not as much of the concern of my study and thus will not be treated here.

In summary, the historical roots of *han* have a fourfold dimension as described by Suh Nam-Dong: colonization and invasion by regional powers such as China, Japan, and Mongolia that threatened the very existence of the Korean nation and people; the tyrannical rulers who inflicted

---

328. Korean Central Intelligence Agency. The secret police that were charged with fighting communists and internal enemies/dissidents in South Korea.

329. In my brief, historical overview, I have omitted the role of religion in general, and Christianity in particular, from my discussion of the historical roots of *han*. This is not because the various religions have played no role in fostering or dealing with *han*. This is because the role of many religions in fostering *han* was often part and parcel of their adoption and functioning as a state ideology. The more recent history of Christianity in Korea (introduced around 1777) has played both liberating and oppressive roles in Korean history and I do not have space to discuss it here. See Yu, *Korea and Christianity*.

330. In my brief twentieth-century history of Korea, I do not have sufficient space to touch upon important events such as the March 1st Uprising, Gen. Park's *Emergency Decrees* and amendments to the constitution, nor to the 1980 Kwangju uprising and massacre by Gen Chun that Andrew Sung Park calls the first modern *minjung* rebellion. For more on these events, and among many sources, see Seth, *Concise History of Modern Korea*.

great suffering upon the Korean people; neo-Confucianism's strict subordination and oppression of women, so that "the existence of women was *han* itself"; and the overwhelming number of Korean peasants who were officially registered as hereditary slaves and thus treated as government property throughout Korean history.[331]

A Han-Ridden Theological Interpretation of Korean History: Ham Sok-Hon

To more fully illustrate the *han* of Korean history, I now turn to the work of Ham Sok-Hon (1901–1989). Ham, although not a historian per se, has provided an unconventional yet illuminating history of Korea that makes clear the context that gave rise to *han*.[332] Ham was a unique figure in the modern history of Korea. He was a prolific writer and important social activist for democracy and for an authentically Korean Christianity. He was a Korean Quaker who was influenced by Gandhi as well as traditional East Asian religions such as Buddhism and Daoism. As his biographer Kim Soo-Sung describes him:

> Who was Ham? For the public, he was a writer who knew the East Asian classics as well as the Bible and who was a uniquely inspiring interpreter of both of them. Ham's life could be summed up as a pacifist resister against unjust political regimes. His thoughts could be described as those of a religious nonconformist and a spiritual maverick.[333]

Ham became an important symbol of nonviolent change during the corrupt regime of Syngman Rhee (1945–1960) but most importantly during the military dictatorships of Park Chung-Hee (1961–1979) and Chun Doo-Hwan (1979–1987), both of which imprisoned him on several occasions. Ham was not an official scholar or church leader. Yet, he proved to be a formative influence upon contemporary Korean identity, as exemplified in the writing discussed here.

Ham's is not a conventional history but rather a theological and religious interpretation of the historical development of Korea. Ham's narrative encompasses the entirety of Korean history from time immemorial

---

331. CTC-CCA, *Minjung Theology*, 58.

332. For an additional helpful history of the roots of *han* see Son, *Haan of Minjung Theology and the Han of Han Philosophy*, 18–32.

333. Kim Sung Soo, *Ham Sok-Hon*, 14.

to the time of his writing in the late twentieth century. He describes Korea's history as that of missed chances, victimization, and continually having worldly greatness frustrated by internal and external strife. Kim points out that Ham did not wish to hide the shame ever-present in Korea's history and memory. Instead, Ham connected Korea's suffering with Jesus, the Suffering Servant, and provided the metaphor *Queen of Suffering* (*Ttus-uro Pon Han'guk Yoksa*) to describe Korea, its people, and its history.[334]

Ham is not credited with directly contributing to the Korean theological understandings of *han* (even though he had a strong formative influence on theologians Ahn Byung-mu and Suh Nam-dong), but Ham's work is colored by a sense of frustration and loss that points to *han*, as discussed above. When characterizing his nation and people in *The Queen of Suffering: A Spiritual History of Korea*, Ham writes, "This land, this people, events big and small, its politics and religion, its art and thought—all that is Korean bespeaks suffering. It is a fact, however shameful and painful."[335] For Ham, his Queen of Suffering is one who knows *han* well. He writes:

> In the first place, ours is not a major nation. Never has Korea played a leading role on the world stage. Nor are there historic relics of vast dimensions comparable to the pyramids or Great Wall, no great inventions of worldwide significance. Personalities there have been, but none sufficiently instrumental to effect great change in world history. No Korean thought has even remotely measured up to setting a trend in world philosophy. Korean history is one of oppression and shame, tearing apart and splitting up, losing and lagging behind. Each nation of the world has its gift to bring to God. All Korea has is poverty and suffering.[336]

After this description, Ham then comes to an insight:

> Amid such agony, the Bible pointed me to the truth, and it was faith that came to my rescue: this suffering is none other than the crown of thorns Korea wears. It turned history inside out and showed me the hidden side of world history. When I realized that the path of the world along which humankind is going

---

334. Ibid., 21–22.
335. Ham, *Queen of Suffering*, 22.
336. Ibid.

is basically one of suffering, Korea, which I thought a maltreated slave, was in fact a queen with her thorny crown.[337]

Finally, Ham arrives at a kind of conclusion:

> Why were we made to bear a burden of suffering? . . . I see it as God's way of curing the malady . . . for suffering makes people think and gives depth to life. Suffering purifies history. An easy-going person thinking in only two dimensions will gain through suffering religion which has three dimensions. A history full of oppression and fighting has all the potential for doing good when seen with tearful eyes. Had it not been for high-handed China, fierce Manchuria, bold Japan, and ominous Russia—all hard to bear—Korea might well have gone under. We are plodding the path of suffering for we want to live. We are alive for God permits it. That God lets us be alive is proof that he has work for us to do. Therefore, we have to endure the scourge of suffering in order to complete the work history has entrusted to us.[338]

Ham continues his history into the late twentieth century of a divided Korea where he describes the 38th parallel as a wound and a test. He writes that on the 38th parallel ". . . American democracy and Soviet communism were weighed and found wanting. It is a line along which modern history failed."[339] Ham continues, "the 38th parallel is a test given by God, perhaps the last one for the nation. Pass this test and Korea will live. Failing in this, however, may well lead to its end for all time."[340] In short, Ham's *Spiritual History of Korea* highlights Korea's great suffering, loss, frustration, and disappointment. At the same time, Ham thinks that Korea as the Queen of Suffering has an important role to play in world history, akin to the biblical Suffering Servant.

The Religion of Han: An Overview of Korean Shamanism

Having given a brief overview of the linguistic and historical roots of *han*, as well as Ham's theological interpretation of that history, I now turn to *han*'s religious expression in Korean Shamanism. Shamanism is perhaps the most important cultural-religious phenomenon for an outer-hearer to

---

337. Ibid.
338. Ibid., 35.
339. Ibid., 160.
340. Ibid., 161.

engage in order to apprehend some of the meaning associated with *han*. There are three aspects of Korean Shamanism that I wish to briefly discuss: its history, practices, and role within Korean culture, its ritual (*kut*) in which *han* is resolved, and its particular importance for Korean women.

Shamanism[341] (known as *Mugyo* or *Mudang*) is the oldest known religion in Korea and has a history of approximately 5,000 years. This is in contrast to Buddhism, which was adopted during the Three Kingdoms Period and United Silla (200s to 816 C.E.) and flourished during Koryo (816–1388), Daoism, also called *Son-bi* (Shamanistic Daoism), which was introduced somewhat earlier than Buddhism and played a greater role for the common people than the ruling class,[342] the philosophy of Confucianism that entered during the Three Kingdom Period but wasn't fully embraced until the Yi Dynasty (1388–1910), and the religions of Catholic and Protestant Christianity which entered Korea in the 18th and 19th centuries.[343]

Due to its deep historical roots, Shamanism was the primary religion of Korean culture, society, and government and laid the foundation for Korean religious sensibilities. After the rise of Buddhism, and especially after the rise of neo-Confucianism and Christianity, however, Korean Shamanism became a marginalized religious practice that was looked down upon by the greater society as mere superstition.[344] In the view of the elites, Shamanism was a backwards, and perhaps despicable, remnant of earlier Korean culture. As Hahm Pyong-Choon points out, this negative attitude continues into modern Korea: "The pervasive influence of Shamanistic attitudes on Korean culture is frequently blamed for

341. The word *shamanism* has its roots in the *Tungusic* language of Eastern Siberia (the word *saman*) which literally meant "one who becomes excited." See Youn, "Toward Authentic Partnership for Mutual Ministry in the Korean Catholic Context," 53.

342. This point can be argued, however, due to the philosophy of *Hwarang-do* in which an elite youth corps in Silla was involved in a life of martial arts, *Sonbi* (Shamanistic Daoist) education, practices and philosophy, shamanistic religious practice, and traditional art and dance. For a good account of the inception and influence of *Hwarang-do* upon Korean thought and religion, see Yu, *Korean Thought and Culture: A New Introduction*, 29–47. See also Guisso and Yu, *Shamanism: The Spirit World of Korea*, 98–118.

343. There are other religions that also are present and important within Korean culture and history, for example, *Tonghak* and *Pugryo*, both of which were noted above. For a brief overview of the history of Korean Christian thought, and the influence of traditional Korean religions upon it, see Yu, *Korean Thought and Culture: A New Introduction*, 97–107.

344. Küster, *A Protestant Theology of Passion*, 38.

everything that is, and has been, 'wrong' with Korea."³⁴⁵ Nevertheless, as of 2000, according to some estimates 87% of Koreans still adhere to some kind of shamanistic practices.³⁴⁶

As Il-Sun Youn observes, Korean Shamanism is a religion that intuits spirits in all of creation—villages, mountains, rocks, rivers, wind, harvest, animals, trees, etc.—and assumes that these spirits interact with people in their everyday lives. Therefore, people would offer sacrifices to the spirits in order to appease them, ask protection from them, or obtain favors from them. Shamanism is egalitarian, professes no explicit doctrines, is not based on any specific historical event, and is not organized into an institution, per se, as other religions tend to be. Also, Shamanism does not profess any vision or understanding of 'salvation' in an otherworldly or eschatological sense. This is because it is mainly concerned with the here and now and with obtaining blessings, healing, and protection from the spirits or gods while also avoiding punishment from them.³⁴⁷ When describing the importance of Shamanism in Korean culture, Grace Kim observes that "since its founding, Korean mass culture has been Shamanistic in its basic characteristics and tone."³⁴⁸ Her observation means that a shamanistic outlook on the world, regardless of one's religious affiliation (or lack thereof), remains the primary religious undercurrent of Korean culture and worldview.³⁴⁹

Having discussed the connection of Shamanism to Korean culture and religiosity, I now move to its connection to *han* through ritual. Although shamans historically could fulfill the roles of fortune-tellers, priests, and even rulers on occasion (as in ancient Korea), the role of shamans as healers is of the most relevance for this study. The shaman

---

345. Guisso and Yu, *Shamanism: The Spirit World of Korea*, 78.

346. This number may be outdated. It comes from the 2002 work by Youn, "Toward Authentic Partnership for Mutual Ministry in the Korean Catholic Context," 53.

347. Ibid., 58–59.

348. Grace Kim, "Women's Oppression and Han," 55. This observation is confirmed by Tong-shik Ryu. See Park, "Minjung and P'ungryu Theologies in Contemporary Korea," 99–148.

349. With respect to the historically controversial practice of "ancestor worship" from a Christian perspective, Hahm argues that shamanistic commemoration of ancestors is not worship in the religious sense. He writes, "Just as the shamanistic man bows and offers food to his living parents, he does the same for them when they are dead; they are still his parents, and still are deserving of his respect and affection." See Hahm's "Shamanism and the Korean World-View, Family Life Cycle, Society and Social Life," 78.

can embody the role of healer in order to resolve the wounds of *han*. The Korean word for the leader of a shamanistic ceremony (*kut*) is *mutang*. As *mutang*, the shaman acts as a medium between the spirit world and the world of the people and enables communication and even reconciliation between the two worlds. This mediation happens either indirectly—contact with the gods through visions or auditory communication—or directly—through being fully possessed by the gods who speak through her.[350] There are three major reasons for asking a shaman to perform a *kut*. These include personal healing, soothing a spiteful soul, or gaining prosperity for a family.[351] In addition, the *kut* was not only for the living but also for the wandering spirits of the dead who could not rest due to their unresolved *han*.

The shaman, as healer and *mutang*, enables *han* to be accounted for and resolved through the *kut*. As Chung Hyun-Kyung points out, the term for the resolution of *han* that comes from Shamanism is *han-pu-ri*. In Chung's analysis, there are three general movements throughout the duration and various steps of a *kut*. These are *speaking and hearing*, *naming*, and *changing*. Chung describes the first as the shaman enabling the *han*-ridden person(s) or ghost(s) to speak. This often occurs through a dialogue with or even possession of the shaman. This allows the ghost or person to break her/his silence and tell the story of her/his *han* that was never brought to light. In the second step, the shaman enables the *han*-ridden person(s) or ghost to name the source that caused the unresolved *han*. In the third step, the community and hearers are emboldened to change the structures of whatever caused the *han* in the first place.[352]

Korean Shamanism has played and continues to play an important role in the lives of Korean women. Scholars estimate that of all Korean shamans (or *mutangs*) upwards of 85% of them are women and it is primarily women who are the patrons of shamans. As Youn argues, in

---

350. Küster, *A Protestant Theology of Passion: Korean Minjung Theology Revisited*, 37–38.

351. Youn, "Toward Authentic Partnership for Mutual Ministry in the Korean Catholic Context," 58.

352. Chung, "*Han-Pu-Ri*: Doing Theology from Korean Women's Perspective," 35. For an interpretation of the Shamanistic *kut* through an engagement with contemporary psychology, see Guisso and Yu, *Shamanism*, 131–61. It is important to point out, however, that Chung's description offers guidelines and a trajectory for healing based on the structure of the *kut* and is more theological than phenomenological. She omits the sometimes radical (and perhaps dangerous) elements of the *kut* that include exorcisms and possessions.

a similar vein with Chung, the ongoing existence and practice of Shamanism and *kut* for healing is, primarily, a way for women to overcome gender and sexual oppression. This occurs through *han-pu-ri* during the *kut* and is a process that is supposed to result in internal transformation, "leading from repression, to liberation, to reintegration."[353] It is not only a process for women to expel and resolve their *han* and be liberated, but one in which liberation leads to a reintegration of mind, body, and spirit in order to lead a renewed life. The heart of Shamanism is centered upon women's *han* through women being both the shamans and the patrons.

As Youn also points out, Shamanism should be understood as a household religion. Not only were there spirits in the natural world, but in the household as well, such as spirits of the kitchen, gate, birthing, etc. This became particularly apparent during the Yi Dynasty, in which both Buddhism and Shamanism were suppressed and confined to the private spheres. The traditional Korean household became a sanctuary in which Shamanism survived and was practiced. Since it was a household religion, and women were the dominant force in the home, Shamanism became a religion of women.[354]

Concluding this overview, Shamanism has been the religion to which the *han*-filled people turned in order to be relieved of suffering. As David Kwang-Sun Suh has argued, Shamanism is the true religion of the suffering *minjung* because only it can understand the depth of their *han* and relieve them from its oppression.[355] This is the role that Shamanism has served for thousands of years and why it can be understood, loosely, as a religion of *han* within Korean culture.[356]

In this first section, I have attempted to contextualize the theologies of Park and Joh within the larger understandings of *han* that lie deep within Korean language, history, and religion/culture. It may seem somewhat arduous to have done so, but I would argue that it is very difficult for an outer-hearer to understand the breadth and the depth of *han* without

---

353. Youn, "Toward Authentic Partnership," 55–56.

354. Ibid., 53.

355. As referenced in Park, "Minjung and P'ungryu Theologies," 34–35.

356. There are many criticisms of Shamanism, such as it being too personal, inward-focused, and lacking a sociopolitical component. Moreover, there often has been an uncritical embrace, romanticization, and celebration of Shamanism by Westerners, perhaps a product of an orientalist mentality and legacy. I need not get into that debate here. For a helpful, contemporary treatment of Korean Shamanism, see Chong-Ho Kim, *Korean Shamanism: The Cultural Paradox*.

engaging its roots in language, history, and religion. Otherwise, a distortion of *han* as it crosses the cultural boundary is highly likely.

Section Two: Minjung Theology and Han: Four Thinkers

The retrieval and re-articulation of *han* in the twentieth century accompanied the rise of the *minjung* movement that sparked Christian *minjung* theology. As David Kwang-sun Suh recently described the term *minjung*, although an essentially untranslatable term it points to those who have been "politically oppressed, economically exploited and culturally alienated."[357] Or, as Hyun Young-Hak has described it, the *minjung* can be loosely associated with the "politically oppressed, economically exploited, socially alienated, culturally despised, or religiously condemned."[358] The *minjung* are the suffering masses of Korea who are present throughout Korean history in general and during the regimes of Rhee, Park, and Chun in particular.[359] Thus, *minjung* theology's inception was not in the church per se, but rather in Korean society in which Christianity was planted in the eighteenth century. It was a movement calling for salvation and liberation for the suffering *minjung* in the here and now in which the Christian churches played a role, to greater and lesser extents.[360] *Minjung* theologians were not only professors in the halls of academia. They also lived and worked among the *minjung* and began ministries and institutes to support the healing and emancipation of the *minjung* from socio-political *han*.

---

357. David Kwang-sun Suh, "Forward," xii–xiii. The term *minjung* consists of two Sino-Korean characters, *min* meaning people and *jung* meaning the masses.

358. Hyun Young-Hak as quoted in Andrew Sung Park, *The Wounded Heart of God*, 202n114.

359. For an excellent overview of the *minjung* cultural movement, see Küster, *A Protestant Theology of Passion*, 27–54. For an excellent dramatic rendering of this time period, the student uprisings, the dictatorships, and the Kwangju massacre and its impact on Korea, see the 1995 Korean television series *Sandglass (Moraesigye)*.

360. For an overview of the social and theological cross-pollination that led to the rise of *minjung* theology, see Küster's *A Protestant Theology of Passion*, 1–58. For a specific account of Christian history in Korea from a *minjung* perspective, see CTC-CCA, *Minjung Theology*, 38–121, 155–82.

The Articulation of the Han of the Minjung: Kim Chi-Ha

There are two representative figures from this time period that are important for my discussion of the retrieval and re-articulation of *han*: the poet Kim Chi-Ha and *minjung* theologian Suh Nam-Dong.[361] I will begin with Kim and there are three aspects of Kim's work that I wish to highlight: the roots of his writings in the experiences of the *minjung*, his understanding and description of *han*, and his philosophy of *dan* that is to overcome and resolve *han*.

The first generation of *minjung* theologians has expressed a great debt in retrieving and rearticulating *han* to the Roman Catholic lay writer and activist, Kim Chi-ha (b.1941).[362] Kim's life has been tumultuous and has mirrored the *han* of the *minjung* in many ways, which led to his writings being deeply connected to the *han* of the *minjung*. He was involved in the 1960 student protests that toppled the Rhee regime and was forced to go underground when the Park dictatorship began, due to illness and political pragmatism. His poems first were published in 1969 and after sensing a revolutionary potential in Christianity for liberating the *minjung* from oppression, he was baptized into Catholicism in 1971. Many times during the Park and Chun dictatorships he was imprisoned and tortured for his anti-regime plays, poems, and essays. During his 1974 imprisonment, Kim was sentenced to death by a military tribunal because of his anti-regime writings. Not long after, however, his sentence was commuted due to the outcry of the international community. During another imprisonment in 1975, Kim wrote his "Declaration of Conscience" as a refutation to his forced confession to being a communist that was obtained through torture. He was not released from prison until 1980 and has continued to write since

---

361. I focus upon these two figures due to their historical, cultural, and theological importance in tracing the roots of *han*. This is not meant to downplay the important work of other first-generation *minjung* theologians, such as Ahn Byung-Mu, Hyun Young-Hak, Kim Yong-Bock, and David Kwang-Sun Suh, to name but a few. In particular, Ahn's work on the Gospel of Mark and the meaning of the Greek term *ochlos* and its correlation to the suffering *minjung* of Korea, along with Kim Yong-Bock's work on *minjung* theology as social biography are important. Nevertheless, their work is beyond the scope of this chapter. For a good overview of these theologians, see Küster's *A Protestant Theology of Passion*, as well as Ahn's, Kim's, Suh's, and Hyun's essays in *Minjung Theology*. See also Ahn Byung-Mu's posthumously published *Jesus of Galilee*.

362. *Chi-Ha* is Kim's pen name and carries a twin meaning, based on its Sino-Korean characters, of "grass stream" and "underground," both of which are pronounced identically but the latter of which is Kim's intent. Kim's given name is *Yong-Il*. See McCann, *The Middle Hour*, 2–3.

his release.³⁶³ In light of the travails of Kim's life, it is no surprise that many of Kim's writings on *han* occurred in prison or used his prison experience as a reference point, location, and motivation.

Kim's writings show his yearning for solidarity with the *minjung* and his attempt to be a mouthpiece for their *han*. For example, Kim wrote in "Declaration of Conscience," "I want to be identified with the oppressed, the exploited, the suffering, and the despised common people. I want my life and my love to be dedicated, passionate, and manifested in practical ways. This is the sum of my self-imposed task for humanity . . . I hope my odyssey will be understood as a love for and faith in humanity."³⁶⁴ This sensibility led Kim's poetry, drama, and political writings to lay at the foundation of much of what became *minjung* theology's understanding of *han*. This is confirmed by theologian Suh Nam-Dong who argued that Kim is "the person who has done the most to develop *han* as a theme in Christian theology."³⁶⁵

Kim's understanding of *han* is found not only in his essays but also in his poems and plays. For example, literary scholars Chong-Sun Kim and Shelly Killen examine Kim's 1972 poem *Groundless Rumors*, which led to one of his imprisonments by the Park regime. They point out that two Korean words that Kim employs frequently are *t'onggok* ("lamentation") and *han* ("grudge" from the heart).³⁶⁶ They observe that in this poem Kim shows, "*Han* and *t'onggok* are sacred impulses that embody Korea's history of repressed suffering and rage. By stifling these cries, the law stifles what the ancients called the 'Will of Heaven.'"³⁶⁷ This poem demonstrates that, for Kim, *han* is inseparable from the cries of the Korean people and their embodiment as the *minjung*. When the governing powers neither listen nor attend to this *han*, they are not only continuing to oppress but also violating a foundational element within Korean culture.

---

363. For a representative example of the various kinds of poetry written at various stages of his life, transcribed in Korean and English, see Susie Jie Young Kim, "12 Poems of Kim Chi-Ha," 67–84. For a clear introduction to the development of Kim's poetry throughout his career, and the later *poetics of full emptiness*, see *Heart's Agony*.

364. Kim Chi-Ha, "Declaration of Conscience," 80. This same sentiment is articulated through his poetry. For example, see Kim's "Prayer, Midnight December 25th, 1974," 2.

365. CTC-CCA, *Minjung Theology*, 63.

366. Chong-Sun Kim and Killen, *The Gold-Crowned Jesus*, ix–xx.

367. Ibid., xx.

In his work, Kim describes *han* as a complex entity. Generally, Kim thinks *han* is the *minjung's* experiences of oppression and violation that also carries the energy for revolution and social transformation. Kim writes, "[A]ccumulated *han* is inherited and transmitted, boiling in the blood of the people" and it possesses "the emotional core of anti-regime action."[368] Kim, however, often emphasizes the intense negativity of *han* and one of Kim's sharpest descriptions of *han* is "a people eating monster."[369] For him, *han* is a "ghostly creature" that "appears as a concrete substance with enormous ugly and evil energy."[370]

Kim not only highlights and articulates the problem of *han* in his writings. He also articulates a solution in his philosophy of *dan*. In light of the extensiveness of *han* in Korean history and society, Kim sees himself as a "priest of *han*" through a practice of *dan*. For Kim, *dan* is the resolution to *han*. *Dan* is the cutting off and suppression of *han* in order to break the vicious cycles of suffering, revenge, and unjust violence it perpetuates. As Kim writes, "*Dan* is to overcome *han*. Personally, it is self-denial. Collectively, it is to cut the vicious circle of revenge."[371] This can be seen in Kim's poems and plays, as he acts as a kind of shaman who returns to and retrieves original deeds and memories of violence and suffering—which have created *han*— in order to bring them into the present.[372]

368. Kim Chi-Ha quoted in CTC-CCA, *Minjung Theology*, 64. Without having extensive knowledge of the Korean language, it is difficult for me to pinpoint where in Kim's writings he uses the term *han*.

369. Ibid.

370. Ibid. In Kim Chi-Ha's outline to his play *Sacred Place*, he characterizes *han* as a "metal eating monster" and the full quote on 64 is as follows: "[H]an, separating itself from human emotion, becomes substantial and grows into a ghostly creature. It appears as a concrete substance with enormous ugly and evil energy and rules and commands all of the prisoners. It is a hero, ghost, and a leader of a religious faction; how do I describe all this?"

371. Ibid., 65. In another quote by Kim found on page 179, Kim's definition of *dan* is "to cut all adherence to the secular world in order that one may be for the revolution of the secular world. It is to sever the link which permits circulation. There is a terrible accumulation of *han* which will burn in endless hate, massacre, revenge, and destruction. Therefore we need the repeated cutting which stops the vicious circular explosion and sublimates it to a higher spiritual power."

372. See, for example, Kim Chi-Ha's poems "The Plain" and "Chirisan" in "Twelve Poems of Kim Chiha," 67–69. See "April's Blood," "By the Sea," "Your Blood," and "Never Forget," in *The Middle Hour*, 18, 69–70, 72, 74, along with Kim's prison-writing, "Declaration of Conscience," in *The Middle Hour*, 77–87. See also his play "The Gold Crowned Jesus" and his poem "Seoul," in *The Gold-Crowned Jesus and Other Writings*, 85–131 and 6–7. Finally, see Kim's grotesque and evocative poem, "The Story of a Sound," 466–75.

Kim lifts up the *han*-filled victims and events, along with the will for vengeance they engender, in order to dismantle *han,* sometimes through a *violence of love* associated with a socio-political practice of *dan*. As Kim wrote, when reflecting upon Thomas Aquinas' argument people have the right to overthrow a tyrant, "I reject dehumanizing violence and accept the violence that restores human dignity. It could justly be called a violence of love."[373] No bloodthirsty revolutionary, however, Kim continues, "I welcome the violence of love, yet I am also an ally of true nonviolence. The revolution I would support would be a synthesis of true nonviolence and an agonized violence of love."[374]

This *agonized violence of love* is part of Kim's understanding of the socio-political practice of cutting off the cycle of *han* through *dan*. Its purpose is to create room for the *han*-ridden person/people to experience justice, renewal, and self-determination through cutting off the sources of *han* within government and society.[375] What underlies this is Kim's conviction that despite its intense negativity, *han* also can be sublimated by the *minjung* in order to foster a more just and peaceful world.[376] This is a reflection of his belief that God and revolution are intertwined. In Christian theological terms, for Kim the *reign of God through Christ* is already here and salvation from *han* is being embraced by the *minjung* through a personal and political practice of *dan*.

373. Kim Chi-Ha, "Declaration of Conscience," 83. For alternate texts and translations (that include his thoughts on *Chang Il-Dam*), see *The Gold-Crowned Jesus*, 13–39; and the *Bulletin of Concerned Asian Scholars*, 8–15.

374. Kim Chi-Ha, "Declaration of Conscience," 83.

375. Kim Chi-Ha and Killen, preface to *The Gold-Crowned Jesus*, xx.

376. See Jung-Young Lee, "Introduction," 9–11. Lee and other theologians see the roots of Kim Chi-Ha's understanding of *dan* as resolving *han* not only in Christianity, but also in the religion of the *Tonghak* movement, later called *Cheondogyo*, that proclaimed, "humanity is heaven." In this vein, Kim himself writes: "I repeat that Chang Il Tam's world is in flux. Religious asceticism and revolutionary action, the works of Jesus and the struggle of Ch'oe Che U (founder of the Tong Hak) and Chon Pong Jun (commander of the Tong Hak peasant army), a yearning for the communal life of early Christianity, and a deep affection for the long, valiant resistance of the Korean people are all part of Chang's kaleidoscopic world. So are Paulo Freire's *The Pedagogy of the Oppressed,* Frantz Fanon's ideas on violence, the direct action of Blanquism, the Christian view of humanity as flawed by original sin, the Catholic doctrine of the omnipresence of God and the Buddhist concept of the transmigration of the soul, the populist redistributive egalitarianism of Im Kok Chong and Hong Kil Tong, and the Tong Hak teachings of *Sich'onju* and *Yangch'onju*. Some of these movements and doctrines combine and coalesce; others clash in mighty confrontation." See "Declaration of Conscience," in *The Gold-Crowned Jesus*, 30–31.

One of Kim's most dramatic illustrations of *dan* is found in his poem *Chang Il- Dam*. As Suh Nam-Dong summarizes the narrative, the protagonist, Chang Il-Dam, is a *han*-filled person both through personal lineage and through socio-political circumstance. Kim characterizes Chang as a Christ-like figure who overcomes his *han* through a religious experience and then begins to preach liberation to the people. He gathers disciples and retreats with them into the mountains to teach them the practice of *dan*. Later, Chang and his disciples march to Seoul in order to proclaim the liberation of the *minjung* from their *han*. Chang is betrayed by one of his disciples, brought to trial before the rulers of Seoul, and beheaded. After three days, he rises from the dead and then the story takes a strange turn. Chang cuts off the head of his betrayer and places the betrayer's head on his own body and his own head on the betrayer's body.[377] In reflection, Kim writes, "It is an expression of Chang's conflicting thought that this is revenge but at the same time also the salvation of vicious men."[378] Or, as Suh Nam-Dong observes, "the head speaking justice and truth is bonded to the body carrying injustice and falsehood."[379] This is one example of *han* being resolved through *dan*.[380]

---

377. The story is recounted in CTC-CCA, *Minjung Theology*, 65–68 and 177–80. As Suh interprets this act on 179, "This peculiar combination of the body of the evil man and the head of truth indicates that Kim Chi-Ha thought that even the most wicked villain will be saved in the end. Through the carrier that is the body of the evil man, Chang Il-Dam's good news of liberation, like a wild and stormy wind, goes everywhere."

378. Kim Chi-Ha, as quoted in CTC-CCA, *Minjung Theology*, 67.

379. CTC-CCA, *Minjung Theology*, 67.

380. See Jung-Young Lee, *An Emerging Theology in World Perspective*, 10. Suh Nam-Dong describes four steps in Kim Chi-Ha's understanding of *dan*, which Kim admits comes from the fusion of spirituality and justice, or what Kim calls the unity of "God and revolution," in Catholic Social Teaching and also the *Tonghak* religion. "The first stage in this process is *Shichonju* (worshipping God in the mind), the second stage is *Yangchonju* (nurturing the body of God), the third stage is *Haengchonju* (practicing the struggle), and the fourth stage is *Sangchonju* (transcending death and living as a single, bright resurrected fighter for the people)." CTC-CCA, *Minjung Theology*, 67.

Towards a Theology of Han and
Minjung Liberation: Suh Nam-Dong

I now move from Kim to *minjung* theologian Suh Nam-Dong (1918–1984).[381] Of the first generation of *minjung* theologians, Suh was arguably the most instrumental in retrieving and utilizing *han* as a fundamental source in doing Christian theology. This focus upon *han* shows his indebtedness to Kim Chi-Ha. As Volker Küster observes, "The confluence of Christian and *minjung* traditions—which is of crucial importance to Suh's theological program—finds its programmatic equivalent in Kim Chi-Ha's dictum of the 'unity of God and revolution.'"[382]

Although born and raised in the Chonum Province of Korea, he received his theological training in Japan (as did many of his generation), returned to Korea in 1941 and was ordained a minister of the Presbyterian Church. He later became a teacher, pursued higher theological education, and embraced the *minjung* movement in 1975 which led to his dismissal from his teaching position at Yonsei University. Like many of the *minjung* movement, Suh was imprisoned and tortured on several occasions. As he writes, when discussing why the Christian churches should support the *minjung* and the theological reflections upon them, Suh writes, "If one does not hear the sighs of the *han* of the *minjung*, one cannot hear the voice of Christ knocking on our doors."[383]

There are two aspects of Suh's work that can contribute to this discussion: his use of *han* to theologically reflect upon the doctrines of sin and salvation and his method of story-telling in doing theology. Regarding sin, Suh thinks that the primary problem for Christian *minjung* theology is to understand and resolve *han*. Suh thinks that *han* is more important for Christian theology because it is the experience of the *minjung* whereas *sin* is the work of the oppressors. Suh thinks that the

---

381. The vast majority of Suh Nam-Dong's writings have yet to be translated into English, so I will rely heavily upon two translated essays of his and the interpretation of his theology by other scholars. I will, however, use Suh's own words whenever possible.

382. Küster, *A Protestant Theology of Passion*, 81–82. Kim Chi-Ha writes, "I've been grappling with that image for ten years. At some point, I gave it a name: 'The unity of God and revolution.' I also changed the phrase 'man [sic] is heaven' into 'rice is heaven' and used it in my poetry. That vague idea of the 'unity of God and revolution' stayed with me as I continued my long arduous search for personal and political answers, and as I became very interested in contemporary Christian thought and activism." See "Declaration of Conscience," 25.

383. CTC-CCA, *Minjung Theology*, 68.

oppressive rulers used the doctrine of sin to dehumanize and control the *minjung* for the purpose of sustaining and advancing their own dominant position in society.[384] As Andrew Park points out, "while the traditional theology discusses a kind of spiritual sin, Suh's *minjung* theology deals with the *han* of the *minjung*."[385]

Suh connects *han* to salvation. For Suh, salvation is realized eschatology; it is the present process of resolving the *han* carried by the *minjung* which was inflicted upon them by the sins of the rulers. When envisioning salvation, the symbol that Suh proposes in order to account for this realized salvation for the *minjung* is the Millennium. Suh finds the roots of this symbol in the millenarian outlook of the earliest church which he thinks disappeared with the inception of the Constantinian church. With the rise of Constantinian Christianity, Suh argues that the Christian understanding of the Messiah and Crucifixion was "depoliticized." Christianity became a tool for the benefit of Roman Empire instead of the revolutionary force to announce and bring salvation to the poor, marginalized, and oppressed that it had been previously.[386]

In light of this understanding of history, and citing the work of Joachim de Fiore and Thomas Müntzer, Suh proposes the symbol of the *Millennium*. He prefers this to *Kingdom of God* because he thinks that the latter has become benign, individual, and overly spiritualized. Suh thinks that the Millennium points to the future of this world whereas God's kingdom points to another realm altogether that is detached from this world.[387] As Suh writes:

> [T]he Kingdom of God is understood as the place the believer enters when he dies, but the Millennium is understood as the point at which history and society are renewed. Therefore, in the Kingdom of God the salvation of the individual person is secured, but in the Millennium is secured the salvation of the whole social reality of humankind. Consequently, while the Kingdom of God is used in the ideology of the ruler, the Millennium is the symbol of the aspiration of the *minjung*.[388]

---

384. Ibid. See also Park, "Minjung and P'ungryu Theologies," 41–45.
385. Park, "Minjung and P'ungryu Theologies," 45.
386. CTC-CCA, *Minjung Theology*, 161–62.
387. Ibid., 163–67. See also Park, "Minjung and P'ungryu Theologies," 45–50.
388. CTC-CCA, *Minjung Theology*, 162–63.

This understanding of the Millennium also plays a role in Suh's Christology. Suh bases his understanding of Jesus on the cross and the Suffering Servant. In this way, Jesus came to serve the *minjung* and to help others understand them. The suffering of Jesus was meant to awaken the *minjung* from their slumber of oppression and enlighten them of their messianic character and mission. Awakened by the suffering of Jesus and the groaning of the suffering Koreans, the *minjung* are commissioned with a messianic vocation to alleviate all that causes *han*.[389] Their work is the creation of a new, *han*-less, more just world.

Second, Suh's methodological use of storytelling is of great importance. Although he employs a three-fold methodology throughout the whole of his writings— socio-economic, pneumatological, and storytelling—storytelling is the most important in this study for understanding a theology of *han*. *Mindam* is the term Suh uses for the storytelling of the *minjung* in which they share their sufferings, frustrations, and affections. As Park describes Suh's understanding, "*mindam* contains the history of the suffering *minjung*, that is, their courageous resistance against their rulers and their hope-filled vision for a new society. The *minjung* through *mindam* lament, accuse, and challenge the injustice and corruption within society."[390] Suh interprets *mindam* as "the collective soul of the *minjung*."[391] Jung-Young Lee, however, makes a distinction between *mindam* and *silhwa*, the former having a more fictitious character to it and the latter having a more factual, biographical character.[392] The *minjung* employ both kinds of storytelling.

One of Suh's more pointed exercises in storytelling—in the vein of what Lee calls *silhwa*—deals with the life and death of Chun Tae-Il. As Park relates, Chun was born into dire poverty (b. 1948) and began working at a garment factory at a young age. The factory had miserable and dangerous working conditions. The average age of the workers was eighteen, and around 40% of the workers were between the ages of twelve and fifteen. The workers labored fifteen hour per day, with only two days off per month, and received pittance wages. The hardship of these working conditions caused the young workers to rapidly deteriorate

---

389. Ibid., 38–39. This awakening of the *minjung* and their messianic vocation given by Jesus the Christ is illustrated in dramatic form in Kim Chi Ha's, *The Gold-Crowned Jesus*.

390. Park, "Minjung and P'ungryu Theologies," 61.

391. Suh Nam-Dong, quoted in Park, "Minjung and P'ungryu Theologies," 61.

392. Jung-Young Lee, "Introduction," 16–18.

physically, showing everything from bronchitis, tuberculosis, to irregular menstruation.[393]

To summarize Suh's recounting of Chun's life, one day Chun witnessed a young woman vomiting blood due to overwork. In response, he began to study law and attempted to organize a labor union. This activity led to Chun being fired in 1969. During a subsequent six months of prayer and manual labor at a church in the mountains, he decided to protest against the oppression of the factory workers. He again obtained a job at a garment factory and began to quietly organize a labor union. On November 13, 1970, he and 500 workers peacefully demonstrated against their exploitation. A special police force was dispatched to break up the demonstration. In the ensuing struggle, Chun protested by dousing himself in gasoline and lighting himself on fire. He cried out in support of the workers and for them to not let his death be in vain. As Suh writes, "At the age of twenty-two, Tae-Il presented his body and soul as a living sacrifice before God for the sake of his suffering sisters and brothers at the Peace Market."[394] Suh paints Chun's self-immolation as a Christ-like sacrifice that mirrored the crucifixion of Jesus for the salvation of others. This is because Chun's radical protest unto death became a rallying point for the beginnings of the *minjung* movement. Suh offers other stories (*silhwa*) of the suffering *minjung*,[395] but this one example will suffice.

As Andrew Park summarizes Suh's work, "Suh starts from the presupposition that the theme of his *minjung* theology is not Jesus but *minjung*. He replaces the traditional concept of the problem of sin with the *han* of the *minjung*. He believes that the mission of the Korean churches is to resolve the *han* of the *minjung* caused by feudalism, colonialism, and neo-colonialism."[396] In addition to this content-oriented contribution to a theology of *han,* Suh frequently highlights the importance of story-telling.[397] To this end, Park points out that Suh thinks that it is in

393. Park, *The Wounded Heart of God,* 21.

394. Suh Nam-Dong quoted in Park, *The Wounded Heart of God,* 22. The above summary is a paraphrase of the entirety of Suh's quote in ibid., 21–22.

395. See Suh Nam-Dong's recounting of the stories of the death of young union organizer Ms. Kim Kyong-Suk and the torture and imprisonment of farmworker Mr. Oh Won-Chun in CTC-CCA, *Minjung Theology,* 55–58.

396. Park, "Minjung and P'ungryu Theologies in Contemporary Korea," 65.

397. To be fair, Suh Nam-Dong was not the only *minjung* theologian to highlight narrative. It was a common and defining method for the entire movement. For example, see Kim Yong-Bock's essay in CTC-CCA, *Minjung Theology,* 183–92. See also Küster's *Protestant Theology of Passion.*

stories that *han* is most clearly and fully illustrated and in which *han* can be transformed into a positive and constructive revolutionary consciousness through *dan*.[398]

Two Critiques of the Han of Minjung Theology: Chung Hyun-Kyung and Jae-Hoon Lee

I now move from the retrieval and re-articulation of *han* by Kim and Suh to critiques of *minjung* theologians' work by Chung Hyun-Kyung and Jae-Hoon Lee.

Chung Hyun-Kyung

As a second-generation *minjung* theologian, Chung Hyun-Kyung (b. 1956) plays a very important role in the development of using *han* as a source in Christian theological reflection. Although educated in the U.S., where she received a Doctorate from Union Theological Seminary in New York, I follow the lead of Volker Küster and place Chung in the family of Korean *minjung* theologians. This is because Chung has adopted a third-world, feminist critical hermeneutic in order to critique Christian theology, and in particular Asian-Christian theology, for being patriarchal and denigrating to women. Chung expanded the scope and re-envisioned the focus of *han* in doing theology.[399]

Chung makes two important contributions to my discussion of *han*. First, Chung accounts for the scourge of women's *han* within Korean society (and the wider Asian societies and cultures) by naming Korean women the "*minjung* within the *minjung*" and "the *han* of the *han*."[400] In this way, Chung shows how Korean women should be understood as embodying

---

398. Park, "Minjung Theology," 14.

399. Moving beyond Chung, some have argued that the *han* of women is so pervasive that *han* should be applied almost exclusively to the woundedness of women. See Yani Yoo, "*Han*-Laden Women: Korean 'Comfort Women' and Women in Judges 19–21." In addition, the static, essentialized identity of "Asian" as allegedly embraced by Chung, is now being critqued by a younger generation of feminist scholars. See Brock et al., *Off the Menu*.

400. Chung Hyun-Kyung, *Struggle to be the Sun Again*, 42. See also Chung's earlier "*Han-pu-ri*," 31. In this short essay, Chung also points out the contribution of Letty Russell in describing the "minjung of the minjung." For Chung's contribution to theology, see Phan's essay, "Jesus Christ with an Asian Face," 399–430.

han due to their very existence as women.[401] Chung describes *han* as occurring from a situation of silence and powerlessness that is prevalent among women and the poor. In this way, "... this unexpressed anger and resentment stemming from social powerlessness forms a 'lump' in their spirit. This lump often leads to a lump in the body, by which I mean the oppressed often disintegrate bodily as well as psychologically."[402] Chung points out that in ancient Korea there is some evidence of a matriarchal society and of a more or less equal status among women and men.[403] This, however, changed considerably and by the time of the Yi Dynasty, when the rigid gender norms of neo-Confucianism began to be strictly enforced. Women's sexuality and roles in society became controlled by the dominating males in the family and by the patriarchal society.[404]

In addition, Chung has pointed out that within *minjung* theology (with a few exceptions) there has been scant attention paid to the unique situation of women and women's *han*. Not only are Korean women oppressed and dehumanized through the same socio-economic and political structures that have dehumanized the men of the *minjung*, they have been forced to grapple with the rigidly patriarchal social structure and values of Confucianism that have limited their life-possibilities, identities, and overall well-being. They have been forced to deal with male violence within their families and larger society as well as their marginalization in the movements for liberation. Chung argues that even well-intentioned male theologians of the *minjung* have been oppressive to women due to their bias against women's liberation movements in general and against feminism, in particular. This is because they interpreted feminism as little more than a neo-colonial Western import that was antithetical to "traditional" feminine traits and values in Asian cultures.[405]

---

401. Suh Nam-Dong as quoted in Jae-Hoon Lee, *The Exploration of the Inner Wounds*, 141.

402. Chung Hyun-Kyung, *Struggle to be the Sun Again*, 42. For a brief connection between women's *han* and Confucianism, see also pages 65–66.

403. Chung Hyun-Kyung, "*Han-pu-ri*," 31–32. This is confirmed by Grace Kim who states that there were at least three women rulers of Silla. See "Women's Oppression and Han," 57. See also Hwang Kyung-Moon, who gives more information on these three queens of Silla, *A History of Korea*, 12–23. The life of one of Silla's queens has been dramatized (fictionalized and embellished) in the 2009 Korean television series, *The Great Queen Seondeok* (*Seondeok Yeowang*).

404. Chung Hyun-Kyung, "*Han-pu-ri*," 31–32.

405. Chung Hyun-Kyung, *Struggle to Be the Sun Again*, 22–36.

Chung's second important contribution to this discussion of *han* is her proposal and description of *han-pu-ri* (as discussed above) as a way to resolve the *han* of women. She adopts this term from Shamanism as the traditional term for resolving *han*. In particular, Chung points towards the *kut*'s focus upon the unresolved *han* of the ghosts and spirits in Korea, particularly that of women. Chung observes that the *kut* gave the disgruntled spirits a chance to articulate their *han* and the community an opportunity to listen and respond to the cry for justice and healing. The community, then, could resolve to act to eradicate all that caused the *han* in the first place. As Chung writes, "Han-pu-ri has been an opportunity for collective repentance, group therapy and collective healing for the ghosts and their communities in Korean society."[406]

For Chung, *han-pu-ri* becomes one of the normative criteria for doing theology from an Asian (Korean) woman's perspective. For her, if a theology enables *han-pu-ri*, which she also links to liberation, it is good theology. If it does not untangle but deepens the *han* of women, it is bad theology.[407] By invoking *han-pu-ri*, Chung places *han* in general, and women's *han* in particular, at the heart of doing Christian theology. A norm for Christian theology for Chung becomes the resolution of *han*. This is similar to Kim Chi-Ha's and Suh Nam-Dong's emphases upon resolving *han* as an inherent part of Christian theology. But Chung deepens its connection to Korean culture through focusing on women, engaging shamanism, and making *han-pu-ri* a normative criterion in doing theology.

Jae-Hoon Lee

Before moving on to the next section, in which I will discuss Park's and Joh's theologies in-depth, I must briefly discuss the work of Jae-Hoon Lee who critiques *minjung* theology while attempting to further its development and praxis.[408] There are two aspects of Lee's work that are important to highlight here: his critique of *minjung* theology that leads him to seek to enhance its understanding of *han*; and his description of three distinct facets of *han* that informs his critique.

---

406. Chung Hyun-Kyung, "Han-pu-ri," 34.

407. Ibid., 36.

408. Jae-Hoon Lee is a relatively unknown scholar who biographical information remains unclear. Thus, I have not given a summary of his life and influences.

Lee argues that although *minjung* theology has called itself a theology of *han*, its expositors have offered an inexplicable understanding of *han*. In this way, *han* has remained a mystery to the theologians themselves as well as to the powerless with whom they sought to be in solidarity.[409] Lee argues that this inexplicability of *han* arises from a lack of depth in engaging the concept. For example, Lee points out that the *minjung* theologians were rightly concerned primarily with the socioeconomic structures of Korea, created and sustained by its rulers and colonizers, as well as the larger economic system, that resulted in the oppression, exploitation, and marginalization of the powerless—the *minjung*. At the same time, Lee argues that this focus describes only one side of *han*. Lee argues that most *minjung* theologians—other than Kim Chi-Ha—have over-emphasized the positive side of *han* while ignoring its deep negativity. In response, Lee attempts to provide a psychological understanding of *han* that can augment the primarily socioeconomic understanding that was prevalent in *minjung* theological discourse.

Lee argues that *han* is unique and particular to the Korean mind, soul, and culture but he also argues that *han*, through a psychological understanding, can speak not only to Koreans but to all humankind.[410] He writes that "in a deeper level it speaks to all people, oppressed and oppressor" and also that *han* can speak to the human psychology "about the mysterious source of both suffering and creativity."[411] Lee develops a cultural-psychological method in order to develop a richer and more complete picture of *han*. To do this, Lee brings traditional Korean understandings of *han* that arise from folklore, shamanism, history, and language into dialogue with the depth psychology of Melanie Klein and Carl Jüng.

Using this method, Lee arrives at three facets of *han* that are distinct, yet always interwoven: *won-han, jeong-han,* and *hu-han*.[412] Although these three kinds of *han* are always mixed, Lee argues that one of the three tends to dominate. For this reason, Lee treats them separately

---

409. Jae-Hoon Lee, *The Exploration of Inner Wounds*, 5.

410. Ibid., 5–6.

411. Ibid. Both quotes from page 6.

412. See ibid., 35–49. It is important to point out that Chung Hyun-Kyung has discussed *won-han* and *jeong-han*. Chung's description of it, however, argues that *jeong-han* is only negative and has been the lot of oppressed women. She argues that women must embrace the aggressive and self-asserting nature of *wonhan* to overcome their oppression. See Chung Hyun-Kyung, *Struggle to Be the Sun Again*, 42–47.

even though admitting that in reality they are not ever fully separated. Together, they comprise the totality of *han*.

Lee describes *won-han* as persecutory, paranoid, and aggressive. It is primarily outwardly-oriented and can manifest in rage, revenge, violence, and sadism. Historically, Lee connects *won-han* with the duration of the Yi Dynasty, with all of its internal coups, killings, corruption, and oppression of the poor and women. He also uses the example of the murderous and paranoid King Yonson to illustrate *wonhan*.[413]

Lee describes *jeong-han* in two stages. Its immature form tends to manifest in the depressive tendencies of masochism and melancholy. In contrast to *won-han*, immature *jeong-han* tends to be inwardly-oriented and to mourn for a lost love-object. If the emotions of *jeong-han* become unbearable, the person regresses to *won-han* in order to defend the ego against pain. If the person remains in this regressive *jeong-han* turned *won-han*, he or she will continue to suffer pain for unknown reasons.[414]

In its mature form, however, Lee argues that *jeong-han* becomes a creative and loving energy. In this manifestation, self-affliction turns into a reparative wish. That is, melancholy becomes sympathy for others and the basis for social concerns and activism. The eros-like love (*jeong*) overtakes and contains one's hate (*won*) without destroying it and one's longing for a love object becomes the power for creativity. *Jeong-han* becomes sympathy for others who are possessed by *han* and is the basis for the energy to fight injustice and create a more just world.[415] To quote Lee:

> A true form of energy for social change or revolution cannot be expected from *wonhan*. Only the aggression based on love can be used for the creation of a more humane community. *Wonhan* destroys the individual and society, and calls for more *wonhan*; but *jeong-han* in its mature form heals the wounds of individuals and society and builds a community. When *jeong-han* becomes fully mature it is no longer *han*, but love, which is the genuine power of healing.[416]

---

413. Jae-Hoon Lee, *The Exploration of Inner Wounds*, 57–67.

414. Ibid., 48.

415. Ibid., 48–49.

416. Ibid., 49. On 37, Lee points out that this kind of "love" isn't a sentimentalized kind but rather one that connotes erotic, libidinal love. Lee employs the Western notion of "eros" not in an exclusive sense but in a sense that it is the life instinct and power of life that overshadows the death instinct. This may be similar to the Korean understanding of *ki* (Chinese, *ch'i*).

Historically, Lee connects the aftermath of the Fall of the Yi Dynasty as a period of *jeong-han*, particularly in its immature form. He also uses the example of the poetry of the Korean poet Sowol to illustrate *jeong-han*.[417]

The third facet of *han* that Lee proposes is *hu-han*. This comes from the Korean word for "emptiness" (*hu*) and is expressed through a feeling of emptiness and a sense of nihilism. Lee describes it as a flight from external and internal realities of pain to a deep place within the self where one cannot be harmed. He argues that people of *hu-han* often withdraw so deeply into themselves in order to escape pain that they can lose touch with the external world.[418] Lee goes on to assert that *hu-han* can often lead to suicide. Thus, for Lee it is unclear whether *hu-han* can result in death or rebirth for a person. Historically, he connects the oppression of the Korean people by the military dictatorship in the 1970s as a period of *hu-han*. He also uses the example of Korean writer Eun-Ko as an example of *hu-han*.[419]

It is on account of *hu-han* that Lee levels his strongest critique against many *minjung* theologians. Lee argues that even though *minjung* theologians have made an inestimable contribution by highlighting the positive and creative aspects of *han* to point to the coming emancipation of the *minjung*, their neglect of its darker side is a glaring deficiency. Lee argues that when articulating *han* in socio-political and religious symbols, *minjung* theologians have lacked a concern to distinguish between healthy and unhealthy symbols; that is, whether or not symbols have revitalizing or pathological roots.[420]

This becomes clear in Lee's reference to Suh Nam-Dong's glorification of the death of Chun Tae-Il (as mentioned above). Chun's death was interpreted by Suh as a Christ-like, sacrificial death to bring life and liberation to the *minjung*.[421] Lee, however, is troubled by this glorification of Chun's suicide. He argues that Chun's action should be understood as a manifestation of the negative energy of *han*, and in particular of *hu-han*.[422] Lee thinks that due to its predominant feeling of "emptiness," it is *hu-han* that poses the greatest social risk. To quote Lee at length, the people of *hu-han*:

417. Ibid., 67–77.
418. Ibid., 51.
419. Ibid., 77–92.
420. Ibid., 144.
421. Ibid., 143–44.
422. Ibid.

suffer boredom, dullness, futility, and meaninglessness in their everyday lives. As a desperate attempt to escape from the psychological predicament they often find solution in devoting themselves to a great social cause or ideology and thus become members of a collective social force. The collective social force rooted in "hu-han" expresses itself in violent and destructive activities, because "hu-han" by its very nature seeks out destruction. People of "hu-han" are nihilists who value nothing in themselves and society, though they worship a great social cause or ideology expressed in their slogans and statements. . . .

It is an illusion to build a humane, healthy society based on "hu-han" type social activities, no matter how beautiful their slogans and statements. At the center of these "hu-han" people exists an empty shell in which no value, beauty, authentic feeling, or hope can be contained. Therefore, a discernment is needed to distinguish between social activities that are based on genuine and healthy personal values, and those that are based upon false, sick, and nihilistic tendencies of destruction. The lack of discernment of the categories of *han* is responsible for the one-sided romanticization of *han* in Minjung Theology, in which symbols arising from [it] are used indiscriminately as political metaphor for the purpose of bringing about social change, as is shown in the deification of Tae-Il Chun's self-immolation.[423]

This is a strong indictment from Lee against *minjung* theologians such as Suh. For Lee, however, it is paramount to always account for the fact that *han* possesses the power of life *and* death. He is appreciative of the *minjung* theologians' work and contributions to liberating the oppressed. Thus, his critique is meant to further enhance their work on behalf of the *han*-ridden *minjung* rather than detract from it.

In this second section, I have discussed the re-embrace of *han* within Christian theology in Korea in the mid to late twentieth century by Kim Chi-Ha and Suh Nam-Dong. I also have discussed the critiques by Chung Hyun-Kyung and Jae-Hoon Lee that offer correctives and developments. Through this examination of four theologians of *han*, the complexity, nature, and characteristics of *han* have become somewhat clearer. Again, from an outer-hearer's location, it is necessary to explore the deep roots and articulations of the essentially untranslatable word *han* in order

---

423. Ibid., 160–61.

to approach a relatively adequate understanding of the theologies of *han* that will be discussed below.

Section Three: Han in the Work of Andrew Sung Park and Wonhee Anne Joh

In Section Three, I now turn to the work of Korean-American Protestant theologians Andrew Sung Park and Wonhee Anne Joh who have continued to articulate Christian theologies based on *han* in the late twentieth and early twenty-first century. Park and Joh are two of the most important U.S. Christian theologians who use *han* as a fundamental theological source.[424] Park, a long-established scholar, and Joh, a relatively new scholar, both have used *han* in order to construct theologies connected to understandings of human salvation from sinning and being sinned-against.

I will first discuss the established work of Park in which he offers an understanding of *han*, constructs a theological reflection upon it, and offers a vision of how Christian salvation from sin and *han* are to be envisioned, particularly through re-envisioning atonement theory. Second, I will discuss the emerging work of Joh who is retrieving and employing the Korean understanding of *jeong* as complementary to *han* in order to articulate a theology of the cross and a revision to atonement theory from a feminist and post-colonial perspective. Third, I will draw out three shared contours of Park's and Joh's understandings of *han's* role in envisioning salvation for the sinned-against creature: an anthropology of woundedness, a focus upon narrative and praxis, and a soteriology based upon the cross.

---

424. Three additional rising Korean-American theological voices with whom I do not engage are Grace Ji-Sun Kim, Jung-Eun Sophia Park, and Hoon Choi. Kim's work also deals with *han* and attempts to constructively respond to women's *han* through re-thinking Christian doctrine in such works as *The Grace of Sophia*, *The Holy Spirit, Ch'i, and the Other*, and *Colonialism, "Han," and the Transformative Spirit*. Although Kim's work is important, she does not provide an extended treatment of *han*. For the purposes of this study, Joh's work is more germane for attempting a cultural outsider's reception and interpretation of *han*. Similarly, Park's and Choi's work thus far is not rooted in *han* in the same way as Andrew Park and Wonhee Anne Joh. See Jung-Eun Sophia Park, *A Hermeneutics of Dislocation as Experience*; and Choi, "Brothers in Arms and Brothers in Christ?"

A Korean-American Theology of Han: The Work of Andrew Sung Park

Andrew Sung Park, Professor of Theology and Ethics at United Theological Seminary in Dayton, Ohio, has written extensively on the nature of *han* and the ways in which it can correct, develop, and shape Christian theology and doctrine. Park is a Korean-American Protestant who has attempted to bring Christian doctrine and theology into a mutually critical dialogue with East Asian and Korean cultural and intellectual sources. His received his PhD in Theology in 1985 from the Graduate Theological Union and his dissertation explored the similarities and differences between Korean *minjung* theologies and Korean *pungyro* theologies. His subsequent work has included mapping the Korean concept of *han* and its connection to the Christian doctrine of sin, theologically addressing racial reconciliation from an Asian-American perspective, envisioning a theology of woundedness in which the Christian church puts victims first, and rethinking the Trinitarian work of atonement.[425] There are three aspects of Park's work that contribute to my study: his exegesis of *han;* his theological reflection upon the connection of *han*, sin, and evil; and his re-envisioning of a theology of the cross as a Triune Atonement for the liberation of the sinned-against and the salvation of the sinners.

Park's Interpretation and Exegesis of Han

First, Park offers a helpful exegesis and understanding of *han*. In the breadth of his work—from his dissertation to his most recent writings—Park has continued to attempt to translate *han* into English through definitions and stories. Park offers various phrases such as "frustrated hope," "collapsed feeling of pain," "resentful bitterness," and "wounded heart."[426] He also remarks, "When the suppressed experience of people accumulate, *han* appears."[427] Or more viscerally, "*Han* is the division of the tissue of the heart caused by abuse, exploitation, and violence. It is

---

425. Some of Park's more recent work has investigated a Christian theology informed by Daoism (which he sometimes calls *Theo-Dao*) as well as investigating what he has termed a theology of *transmutation* and a theology of *enhancement*. See, for example, Park's "A Theology of the Way (Dao)," 389–99.

426. Park, *The Wounded Heart of God*, 1–19.

427. Ibid., 19.

the wound to feelings and self-dignity."[428] In this definition, *han* is correlated to the human body. Like other emotions and states of being that are connected to internal organs in some East Asian cultures, *han* has a bodily correlate—the human heart.[429] To quote Park at length from his most recent monograph:

> In Korean, *han* is a deep, unhealed wound of a victim that festers in her or him. It can be a social, economic, political, physical, mental, or spiritual wound generated by political oppression, economic exploitation, social alienation, cultural contempt, injustice, poverty, or war. It may be a deep ache, an intense bitterness, or the sense of helplessness, hopelessness, or resignation at the individual and collective levels.[430]

Park confirms that the Korean understanding of *han* finds its deepest roots in the centuries of oppression and violence experienced by the Korean people at the hands of the other powers in the region such as China, Russia, and Japan. Moreover, he confirms that the more immediate source, however, is in the Korean protest and *minjung* movement in the mid-twentieth century that opposed the military dictatorships.

To better illustrate *han*, Park offers the metaphor of a black hole theory in astrophysics.[431] Park explains that, in black hole theory, a large star expands to become a red giant and its core compresses greatly. When it cannot expand anymore, the core implodes and a giant explosion—a supernova—occurs. Afterwards, the core has so collapsed in on itself that it distorts time and space and becomes a black hole. The gravity created from this is so powerful that even light cannot escape. Like a black hole, for Park, *han*, becomes an abyss from which little can escape. It is a "deep, dark, abyss" and its "collapsed inner core swallows everything, dominating the victim's life agenda."[432] This is because there is a tipping point at which an individual's or group's suffering becomes too much to bear.

---

428. Ibid., 20.

429. Another helpful description Park borrows from Soon Tae Moon: "'[H]an is the wound of the heart in a passive term and the blood occlusion. The former is the knot of the mind and the latter is the knot of the spirit.'" See ibid., 181n26.

430. Park, *Triune Atonement*, 39. Park also connects the Korean folk song "Arirang" to the crucifixion of Jesus. He observes that if Jesus lived in Korea he would have sung "Arirang" on the way to Calvary. See pages 40–41.

431. Park, *Wounded Heart of God*, 17. See also Park's "Theology of Han (the abyss of pain)," 50–51, as well as Park's "God who Needs Our Salvation," 82–83.

432. Ibid., 82.

At this point, this suffering implodes into a "condensed feeling of pain" which Park links to *han*. It is connected to one's entire being—mind, body, and spirit. Similar to the *minjung* theologians described above, Park thinks that the concurrent explosion associated with *han* can lead to constructive protest and social change. At other times, he thinks it can lead to destruction, both personally and collectively.[433]

In order to clarify the nature and inner-workings of *han*, Park interweaves psychological and socio-economic descriptions and offers a rough map for understanding *han*. He argues that *han* can fester in individuals or groups, manifest as active or passive, and be working either in the conscious or unconscious. Although he makes a distinction between the functioning of *han* in individuals and groups, there are enough similarities to allow me to discuss them together. For Park, the active aspect is explosive—akin to *won-han*—whereas the passive aspect is implosive—akin to *jeong-han* or *hu-han*. In the conscious realm, *han* is more visceral and can be acted upon. In the unconscious realm, it is hidden and manipulates the interior structures of the body, mind, and spirit. For the wounded, conscious active *han* can be unleashed against others whereas its passive version is unleashed against one's self—body, mind, and spirit. On the other hand, unconscious active *han* is often expressed in a simmering bitterness or resentment and its passive counterpart is expressed in lamentation and despair.[434] In all these ways, *han* is a deep woundedness that simmers and that can be harmful to the self and others. It has become part of being human for many—an anthropology.[435]

Park further describes *han* through three levels and through the means by which it is transmitted to posterity. Regarding the former, Park argues that the three levels of *han* are: personal, collective, and

---

433. Park, "Theology of Han (the Abyss of Pain)," 51.

434. See Park, *The Wounded Heart of God*, 31–44. I should point out that Park does not explicitly engage with the technical categories of *won-han, jeong-han,* and *hu-han*. Park's work is meant to make *han* more clear and accessible for the larger Christian theological discourse. I would contend, however, that the understandings of *won-han, jeong-han,* and *hu-han* are implied in the foundation for his descriptions, if not identical with them.

435. It is important to point out that, for Park, nature and the ecological environment and animals also have *han*. Park is not offering a strict, anthropocentric understanding of *han*. Rather, for Park it has ecological dimensions as well. For the sake of my focus on the sinned-against human creature, however, I will not be engaging with Park's development of *han* to include the devastation of nature. Also, I will not be engaging with the *han* caused by natural disasters such as hurricanes, tsunamis, earthquakes, etc.

structural.[436] These three levels are interconnected but can be discussed separately for the sake of clarity. The structural roots of *han* include the global political economy, patriarchy, and racism and ethnic prejudice. On the one hand, structural sin causes *han* in the collective experience of social groups and also in individuals within these groups. On the other hand, individual *han*, whatever its cause, affects the *han* of the collective group, all of whom are influenced and shaped by structural *han*.[437] Regarding the latter, Park argues that the structure of *han* is inherited and passed down from generation to generation. This occurs in four main ways: biologically, mentally/spiritually, socially, and racially. For example, biologically one may inherit genes predisposing a person for heart disease or alcoholism; mentally/ spiritually, one can be formed by the conscious and unconscious *han*—depression, melancholy, violent attitudes—of one's parents and family; socially, one inherits the structural brokenness of one's social context, which include patriarchy, racism, violent lifestyles, but are not limited to these; racially, one inherits the collective wounds and experiences of one's racial and ethnic group that comprise what Park calls an *ethnic ethos*.[438]

In his exegesis of *han*, Park suggests that *han* is not the exclusive possession and experience of the Korean people. He follows the lead of many *minjung* theologians and argues that *han* is particular to its context but that it also can transcend its native context and shed understanding on global suffering. Therefore, Park connects *han* to Jewish survivors of the Nazi Holocaust, Palestinians in occupied territories, those who are the victims of racism, sexism, classism, and homophobia, as well as exploited workers, sexually abused children, and many others.[439] *Han* is an understanding that arises from a particular context but points to—although is not identical with—a general human experience, within a global context, of being sinned-against and wounded.

Park offers a vision of *han-pu-ri*—although he does not employ this term—that is a Christian theological and pastoral response to the reality of *han*. To begin, Park describes *han* as a frozen energy that can and must be unraveled, be it negatively or positively. He gives the example that a

---

436. Park, *Triune Atonement*, 41. This is somewhat of a development from his description in *The Wounded Heart of God,* but it remains consonant with the description offered there that I have adopted.

437. Ibid., 71.

438. Park, *The Wounded Heart of God*, 80–81.

439. Ibid., 20–30.

negative unraveling can take the form of vengeance and violence against the victimizers by the victims. It could also take the form of collapsing in on the *han*-filled person and result in despair, mental illness or suicide.[440] As Park's black hole metaphor above showed, there is a great energy inherent in the creation of *han*. It can be unraveled and resolved positively, but care must be taken.

To avoid a negative or violent unraveling of *han* that causes destruction, Park offers four steps in resolving *han* positively. Park calls this fourfold process a *compassionate confrontation* through awakening, understanding, envisagement, and enactment.[441] First, the sinned-against must be *awakened* to the existence of their own *han* and the root causes of *han*, including its personal, social, and structural roots. Second, the sinned-against must work to live in a place of *understanding*. Park offers three kinds of understanding—rational, intuitive, and incarnational. Rational understanding entails engaging the roots of *han* that have formed both victims and victimizers and to integrate this understanding into a richer picture of the victimizer. Intuitive understanding includes an emotional aspect in which one halts attempting to rationally understand *han* and instead embraces its fullness. In this way, one becomes a wounded healer. Incarnational understanding is akin to praxis. This is an understanding that only comes through active solidarity with the experience of another's *han*. The third step Park proposes is *envisagement*. In short, this is the work of the victims and the victimizers to envision a new world in which the root causes of *han* are no more. This includes economic, social, personal, and ecclesial envisioning. The final step, *engagement*, Park also calls *compassionate confrontation*. In this step, the oppressed and the victims confront and challenge the oppressors and the victimizers to repent and change their lives. They are to stop inflicting *han* on others and work with them to alleviate all that causes *han*. In this final step, conscious *han* can be transformed into constructive action and unconscious *han* can be transcended so that it no longer dominates the lives of the *han*-ridden.[442] This process illustrates the human, earthly process of *han-pu-ri*. Unconscious *han*, however, is often too deeply planted in the unconscious for this process of *han-pu-ri* to occur in this life. In his earlier work, Park

440. Ibid., 31–44.
441. Ibid., 137–38.
442. Ibid., 170–76.

argues that this kind of *han* can only be transcended, not dissolved.[443] In his later work, Park connects this deepest level of *han* with the Triune Atonement associated with the cross. This means that the ultimate *han-pu-ri* is God's work of healing through Christ and the Holy Spirit.

Park's Critique of the Doctrine of Sin— Preferential Option for the Han-Ridden

Having discussed Park's understanding of *han*, I now move to the ways in which he envisions the connection between *han*, sin, and evil. Among these, Park's focus is primarily upon the connection between sin and *han*. Park argues that sin is the experience of the oppressor and *han* is the experience of the oppressed.[444] *Han* is the wound carried by the victims and the oppressed, both individually and collectively, and caused by the victimizers and oppressors. Park, however, is careful to nuance his binary understanding of sin vs. *han*, oppressor vs. oppressed. As he writes, "Although for convenience I have divided the sin of the oppressor and the *han* of the oppressed, most people experience both sin and *han*. This is not to play down the difference between the oppressed and the oppressors, but to point out the complete entanglement of sin and *han* in the reality of life."[445] Park argues that sin produces *han*, and then *han* produces more *han* as well as sin. The interweaving of sin and *han* is a vicious cycle that continues to reproduce unless confronted and unraveled.

Park contends that the traditional concept of sin has focused too much upon the sinners and too little upon the sinned-against.[446] In other words, the way in which the traditional Christian doctrine of sin is understood and articulated is insufficient because it focuses almost exclusively

---

443. Ibid., 171; 174–76. Here, Park illustrates this transcendence of *han* through the *kut* that leads to *han-pu-ri* in Shamanism. He also cites Hyun Young-Hak's description of the critical transcendence of *han* that can occur in the traditional Korean mask dance in which the *minjung* laugh, dance, and mock their oppressors.

444. Ibid., 69–70. As Park continues on page 70, "The sin of the oppressor may cause a chain reaction via the *han* of the oppressed. The *han* of the oppressed in its active mode can seek retaliation against the oppressor in a form which is often itself unjust. The oppressor will in turn react in a way that is yet more harsh and unjust. As a consequence the vicious cycle of violence continues. Since the *han*-ful reaction of the oppressed is not sinless, the line between sin and han becomes blurred in their action and reaction."

445. Ibid., 70.

446. Ibid., 72–77.

on sinners and violators. With a rigid focus upon the guilt, repentance, and forgiveness of sinners, the doctrine of sin leaves little room for addressing the experience and healing of the sinned-against on a doctrinal level. This is why Park thinks that the traditional doctrine of sin within Christianity must be enhanced through a dialogue with *han*. Park thinks that a thorough engagement with *han* complements the doctrine of sin and places a much needed emphasis upon the sinned-against while not forgetting the sinner. *Han* adds another dimension to Christian soteriology that has mostly been ignored or underemphasized.[447]

A focus upon *han* is important in the doctrinal and concrete sense because it points to the different processes of healing for the sinners and the sinned against. Park argues that, for sinners, the process moves thusly:

sin → guilt→ guilt anger→ repentance→ forgiven-ness→ justification by faith→ holiness/sanctification→ Christian perfection.

For the sinned-against, however, Park thinks the process looks different. Their healing involves:

han → shame→ shame anger→ resistance→ forgivingness→ justice by faith→ healing/wholeness→ jubilee.[448]

This is a process of earthly *han-pu-ri* in which the sinner and sinned-against are reconciled to each other in the presence of the Living God of Jesus Christ. Whereas sin calls for forgiveness of sins and guilt, *han* calls for a sense of forgivingness in the sinned-against for the perpetrators who inflicted their *han* and their liberation from the shame inflicted upon them.[449]

Park argues, however, that the victims are never forced to forgive against their will and before they are ready (if ever). Instead, Park characterizes the doctrine of forgivingness as the church's work to create a space where healing can occur through resolving the victims' *han* and where a sense of the power and godliness of forgivingness can be instilled. It means that the church embraces the *han* of the victims not only in counseling and pastoral care, but also in official doctrine. As Park writes,

---

447. This is a current that runs through the entirety of his work. For his earliest observations on the doctrine of sin in dialogue with *han*, see Park's discussion of the theology of Suh Nam-Dong in "Minjung and P'ungryu Theologies," 36–66.

448. Park, *From Hurt to Healing: A Theology of the Wounded*. The entirety of this work is devoted to these parallel processes of liberation and salvation.

449. Park, *The Wounded Heart of God*, 90–93.

"Forgiveness must take place in cooperation with victims and must involve offenders' participation in the dissolution of their victims' *han*-ridden shame. The one-sided forgiveness proclaimed by any authority is not forgiveness, but false comfort."[450]

One implication of his connection between sin and *han* is Park's critique of the doctrine of original sin. Park argues that sin is not passed on from generation to generation. It is *han* that is passed on. Park thinks that the intention behind the doctrine of original sin—human universal solidarity and an explanation for the human proclivity to sin—can be helpful. At the same time, he finds the concept of the guilt of one generation being transferred to the next generation problematic. This is because original sin implies a universal 'original guilt' that is shared equally by everyone and that is equally transmitted to all generations from the first parents.[451]

Park thinks that such an understanding results in the wrongful dismantling of any distinction between sinners and their victims. If all humankind shares in the same guilt, then the sinned-against are as responsible for their wounds as the ones who sinned against them. The guilt of the oppressors is not their own but belongs to all of humankind.[452] With this understanding in mind, Park argues that original sin should be superseded by a doctrine of original *han*. That is, a doctrine that accounts for the unfair transmission of human sinful nature, and the consequences of this sinfulness through *han*, from one generation to the next.[453]

Park offers a helpful illustration of this critique of original sin. He argues that the sins of the parents are not the sins of the children because the children cannot be held responsible for the actions of their parents. Guilt cannot be inherited because it accompanies one's own decision-making and sin is often the consequence thereof. Sin requires volition and thus incurs guilt. Subsequent generations, then, do not inherit guilt. They inherit *han*. They are responsible before God and others only for their own misdeeds, not those of their forebears.[454] The brokenness and oppression that is passed down from generation to generation takes the form of *han*.[455]

450. Ibid., 84.
451. Ibid., 79–81.
452. Ibid., 79.
453. Ibid., 81.
454. Ibid., 74. As he points out on the same page, "*Han* can be engendered within one generation by the sin and han of the previous generation."
455. Ibid., 80.

It is also important to point out that Park's theology of sin and *han* is related to his understanding of God. For Park, God has *han* and, in a way, needs our salvation. This is because the intertwining of sin and *han* creates a vicious reality that causes destruction to creation and is a wound to God. He is careful to make the distinction between God having *han* and the heresy of patripassionism. Park unequivocally denies patripassionism while also proposing that God has *han*. He thinks that the traditional doctrine of God's impassibility is one particular inculturation of Christian theology into a Greek philosophical mindset and is no longer useful. Park argues that the Old Testament, Mark's Gospel, John's Gospel, and the work of St. Anselm and Martin Luther, for example, provide ample evidence against impassibility and display an anguished and wounded God. To describe his conviction, Park writes, "Our God is not the aloof one who does not want to prevent evil but the passionate one who endures unbearable evil with the victims, not because God is not powerful, but because God is strong enough to love the sinned-against and to forgive the sinners."[456]

Moreover, Park observes that God's *han* has nothing to do with impotence or deficiency. Instead, God's *han* is a consequence of God's love that "is too strong to be apathetic toward human suffering. No power in the universe makes God vulnerable, but a victim's suffering, a victim's *han*, breaks God's heart."[457] Park argues that God needs salvation because salvation is the reconciliation and reunification among estranged parties. God doesn't need salvation from sin. Park thinks that God desires the wholeness and *shalom* of all creation and, until this is realized, carries *han*. God desires reconciliation and reunification with humankind but will not force it upon them. Thus, for Park, humans must choose into God's offer of salvation from sins, return to God, and alleviate God's *han*.[458]

---

456. Park, "God Who Needs Our Salvation," 91.

457. Ibid., 85.

458. If this study focused solely on Park's theology, I would offer a critical appreciation of his understanding of God as having *han*, particularly as an analogical statement. There are many questions, however, to be answered, particularly in the Roman Catholic tradition with strong and convincing critiques of a God who suffers by Karl Rahner and J. B. Metz. See, for example, Metz, *A Passion for God*, 54–71 and 107–20.

Park's proposal of God as having *han* is not the same as a proposal for patripassionism, although he is skeptical of the traditional attribute of impassibility to God. I cannot treat this entire discussion here, so it must suffice to say that Park's vision is complex but rooted in the tradition. His argument would benefit from an engagement with Cyril of Alexandria and Maximus the Confessor. Cyril, against Nestorius, argued

Moving on, Park realizes that one cannot connect *han* to the doctrine of sin without exploring its implications for understanding evil. After connecting sin and *han*, Park then connects these to evil. Evil, for Park, is not an ontological entity but a dark and wounding reality within the world that is almost indescribable.[459] Having his roots in process theology, Park envisions evil as a relative concept and as "the cosmic element that gives rise to sin and *han*."[460] He argues that when the cycle of sin and *han* continues to thrive, a darker state of affairs called evil arises.[461] Park thinks that *han* that is left to fester gives rise to evil, which then can regenerate both *han* and sin. As the cycle continues, sin and *han* collaborate to engender more evil, and so on.[462] Park argues that both sin and evil produce *han*. He uses the story of Job to illustrate this relationship and writes that Job is an innocent man who is suffering through no fault of his own and from the fault of no clear sinner. The ambiguous cause of Job's *han* isn't sin but evil.[463] In a somewhat complicated description, Park writes, "Evil in absence of sin is *han*; *han* in absence of sin is evil. Sin causes *han* and evil. Evil can produce *han* and sin, and *han* can regenerate evil and sin."[464]

---

that the "Word can be said to suffer" on the cross, but how that happens remains a mystery. Maximus offered an account of Jesus, in full union with the divine, undergoing his agony in Gethsemane. See McGuckin, *Saint Cyril of Alexandria and the Christological Controversy*, and in particular the primary documents "Cyril's Letter to the Monks of Egypt," "The Second Letter of Cyril to Nestorius," and "The Third Letter of Cyril to Nestorius," 245–75. See also St. Maximus the Confessor's *On the Cosmic Mystery of Jesus Christ*, and in particular "Ad Thalassium 42," 119–22, and "Opusculum 6," 173–76.

In my opinion, Park is making an analogical statement that points to God's solidarity with the victims and God's preferential option for the *han*-ridden. This may be a questionable interpretation, but I think it is valid nonetheless. It is also important to point out that the statement that God has *han* is not the same as to state that God suffers. As shown above, the two ideas are similar, but far from identical. Again, an intercultural communication problem arises: how exactly does an outer-hearer understand and interpret what Park means by God having *han*? This is because, as shown above, there is no easy translation of *han* into English. But this and other questions are not the focus of this study.

459. Park's non-ontological understanding of evil comes from his appreciation for process theology and philosophy. See *The Wounded Heart of God*, 185n1.

460. Park, *From Hurt to Healing*, 21.

461. Park, "God Who Needs Our Salvation," 83.

462. Park, *From Hurt to Healing*, 16.

463. Ibid., 21.

464. Ibid.

Park's Soteriology of the Cross—Triune Atonement

Having discussed Park's understanding of *han* and his theological reflection upon the connection between sin, *han,* and evil, I now move to the way in which Park uses *han* to articulate his theology of the cross. This theology is most explicitly articulated in his recent monograph, *Triune Atonement: Christ's Healing for Sinners, Victims, and the Whole of Creation* (2009). Here, Park argues that the symbol of the cross, when interpreted in conjunction with the Trinitarian God, manifests the brokenness of humankind and all of creation and its need for atonement. Park argues that in the Christian symbol of the cross sinners find salvation from their sins, the sinned-against find liberation from their *han,* and the ecological environment healing from its disruption by humankind. In other words, Park argues that sinners are saved because of the cross and the sinned-against despite the cross.

To clarify, Park is employing a very specific vocabulary when proposing this Trinitarian theology of the cross. He uses the term *atonement*, not in the sense of sacrifice but in its literal sense of *at-one-ment*. In short, atonement, for Park, implies the Triune God's action of healing the brokenness in the world. It is a reconciliation of the rupture among God with humans, humans with each other, and humans with the whole of creation and the reunification of all things. In further elaborating upon his terminology, Park intentionally draws a distinction between the relation of the cross to sinners and to the sinned-against. He argues that *salvation* is a term reserved for the sins of the violators and *liberation* is the term reserved for the *han* of the victims.[465] As he pointed out as early as his dissertation and in the *Wounded Heart,* all human beings have an amalgamation of sin and *han*. The *han*-ful people of the world sin and the oppressive and violating sin-ful people of the world have *han*. Nevertheless, as discussed above, Park finds the distinction between sin and *han* in theological discourse very useful, as long as used with the basic interconnectedness of sin and *han* in mind. Atonement, through Christ, is for victims to be free from *han* and violators to be free from sin.[466] As Park observes, Jesus carries the *han* of the victims and the marginalized—"Jesus shed his blood to bear our *han*."[467]

---

465. Park uses this distinction in *From Hurt to Healing* as well as *Triune Atonement*.
466. Park, *The Wounded Heart of God*, 101.
467. Park, *Triune Atonement*, 43.

For Park, the cross by itself may symbolize liberation and salvation, but it does not do so in isolation. Rather, it is the connection of the cross to Jesus' life, resurrection, and post-resurrection atoning work through the Paraclete.[468] The foundation for Park's Triune Atonement theology of the cross is the Holy Spirit, or the Paraclete as John's Gospel designates him/her. Park thinks that the concrete healing of the victims and the victimizers in this world is rooted in the ongoing, post-resurrection work of the Paraclete. The Paraclete is the Spirit of the Risen Christ. The Paraclete knows *han* well because s/he, as part of the Trinity, was united with Jesus and experienced his life, crucifixion, and resurrection. The Paraclete has been sent by Jesus into the world and makes Jesus present in a ministry of post-resurrection healing. The Paraclete has experienced the depths of *han* and s/he knows the wounds of the victims almost better than the victims themselves. This is because much *han* is too deep for the victim himself/herself to recognize, yet, the Paraclete searches the depths of all creation and encounters and attends to this *han*. Much *han* is too deeply embedded in humankind and creation for humans to resolve.[469] Therefore, in the atonement it is the Triune God who ultimately performs *han-pu-ri*. This occurs principally through the ongoing work of the Paraclete, although human beings participate in this work. In Park's view, the Paraclete is the key for understanding the way in which the cross symbolizes atonement, salvation, and liberation.

In Park's theology of the cross, one finds what could be referred to as a preferential option for the *han*-ridden. God's love is universal and includes all of humankind. But God's love is experienced differently by the sinners and sinned-against, oppressors and oppressed. This means that the cross, as a central Christian symbol, must apply not only to the sinners but to the sinned-against. Mindful of feminist, womanist, and other critiques of the interpretive abuses of theologies of the cross in general, and atonement theories in particular, Park intends to articulate a theology associated with the symbol of the cross that can be life-giving to victims. In the symbol of the cross, the sinned-against find liberation from their *han*.

Park argues that this liberation, symbolized by the innocent and needless execution of the Messiah, emancipates the oppressed from the weight of *han* itself, as well as from theologies of retribution that have

---

468. Ibid., 71–72.
469. Ibid., 68–69.

condemned the sinned-against by convincing them that they are only sinners. Park thinks that, on the cross, Jesus' blood does not pay a debt to God but rather is meant to restore the dignity of the victims through demanding justice and compassion.[470] When describing the blood-soaked imagery of the cross, he writes:

> For the oppressed, Jesus' blood as a symbol participates in the agony of their suffering under unjust persecution, exploitation, oppression, and violence. The blood of Jesus is the violent symbol of human cruelty against fellow humans, particularly against the powerless and the helpless . . . his blood signifies the intermingling of God's woundedness, sorrow, grief, and God's neverending hope for them. Jesus' blood represents God's pierced heart for the sinned against.[471]

Park begins his theology of the cross with a preferential option for the *han*-ridden. But it is not exclusively for the benefit of the sinned-against. God's love is truly universal and therefore the sinners also are included in the atonement symbolized in the cross. In the symbol of the cross and Jesus' blood, they find salvation from their sins. The cross is not the totality of Jesus' atoning work because this work continues post-resurrection through the Paraclete. Rather, the cross calls sinners to repentance through Jesus' blood. Jesus' blood is a glaring symbol of the *han* of the victims and of God's offer of forgiveness to sinners. When describing this in terms of Christ's blood, Park writes:

> To the oppressors, Jesus' blood symbolizes the protest, confrontation, and challenge of the oppressed and of God. It participates in the outcries of the victims. Like Abel's blood, Jesus' blood cries out from the ground until its voice is heard. It has the extraordinary strength to open up the cruelty of injustice, violence, vice, and evil—to unlock the oppressors' hearts of stone.[472]

The cross issues a call to *metanoia* and to live a new life, embodying a preferential option for the *han*-ridden and participating in their healing. For Park, this salvation is nothing other than living with God, or "the freedom to choose to be with God."[473] It is a chance for a reunited fellowship with the Creator and with all of creation. The Paraclete, as

470. Ibid., 70.
471. Ibid., 36.
472. Ibid.
473. Ibid., 92.

another Jesus, calls the offenders to own their sins, confess them, change their hearts, and work for the healing of victims while participating in God's in-breaking reign on earth.[474]

Summary of Park

To close this discussion of Andrew Sung Park's theology, I wish to again highlight three important contributions that he offers to my discussion and that I have shown above: his detailed understanding and development of *han*, his theological reflection upon the doctrine of sin through the lens of *han*, and his theology of the cross in which the cross symbolizes the salvation of the sinners and the liberation of the sinned-against through a Triune Atonement.

In discussing and interpreting *han*, Park has attempted to move away from more technical discussions and translate *han* in a way to make it more accessible to a general theological audience while preserving its integrity of meaning. Park has offered a constellation of signifiers—from phrases and definitions to metaphors such as the black hole to stories of the Korean *minjung* and Jewish Holocaust survivors—in order to illustrate the reality of *han*. Furthermore, he has offered a clear description of the structure of *han*, the way it is transmitted to posterity, its major structural roots, and a fourfold process by which it can be resolved. In all of these, Park has greatly assisted an outer hearer to apprehend some of the meaning associated with *han*.

Second, Park has reflected upon his understanding of *han* in order to critique and re-envision the doctrine of sin and salvation. Park argues that the doctrine of sin focuses almost exclusively on the salvation and well-being of the sinners and does not account for the experience or woundedness of the sinned-against. In this way, the doctrine of sin is not assisting in Christ's work of healing and *han-pu-ri* that continues in the world. Rather, it is assisting in the continued denigration and dehumanization of the victims by obscuring the particular guilt of the sinner and ignoring the *han* of the sinned-against. Park finds this active in the doctrine of original sin, which he thinks should be superseded by a doctrine of original *han*. For Park, it is *han* that is passed on to posterity and it is *han* that requires the church's pastoral and theological attention in order to correct a one-sided concern with the sin. Park points out that

---

474. Ibid., 74–75.

sin produces *han*, which then enables more *han* and sin, which if left unresolved leads to the rise of evil. Moreover, Park argues that even God has *han* due to the enormity of divine love for humankind and yearning for reconciliation with them.

Third, Park has attempted to re-envision a theology of the cross through atonement—reconciliation and reunification—among God and humans, humans and each other, and humans and the ecological environment. He argues that the cross symbolizes the liberation of the sinned-against from *han* and the salvation of the sinners from guilt and death. For Park, the cross and the blood of Christ have an excess of meaning that are connected to sinner and sinned-against but in different ways. The foundation for Park's theology of the cross is his contention that the atoning work of Jesus is not exclusively tied to the cross, but also to Jesus' life, resurrection, and post-resurrection work. To further this claim, Park highlights the presence and work of the Holy Spirit—the Paraclete—in the continuation of Christ's atoning work within history and society. As united with Christ in the Trinity, the Paraclete experienced Christ's life, death, and resurrection and knows the depths of *han* within creation. This enables the Paraclete to carry on the divine work of salvation for sinners and *han-pu-ri* for the sinned-against in this world. Finally, the Paraclete is the guarantor of the ultimate resolution of *han* that is so deep within the person and creation that human activity cannot reach it.

The Confluence of Han and Jeong: The Theology of Wonhee Anne Joh

Having discussed the established, yet ongoing, work of Andrew Sung Park, I now turn to the emerging work of Wonhee Anne Joh. Joh, Associate Professor of Systematic Theology at Garrett-Evangelical Theological Seminary, has focused her work upon the connection between *han* and *jeong* in order to correct, develop, and re-articulate Christian theology. She obtained a Ph.D. in Theological and Philosophical Studies from Drew University in 2003, and her dissertation became the foundation for her monograph *The Heart of the Cross: A Postcolonial Christology* (2006). She also has published a number of essays, chapter-length contributions to larger projects, and has several books either forthcoming or in progress. There are two aspects of Joh's emerging theology that are important for my discussion of Korean-American theologies of *han*: Joh's proposal of *jeong* as complementary to *han* and Joh's Christology that uses *jeong* as a fundamental theological source in envisioning salvation through a theology of the cross.

W. Anne Joh is one of the few, and perhaps the only, Korean-American theologian to retrieve and re-articulate a thick description of *jeong* as a source in doing Christian theology. Like *han*, *jeong* is ultimately untranslatable into English. At the same time, similar to my discussion of *han* above, it is possible to arrive at a relatively adequate interpretation of the meaning associated with *jeong*. It is beyond the scope of this chapter to offer as deep and thorough an exegesis of *jeong* as I have attempted with *han*. Instead, I will highlight the ways in which Joh has attempted to describe and unlock some of the meaning associated with the Korean understanding of *jeong*.

Joh's understanding of Han

In order to understand *jeong*, however, it is important to briefly summarize Joh's understanding of *han*. Joh embraces a general definition very much in line with what I have presented above and is indebted to the work of Kim, Chung, Lee, and Park. In her general definition, Joh quotes the work of Han Wang-Sang: "*Han* is a sense of unresolved resentment against injustices suffered, a sense of helplessness because of overwhelming odds against one's feeling of total abandonment, a feeling of acute pain and sorrow in one's guts and bowels."[475]

The roots of her more specific definition of *han*, however, are found in Joh's examination of the work of Jae-Hoon Lee (who was discussed above). Joh wants to make it clear that *han* is not innocent.[476] Following Lee and Park, Joh argues that *han* causes evil and the will to revenge as much as it can provide the energy for positive social change. Joh also embraces Lee's critique of an exclusively socio-political interpretation of *han*, which has been prevalent in Korean *minjung* theology. She references Lee and argues that there is a layer of original *han* in everyone to

---

475. Han Wang-Sang quoted in Joh, *Heart of the Cross*, xxi. The source for this quote of Han's is Park's *The Wounded Heart of God*, 120.

476. Joh, *Heart of the Cross*, 25–26. This is her embrace of the critique of *minjung* theologians such as Suh Nam-Dong who are seen as idealizing the *minjung* and their *han* while overlooking the sinfulness of the *minjung*, despite the infliction of *han* upon them by the oppressors. For a summary of this critique of Suh, see Park's "Minjung and P'ungryu Theologies in Contemporary Korea," 91–93.

greater or lesser degrees. This original *han* is a psychological wound that is caused by an original fragmentation of the ego in early childhood.[477] In short, it is the original wound at the core of a human being.

Joh observes that this original *han* is formed during the earliest childhood experiences and remains in the unconscious while also wielding a very strong influence over one's life. This particularized, psychologically painful ego-fragmentation affects the ways in which one copes with, resists, or is overwhelmed by external *han*. Joh embraces Lee's conception of original *han* that resides in the deepest recesses of the unconscious.[478] In this way, original *han* is a general human phenomenon and not the exclusive experience of the *minjung*.

There is a distinction to be made, however, between this original *han* and the *han* of the suffering *minjung*. Joh goes on to argue, along with Lee, that the *han* of which Korean *minjung* theology speaks is secondary *han*.[479] It is neither secondary in importance nor is it meant to downplay the material and socio-political causes of *han*. It is secondary because it is externally, rather than internally, inflicted and is connected to and influenced by original *han*. This secondary *han* is the result of external factors, such as socio-political oppression and violence, whereas original *han* arises from the original formation of a human person.[480] This distinction between original and secondary *han* becomes important in Joh's understanding of *han-pu-ri*, or the resolution from and healing of personal and collective *han*. Unless this original *han* is healed, for Lee and Joh, it is impossible to fully heal the secondary *han* upon which Korean *minjung* theology is focused.[481] This will be discussed in more detail below.

In addition, Joh connects *han* to Julia Kristeva's notion of *abjection*. In summarizing Kristeva, Joh writes:

> abjection can be loosely defined as an operation of the psyche that requires the expulsion and exclusion of that which threatens the formation of one's identity. This process assumes that identity, especially the subject of the dominant West, is shaped and formed in opposition and as antagonistic towards the other . . . the abject is that which the self perceives as unclean, foreign,

---

477. Joh, *Heart of the Cross*, 21–22.
478. Ibid.
479. Ibid., 21–23.
480. Ibid., 21–27.
481. Ibid., 22.

and improper . . . the abject is everything the subject feels it needs to expel in order to create its own subjectivity.[482]

In short, the *abject* haunts the subject at the boundary of its identity and self-understanding.[483] Joh uses Kristeva's psychological understanding and applies it to a more socio-political understanding. This means that *han* is not only a wound but also the marginalization of the unwanted, both within oneself and in society at large. The abject is what is expelled but that always returns to threaten the subject at the margins and boundaries. It refers not only to internal psychology and identity but to people within society. They are the garbage expelled from the center of society but who never truly disappear.[484]

Joh's Understanding and Proposal of Jeong

This is the foundation upon which Joh begins to offer an understanding of *jeong*.[485] Underlying the word *jeong* is a Sino-Korean character that signifies "heart, clarity, vulnerability" and is "a character that means life when used as a noun and 'something arising' when used as a verb."[486] Joh offers a constellation of signifiers that can help point to some of the meaning associated with *jeong* in Korean and Korean-American culture. To begin, for Joh there is no discrete separation between *jeong* and *han* in human life and relationships. The distinction is for the purposes of theorizing and clarity. Joh thinks that *jeong* and *han* are always interconnected in a messy web, one example of which is the name *jeong-han*.[487]

Joh argues that *jeong* points to the "stickiness" in human relationships. Due to the relational nature of the human person, *jeong* is always,

482. Joh, "Loves' Multiplicity," 172–73.

483. Ibid., 173.

484. Ibid.

485. True to the theological tradition to which she is rooted, Joh also engages in storytelling and narrative to illustrate *jeong*. To do this, she describes the Korean film *Joint Security Area* (2000, directed by Park Chan-Wook) and the documentary *Sa-I-Gu* (1993) that treats the experience of Korean-American immigrants and businesses in the aftermath of the 1992 L.A. riots. Park Chan-Wook's other films also offer visceral and often disturbing illustrations of *han*, as can be seen in his vengeance trilogy, particularly *Sympathy for Lady Vengeance* (*Chinjeolhan geumjassi*—literally, "Kindhearted Ms. Geum-Ja," 2005).

486. Joh, *Heart of Cross*, 120.

487. Ibid., 22–23.

already present. It can be related to the English word *love*, but not too closely. When comparing it to traditional Western Christian theological understandings of love, she writes, "*jeong* combines agape, philia, and eros—all three interweaving to form a kind of love that is difficult to define and conceptualize, but often practiced in the everyday relations with the other."[488] Joh writes:

> Many Koreans often feel that *jeong* is more powerful, lasting, and transformative than love. *Jeong* makes relationships 'sticky' but also recognizes the complex and dynamic nature of all relationalism. While *jeong* works to resist oppression and suffering, it does not have elements of retaliatory vengefulness. When *jeong* is present among sufferers and the oppressed who do not forget justice, they preserve an element of forgiveness even for those who participate in the structures of oppression.[489]

To illustrate *jeong*, Joh gives two examples.[490] The first is a Korean saying "You die—I die; you live—I live," which describes the deep relationality and connection between persons. The second example she gives is *mi-eun jeong* versus *go-eun jeong*. The former is applied to relationships that are full of discontent while the latter applies to mutual and satisfying relationships. After making this distinction, Joh observes that there is a Korean saying—"It's better to have *mi-eun jeong* than no *jeong*."[491]

Jeong, no matter what its manifestation, is of great importance. It carries a connotation of the deep, transformative energy of relationality that Joh argues has often been linked to a "feminization" of *jeong* and thus a patriarchal disregard for it. *Jeong* is seen as too passive or impotent to be of any use in the struggle of the oppressed for freedom and dignity. In response, Joh hopes to liberate *jeong* from these patriarchal distortions and retrieve it as an understanding that indicates true transformation of oppressive and victimizing structures and people into being in solidarity

---

488. Joh, "Loves' Multiplicity," 169. In *Heart of the Cross* on page 120, Joh writes, "*Jeong* connotes agape, eros, and filial love with compassion, empathy, solidarity, and understanding that emerges between hearts of connectedness in relationality."

489. Ibid., 179. On 181, she continues, "[P]ractice of *jeong* in the praxis of liberation holds love and justice together with a fierce commitment that also embraces a sense of playfulness."

490. Joh, *Heart of the Cross*, 122–123.

491. She uses this example in several writings. One example is "Violence and Asian American Experience: From Abjection to *Jeong*," 156.

with the oppressed and the victims.[492] Joh warns that *jeong* can be employed to disempower the sinned-against in a patriarchal understanding. Through a thorough feminist critique and retrieval however, Joh thinks that *jeong* can be a fundamental understanding to bring about true justice and positive transformation.[493]

One of the more important aspects of Joh's discussions of *jeong* and *han* is her conviction of the deep connection between oppressed and oppressor, victim and victimizer.[494] She is serious about resisting and unmasking oppression. At the same time, she is offering an understanding of the interconnected wounds among oppressed and oppressor in the power-dynamics of their relationship. As she writes, "I would argue further that *han* itself is also double-edged because it is present not only in the oppressed but in the deeper psyches of the oppressors. Recognizing the prevalence of *han* in both oppressors and the oppressed allow us to admit that a dichotomy can no longer function as the only critical hermeneutics of resistance."[495] Additionally, Joh argues:

> *Jeong* manifests itself in unique combinations of different dimensions of love, justice, and restorative dignity, transgressing boundaries between oppressor and the oppressed, finding ways to mix resistance and embrace amid oppressive relations, and giving birth to new forms of love and justice. *Jeong* does not compromise with those who perpetrate violence and oppression. Rather, the power of *jeong* allows us to recognize the seriousness of the suffering of the oppressors even as we resist their oppressive practices.[496]

---

492. Joh, "Loves' Multiplicity," 180–82.

493. See also Joh, *Heart of the Cross*, 127.

494. To illustrate this connectiveness, Joh describes how *jeong* is what gives the power of victims and the oppressed to retain their dignity and humanity, even by recognizing it in the other. She writes, "A woman who experiences domestic violence does not *love* her abuser, but she might hold on to *jeong* for that abusing other and not only because it is about holding onto the kernel of the abuser's humanity; more importantly, *jeong* preserves her in that situation from the abyss of inhumanity and restores to her a certain valuable dignity and agency. *Jeong* does not discourage separation and autonomy, but *jeong* works to help us to be mindful that we are always in relation to the other." See "Loves' Multiplicity," 182.

495. Joh, *Heart of the Cross*, 21.

496. Joh, "Loves' Multiplicity," 181. On 182 and 183, Joh goes so far as to speculate, "Sometimes, even in relationships of animosity, as in the case between the colonizer and the colonized, *jeong* emerges despite our best efforts to block it out because we cannot prevent glimpsing the image of oneself mirrored in the other. When one sees

Joh's vision of the relationship between *jeong* and *han* undergirds her understanding of the practice of *han-pu-ri,* or the resolution of *han.* She questions the traditional practice of *dan* as proposed by Kim Chi-Ha and adopted by Korean *minjung* theologians. Joh thinks that Kim's understanding of *dan*—a severe cutting off of all that causes *han* and a radical break from these causes, relationships, structures, etc.—is an insufficient way to address *han.* This is because Joh thinks that *dan* does not account for the complex relationships in which one is already always enmeshed, even between oppressed and oppressor, as signified by *jeong.*[497] Joh argues that Kim's call for an agonized, but necessary, violence of love retains too much patriarchal pathology to be useful.[498] Joh is not attempting to fully eradicate *dan* from the process of resolving *han.* Instead, she is pointing out that *dan* in and of itself is insufficient for transforming oppressive structures and relationships. Cutting off is not the same as giving life. If necessary, *dan* is merely one step within the larger process of liberation, transformation, and life-giving for the *han*-filled peoples of the world.[499] Joh argues:

> *Jeong* is what is needed to bring wholeness and healing from abjection and *han.* The practice of *dan* is crucial in dismantling individual and collective experiences of *han;* however, healing can only come through the power of *jeong.* We might be able to wrestle some justice out of the unjust, but we cannot extract the profound transformation of the causes of injustice that come only through love/*jeong.*[500]

---

one's very self mirrored in the face of the other, one knows in the deepest recess of one's heart that complete severing is not the solution. In this way, *jeong* is even more expansive and generous that love even in the context of relational complexity, for it inherently believes in the possibility of the impossible."

497. Joh, *Heart of the Cross,* 26–27. Joh points out that in his work Kim moves away from a hyper-masculinized understanding of *dan* and love to a stance of desiring mutual transformation. She writes, on page 27 that "his image of the revolutionary is changed from the fighter to the caring mother."

498. This is similar to Jae-Hoon Lee's argument that *won-han, hu-han,* and immature *jeong-han* cannot be the foundation for positive social change. These aspects of *han* are either destructive (*won-han, hu-han*) or they are not useful (immature *jeong-han*).

499. Joh, *Heart of the Cross,* 26–27.

500. Ibid., 106.

Joh's Christology and Theology of the Cross

Joh's second main contribution to my discussion is her emerging Christology that uses *jeong* as a fundamental theological source in envisioning salvation through a theology of the cross. Joh envisions the cross as a site of *han-pu-ri* through the lens of *jeong*, feminist theory, and postcolonial theory. In short, Joh argues that on the cross Jesus makes a "double gesture," so to speak, one with its source in *han* and the other in *jeong* in order to embody salvation. That is, the cross is both *homage* and *mockery* towards the oppressive powers for the benefit of the victims and also for the salvation of the victimizers. This double gesture of the cross is somewhat similar to Park's theology that proposes a double-meaning of the cross: atonement through liberation from *han* for the oppressed and salvation from sin for the oppressors.

At the foundation of Joh's theology of the cross is her embrace of a general feminist critique of what has become known as atonement theory, a theology whose roots are found in the work of Anselm of Canterbury (c.1033–1109). Joh argues that traditional Anselmian atonement theory enables and furthers the suffering of the victims, and particularly women, due to its glorification of the death and suffering of the sinless Son of God. In her interpretation, atonement theory proposes that God the Father willed Jesus' death on the cross as a payment for the sins of humanity against God. In this way, God demands satisfaction through blood and sends the Son to die. She argues that this theology often results in the passive and redemptive suffering of the innocent as being part of God's will.[501]

Joh contrasts this with Mark Lewis Taylor's Christology that focuses on Jesus' crucifixion as an execution. Joh wants to follow Taylor and focus upon the historical context in which the Roman Empire considered this marginal Jew an enemy of the state and thus used the most horrible, state-sanctioned form of punishment against him. Joh embraces this historical-contextual focus because it brings out the more liberative aspect of Jesus' death, whereas she thinks atonement theory adds to oppression and victimization.[502] A historical-contextual execution of Jesus

---

501. Ibid., 95–96.

502. Ibid., 72–73. Although Joh may be offering an adequate interpretation of the tradition of atonement theory that is derived from Anselm, hers is a questionable interpretation of Anselm's work itself, particularly in *Cur Deus Homo*. Her claim that "traditional atonement theory depicts Jesus as passively suffering for the sake of the world" speaks more to the interpretations of atonement than to Anselm's work itself. The question for Anselm, in brief, was how God's love and justice can both be upheld

reminds Christians that Jesus was seen as a menace to the status quo. In this light, Joh thinks "his death then might be construed as the result of the liberative *jeong* that is at the heart of liberative action, a living by the way of the cross."[503]

Joh embraces this critique but does not want to eliminate the Christian symbol of the cross and crucifixion altogether. Similar to Park, she wants to interrogate and reinterpret this symbol. To do this, Joh employs feminist and postcolonial sources and argues that in the crucifixion of Jesus the cross becomes a *third space*, or what postcolonial theory calls *interstitial space*. That is, an ambiguous, liminal space in which something new is emerging that opposes and deconstructs a previous binary or dichotomy.[504] It is an "in-between" space that is a womb for recreation and healing.[505]

As an interstitial space, Joh interprets the cross as a messy, ambiguous space that is one of hybridity. This means that it is not the exclusive space of the executed or the executioners, victims or victimizers, but the space of interconnected *han* and *jeong* that includes each while allowing each to function differently. As she writes, "It is at this interstitial space that *jeong* arises between the hearts of the oppressed and the oppressor, in between the harrowing and the vulnerable and often tortuous space, the utter abyssal space between the executed and the executioner, victim and the victimizer."[506] Interstitial space, for Joh, is the site in which *jeong* is most manifest. She argues that *jeong* is the glue that holds together the creativity and hybridity within this space. As an interstitial space of hybrid-

---

in light of the grave reality of sin, while still safeguarding God's love. Anselm's answer is that God gives God's self, through the Son, as a means for atoning for the infinite offence caused by humankind. Humankind could not pay the debt, and God continued to will the flourishing of humankind, so God offered God's self to atone for sin instead of exacting payment from humankind. This debate over Anselm, however, is beyond the scope of this study and also is not the focus of Joh's work. But her uncritical embrace of this interpretation of Anselm and her lack of a treatment of the primary source remains a weakness within her Christology. Joh offers a summary of Anselm on 95 that is incomplete and does not reference the text of the primary source. She misses the crucial concern of Anselm for sin in the context of both God's justice and God's love/mercy. This does not invalidate her larger point, but is a weakness at the base of her argument.

503. Ibid., 73.

504. Ibid., 62.

505. For a discussion of the terms *in-between* and *in-beyond*, see Jung Young Lee's *Marginality: The Key to Multicultural Theology*.

506. Joh, *Heart of the Cross*, 88.

ity, Joh argues that the cross is the location where "death and life coexist, and where suffering/*han*/abjection, liberation/love and *jeong* challenge one another... The cross embodies *han* and *jeong*, abjection and love."[507] As the cross painfully and uncompromisingly manifests the reality of *han*, it also manifests the reality of *jeong* that always accompanies *han*.[508]

Two other terms that Joh adopts from postcolonial theory to better articulate her theology of the cross, in which both *han* and *jeong* are active, are *mimicry* and *hybridity*. Regarding the former, Joh argues that it describes a socio-political move that simultaneously acknowledges and resists an oppressive or dominating power. Referencing Homi Bhabha, Joh observes that mimicry simultaneously pays homage to and menaces the oppressor's identity and power. It is a move of destabilization of a given power structure through affirmation and negation while also acting as a means for asserting subjectivity (or having it denied).[509] Regarding the latter, Joh prefers to envision hybridity as a "thick description of historical and geographical situations... this framework suggests mutual agencies on all sides. Here power flows in multidimensional directions."[510] It is an ambiguous mixing that has a destabilizing effect upon set power structures. For Joh, hybridity and mimicry are connected to the interstitial space in which something new arises from the ambiguities of what came before.

The cross performs mimicry in that it pays homage to the Roman violators while also menacing their self-understanding and power structure. For Joh, the cross is the third space in which original *han* can be resolved through engaging hybridity, the entry to which is the hybridity and double gesture of Jesus on the cross.[511] "The cross intimates the significance of *jeong* but it is not immune to the horror of *han*. The cross therefore transgresses doctrinal self-enclosures and instead privileges *jeong* as the divine presence between the divine and the world . . .

---

507. Ibid., 111. Or, as she writes on 74, "I suggest that the cross, when understood in light of *jeong*, works effectively to encompass incommensurable aspects of life: mainly the coexistence of both life and death, hate and love. The cross, with its powerful love ethic, is the symbol of the inclusive relationalism embodied by *jeong*. *The way of the cross must be sustained by living with, in, and through the power of jeong*" (Joh's italics).

508. Ibid., 99–100.

509. Ibid., 55–56.

510. Ibid., 53.

511. Ibid., 115.

the transgressive and transformative power of the cross lies in its very complex messiness."⁵¹² The cross is salvific for both the victims and the victimizers, the oppressed and the oppressors, due to its embodying a third space that includes *han* and *jeong*, suffering and transformative love, sinners and sinned-against.

Joh concludes that even though the cross is best envisioned as an interstitial space in which all binaries fall apart and a new creation occurs, she argues that in the end the cross in itself does not save. Neither is the cross a symbol of love, per se. Instead, Joh contends that the cross is a symbol of the risk taken by love and through living a life in the fullness of *jeong*. She writes, "What is significant about the cross, then, is not that Jesus died on it but that because of his living out of *jeong*, he ends up de facto on the cross."⁵¹³ Moreover, the cross also points to the resurrection by embodying the return of the abject: that is, the return of all who have been repressed, marginalized, executed—the *han*-ridden people. It becomes a confrontation between love and violence, and a location of *jeong* and *han*.⁵¹⁴

The cross and the life of Jesus become, for Joh, a location of *han-pu-ri*. It is the resolution of *han*, both original and secondary, of both oppressed and oppressors, through the work of *jeong*. The cross does not accomplish an atoning, sacrificial death to appease an angry God. So it is not the act of crucifying and dying that is salvific. Instead, it is the creation of the interstitial space despite the violence in which both *han* and *jeong* are present. The cross has salvific value because it is an extension of Jesus' life. The cross was the inevitable outcome of his life of overflowing *jeong*. It was the consequence of Jesus' life-praxis.

For, as Joh argues, Jesus' life was one not of *dan* but rather of a praxis of *jeong*.⁵¹⁵ This is different from Kim Chi-Ha's play *Chang Il-Dam* in which Chang is portrayed as a Christ-like figure who practices *dan*, teaches it to his disciples, and resolves *han* through placing his own head on his betrayer's body and vice versa. For Joh, Jesus approaches and embraces those who have been cut off, rather than being the one to do the cutting. Joh thinks that Jesus' praxis of *jeong* applies not only to the victims but to the oppressors, as seen in his ministry and in his cross. *Dan*

---

512. Ibid., 118.
513. Ibid., 106.
514. Ibid., 114.
515. Ibid., 119–20.

can occasionally be seen, such as in the cleansing of the temple, but the main thrust is Jesus' radical embodiment of *jeong* in life and death.[516] As an illustration, Joh points out that in Matthew's Passion Narrative Jesus calls his betrayer "friend" and then renounces the cutting off of the Roman soldier's ear.[517] Jesus has no interest in a revolutionary, violence of love associated with *dan*. For Joh, Jesus' concern is to live a life of *jeong* that is fully transformative of all humankind. Ultimately, it is Jesus incarnation in a praxis of *jeong*, with all its consequences, that saves. Jesus' life displayed *jeong*, fostered *jeong*, and even received *jeong* from others.[518]

Summary of Joh's Theology

To close this discussion of Joh's theology, there are two main contributions that I again wish to highlight: her proposal of *jeong* as a correlate and corrective to *han* and her re-interpretation of the cross as an interstitial space in which oppressor and oppressed, *han* and *jeong*, are revealed and in which *jeong* has the final word.[519] First, Joh offers an understanding of *jeong* as a complement and corrective to *han*. Joh engages the work of Jae-Hoon Lee to arrive at a distinction between original *han* and secondary *han*. This distinction allows her to account for the deep *han* not only in the oppressed but also in the oppressor, both of which are in need of healing. She then offers an understanding of *jeong* through phrases, stories and metaphors in order to make it somewhat accessible for an outer-hearer to understand. *Jeong*, as the "stickiness" in human relationships that is always, already present, is the means by which Joh thinks *han* is to be resolved, both original and secondary. It is a positive, creative, transformative energy to counter the negative, disruptive, and destructive energy in *han*. Moreover, Joh contends that *jeong* is the more appropriate lens through which to envision a Christian praxis of *han-pu-ri* than *dan*. This is because she interprets Jesus' life not as a cutting off of the sources of *han* but as a relational transformation of them through *jeong*.

---

516. Ibid., 118–20.
517. Ibid., 235.
518. Ibid., 124–25.
519. Joh's utilization of feminist and postcolonial theory, along with *jeong*, to re-interpret the cross is another contribution to the larger academy. That, however, is beyond the scope of this chapter.

Second, Joh utilizes her understanding of *jeong* to re-envision a theology of the cross in which Jesus performs a double gesture for the benefit of the oppressed and their oppressors. The wounds of the victims and the oppressed are connected to the wounds of the victimizers and oppressors and find a kind of resolution in the interstitial space of hybridity as symbolized in the cross. Rather than interpreting the cross as an atonement/sacrifice in order to restore God's honor through satisfaction—an accepted, if imprecise, interpretation and critique of Anselmian soteriology—she interprets the cross as the horrible, yet inevitable, consequence of Jesus' life that showed a praxis of *jeong*. For Joh, the cross is the third space in which the executed and executioners, sinners and sinned-against, come together in the presence of the Living yet Crucified God. The cross reveals *han*/abjection and points to *jeong*/love. *Jeong* ultimately overcomes *han* not only in the cross but in the life and resurrection of Jesus. Joh argues that although the cross is a necessary symbol of *han-pu-ri*, it is Jesus' praxis of *jeong* that is truly salvific. It is the entirety of Jesus' life, death, and resurrection that saves—and perhaps even despite the cross. Similar to Schillebeeckx's emphasis on hope in God, Joh writes, *jeong* is the "relentless faith that *han* does not have the final word."[520]

Conclusion: Three Characteristics of Park's and Joh's Theologies of Han[521]

To conclude this discussion of Park and Joh, there are three shared characteristics of their theologies that I wish to briefly highlight. These three characteristics will be explored in more detail in the following chapter as I employ them as points of critical dialogue with the theology of Edward Schillebeeckx. But a concise summary is helpful to conclude this chapter. These shared characteristics are: an anthropology of *han* (woundedness), a preference for narrative and praxis, and a reinterpretation of the salvific meaning of a theology of the cross.

The first characteristic that I wish to highlight is a shared anthropology of *han*. In short, Park and Joh agree that *han* is a deep, festering wound

---

520. Joh, *Heart of the Cross*, 120.

521. Although I am in agreement with the distinction that Park makes between God's work on behalf of the victims and victimizers, I will continue to employ the term salvation to apply to the entire divine process of healing and recreating wholeness in the world. This is in line with the Roman Catholic theological tradition and I will continue to employ the traditional theological language.

within the human person that is complex and that resides in the mind, body, and spirit that has both creative and destructive potential. They both reference, and expand upon, the definitions of Han Wang-Sang and Kim Chi-Ha, among others, the former describing *han* as "unresolved resentment against injustices suffered, a sense of helplessness because of overwhelming odds against one's feeling of total abandonment, a feeling of acute pain and sorrow in one's guts and bowels"[522] and the latter as an dark, devouring energy that can either be unraveled negatively or positively. For Park and Joh, *han* finds its primary location in this world within the human being—Park's contention of God having *han* notwithstanding. Both theologians also agree that traditional Christian doctrine has not focused enough on the healing of the sinned-against. For each thinker, *han* is intrinsically connected to human beings, individually and collectively, and is one particular way to articulate the wounds inflicted upon humankind by personal, communal, and structural sinfulness. As one employs human experience as a fundamental theological source, one also can employ *han* as a component of the experience of being human.

Moreover, although each theologian calls *han* (and in Joh's case, *jeong*) a "concept," I wish to suggest that, from an outer-hearer's perspective, it is more adequate to interpret *han* as a facet of anthropology and not as a concept per se. This is because a concept, in the Western intellectual tradition, implies an abstraction[523] from experience and sense data to a rational, abstract, conceptual paradigm that is tidy and pertinent mostly to the realm of academic discourse. It is clear that neither Park nor Joh intend *han* to become such an abstract concept. Their emphasis is on the concrete experiences of *han*—that is a confluence of mind, body, and spirit—both in the victims and the victimizers. This is shown through their use of storytelling and metaphor when attempting to interpret this difficult Korean understanding. It is also shown in the way that *han* functions anthropologically in Korean language, history, and Shamanism.

In light of this evidence, and although Park extends *han* not only to humankind but to animals and nature, it seems most appropriate to interpret *han* as an integral aspect of anthropology and not as an abstract concept. It is a culturally specific understanding of the wounds that are carried consciously and unconsciously but that can transcend that

---

522. Wang-Sang Han quoted in Joh, *Heart of the Cross*, xxi. Joh takes this quote of Han's from Park, *The Wounded Heart of God*, 120.

523. In the general Kantian sense, where one receives data from the senses and through reason organizes this data into rational, more abstract ideas.

culture to some extent to shed light on the general experience of being human. Within theological discourse, *han* as an anthropology calls for a focus on the healing and liberation of the sinned-against while also including the forgiveness and salvation of the sinner. It is not a mere conceptual source for fundamental theology but also an anthropological hermeneutic for articulating doctrine and an integral source for the work of practical theology that partakes in God's healing of humans and all of creation. For the purposes of this study, and with the work of Park, Joh, and others in mind, I wish to suggest that *han* be understood primarily as an anthropology from an outer-hearer's perspective.

The second shared characteristic—preference for narrative and praxis—has been perhaps the least explored in my discussion above. This is because neither Park nor Joh feels the need to discuss this method in great detail. Rather, each theologian is true to the tradition in which he or she is working and their influences—from *minjung* theology and psychology to feminist and postcolonial theory—and demonstrates a preference for narrative in their work. For example, in *The Wounded Heart of God* Park dedicates part of an entire chapter to illustrating *han* in narrative and also uses the metaphor of a black hole to describe it. In Joh's *The Heart of the Cross*, she offers illustrations of *han* and *jeong* from film and also from women's experiences, as well as the Gospels. True to both *minjung* theology and using human experience as a fundamental source in doing theology, each shows that narrative is of great importance.

Furthermore, the centrality of praxis—theory and practice mutually informing and critiquing each other—in their theologies is demonstrated by Park's and Joh's focus on *han-pu-ri* for the victims and forgiveness for the victimizers. The point of bringing *han* (and *jeong*) into the contemporary theological discussion, for Park and Joh, is not only to offer a useful hermeneutic through which to better articulate Christian doctrine in order to account for the experiences and healing of the sinned-against. Each theologian, in addition, hopes to suggest concrete practices in which both forgiveness of sins and liberation and healing from *han* really do occur within history and society in our day. For example, Park offers the fourfold process for undoing *han* that culminates in compassionate confrontation and Joh offers a Christ-like praxis of *jeong* for addressing *han* and transforming both sinner and sinned-against into a new creation that fully expresses the creative and loving power of *jeong*. Each theologian is concerned with concrete salvation within this world—what Schillebeeckx would call moments of fragmentary salvation—while also realizing that ultimate healing and *shalom* will occur only in the eschaton. This focus on praxis may loosely be called a preferential option for the *han*-ridden. A praxis of *han-pu-ri* for the *han*-ridden and a praxis of repentance and participation in God's salvation for the *han*-inflictors are at the core of their methods.

The third aspect of their theologies that I wish to highlight is their shared focus upon crucifixion-soteriology while also seeking to interrogate and rearticulate a theology of the cross. In this way, both Park and Joh wish to enable Christian churches to articulate the cross in a way that is liberating, life-giving, and salvific for the wounded and the perpetrators. That is, a theology of the cross that shows a preferential option for the *han*-ridden but that does not forget the connection between the wounds of the oppressed and the wound of the oppressor. Both Park and Joh think that traditional, and particularly (but not exclusively) Protestant theologies of the cross and subsequent soteriologies are no longer adequate to the contemporary situation. These theologies have been found wanting because of their connotations of God-sanctioned violence and retribution and because of their almost exclusive focus upon the well-being of the sinners and oppressors.

Each theologian argues that the cross is a central Christian symbol that must continue to function and that cannot be eliminated. At the same time, each theologian wants to suggest a crucifixion-soteriology that provides more than an exclusive focus on the cross as the means for salvation. Park highlights the work of the Paraclete in Jesus' life, death, and resurrection in saving sinners and liberating the sinned-against, the work he calls the triune atonement, and Joh wishes to interpret the cross as the inevitable consequence of Jesus' praxis of *jeong*. For both thinkers, the cross is of great importance and remains a central Christian symbol. But the cross, by itself, cannot articulate a full soteriology that includes the sinners and sinned-against in a reconciled life with each other and the Living God of Jesus Christ. A soteriology for humankind and all of creation that remains anchored to the cross of Jesus Christ while not being exclusively defined by it.

As this chapter concludes and this study continues into chapter 5, it is important to make one observation regarding the extent to which I have gone to contextualize Park's and Joh's theologies. Had I not done so, I would not have been true to the method of intercultural hermeneutics that I presented in the previous chapter. As an outer-hearer, it is intellectually problematic, if not culturally arrogant, to assume that the surplus of meaning connected to *han* is immediately apparent and easily accessible to a cultural outsider.

Although Park's and Joh's theologies are intentionally written to be accessible to an outer-hearer and to be adequately received by non-Korean and non-Korean-American theologians, I think that they perhaps concede too much intercultural communication competence on the part of the outer-hearer in his or her ability to adequately receive and interpret *han*. In Park's and Joh's valuable works, which make *han* (and *jeong*) more accessible and intelligible, it is also possible that they have unintentionally allowed for a greater degree of misappropriation and misinterpretation of *han* by non-Korean (particularly white) theologians who have not taken the time to deeply examine the roots of *han* and the way that it is appropriate and inappropriate to use. In my opinion, it is difficult to arrive at a relatively adequate understanding of the meaning associated with *han* without, at a minimum, also delving into a.) Korean language, history, and religion; b) *Minjung* poetry and theology and thinkers who critique the *minjung* Christian theological position while also attempting to enhance it. Park's and Joh's works have not come about within a theological and cultural vacuum. They are beholden to and influenced by a specific cultural-theological trajectory while also employing other sources to critique, reform, or even break from that trajectory. In addition to discussing the theologies of Park and Joh within their larger context, this chapter should have made it clear that a cross-cultural reception and interpretation of *han* does indeed require a thick description. It is an endeavor that should not be taken lightly.

5

Intercultural Dialogue: Toward a Roman Catholic Soteriology for the Sinned-Against

THUS FAR, MY ARGUMENT has unfolded in four chapters:

1. A critique of *Gaudium et spes* as offering a relatively inadequate theological anthropology and soteriology by not focusing sufficiently upon salvation for the sinned-against creature.

2. An examination of the soteriology of Edward Schillebeeckx and the condensation of it into four useful points for dialogue: definition, location, foundation, and encounter of God's salvation for humankind through Jesus the Christ.

3. An overview of a method of intercultural hermeneutics that will facilitate an intercultural dialogue to occur to some degree of relative adequacy.

4. A thick description of the Korean and Korean-American understandings of *han*, with an emphasis on the theologies of Andrew Sung Park and Wonhee Anne Joh and three points of contact with the work of Schillebeeckx: an anthropology of woundedness, a preference for narrative and praxis, and a focus upon the crucifixion as the site for reinterpreting God's salvation for humankind.

My overall argument is that an intercultural encounter with and interpretation of theologies of *han*, through an intercultural dialogue with the soteriology of Edward Schillebeeckx, can offer a reference point and resource for envisioning a more relatively adequate Roman Catholic anthropology and soteriology. That is, an encounter with the surplus of meaning associated with *han* provides a focus upon fragments of salvation for the sinned-against creature in *this* world as a supplement to the traditional soteriological paradigm of sinning creature/Sinned-Against Creator. *Han* holds the possibility for envisioning a Roman Catholic soteriology for the sinned-against creature as well as for the one(s) who have sinned against the person(s) and how this occurs in the presence of the Living God of Jesus Christ in this world.

This chapter will proceed in three sections. First, I will briefly outline the concept of *interstitial space*, also known as *third space*. I will show how I employ this concept as a heuristic device for imagining the space in which this intercultural conversation can occur. A third space, or interstitial space, of hybridity offers a greater possibility for a creative exchange between the interlocutors while also accounting for issues of communication distortion, power dynamics, and asymmetry in the dialogue.[524] Schillebeeckx, Park, and Joh can meet and converse within this space in order for Schillebeeckx's soteriology to act as a receiver of the message of *han* and interpret it in a way that can challenge, inform, and supplement the relatively inadequate soteriology of *Gaudium et spes*. I will discuss this through the observations of Schreiter, Joh, and Fumitaka Matsuoka.

Second, I will commence an intercultural dialogue. I will use the four elements condensed from Schillebeeckx's soteriology as the framing device to structure the conversation. As an outer-hearer, my primary focus is upon receiving and synthesizing the message of *han* into my own Roman Catholic semiotic domain. I will show how Park's and Joh's anthropology of woundedness, preference for narrative and praxis, and focus upon the crucifixion as the site for reinterpreting God's salvation for humankind are consonant and dissonant with Schillebeeckx's soteriology. These points of consonance and dissonance, however, are points of constructive theological dialogue as the inner-speakers of *han* interact with the outer-hearer of Schillebeeckx (and myself) within this interstitial space. From each point of the dialogue, I will show how at least

---

524. An additional resource that is important to highlight and consult is Paul Chung, *Constructing Irregular Theology*. Here, Chung labors to develop Suh's and Ahn's legacy and create a postcolonial *minjung* theology. Much of his work is involved in advancing dialogue between Western theology and Asian cultural and multireligious resources, which differentiates his position from the *han* theologies of Park and Joh. See also Chung's edited volume, *Asian Contextual Theology for the Third Millennium*, his recent book *Hermeneutical Theology and the Imperative of Public Ethics*, and his forthcoming monograph entitled, *Postcolonial Imagination: Archaeological Hermeneutics and Comparative Religious Theology*.

one particular question emerges that is important to address in order for *han* to be received, interpreted, and synthesized into the Roman Catholic semiotic-theological domain. In other words, at least four questions are fundamental for receiving and interpreting *han* as it moves from the interstitial space of dialogue with Schillebeeckx to full engagement with *Gaudium et spes*. These questions focus upon the cross, human experience, grace/creation/sacramentality, and mysticism.

Third, I will address each of the four questions that emerge from the dialogue:

1. Must the meaning associated with *han* be centered around a crucifixion soteriology and theology of the cross?

2. How can *han* be received and interpreted without distorting its meaning and deflating it from a thick description of woundedness to a mere "thin" synonym for suffering; an exercise that becomes little more than theological tourism?[525]

3. Can *han* be infused with a robust theology of grace, creation, and sacramentality, all of which are foundational in Roman Catholic soteriology and anthropology, while remaining intelligible to the inner speakers?

4. Can *han* carry both the political *and* the mystical dimensions of Christianity?

I will address these four questions that are fundamental for attempting to receive, interpret, and synthesize *han* into Roman Catholic soteriology and theological anthropology while retaining some degree or relative adequacy and intercultural communication competence. Again, Schreiter describes the task at hand: "The intercultural hermeneutics challenge would be stated thus semiotically: how does the same *message* get communicated via different *codes*, using a mixture of *signs* from two different cultures?"[526] This is a difficult question that lacks simple, clear answers. Nevertheless, this final chapter will offer a skeleton upon which subsequent work on this topic may be fleshed out.

---

525. Chapter 4 has made it clear that *han* is not identical with the concept of *suffering*.

526. Schreiter, *The New Catholicity*, 30.

Section One: Intercultural Dialogue in Third Space[527]

The purpose of this chapter is to demonstrate how *han* may be brought into conversation with *Gaudium et spes* through an engagement with the soteriology of Edward Schillebeeckx. In chapter 3, I described my approach to intercultural communication as follows: my understanding of culture is *globalized,* my approach to culture is *semiotic,* and my intercultural hermeneutic is *particularist*—one that highlights the relative incommensurability of cultures. Furthermore, I located myself as an *outer hearer* and the theologians of *han* as the *inner speakers* and proposed *intercultural communication competence* as one tool for gauging the relative adequacy of the communication of *han* from one location to the other.

These tools can work together to enable conversation in this chapter through the creation of a liminal, or interstitial space.[528] Both Schreiter and Joh are helpful in briefly discussing this concept of third space. Schreiter has referenced the work of Fumitaka Matsuoka who suggests, ". . . hearers and speakers do not come together in the culture of each other, but in an interstitial zone created out of the liminal experience of both interlocutors interacting with one another. [Matsuoka] suggests that it is perhaps in this specially created zone that intercultural communication takes place."[529] Similarly, as Joh points out, although in a somewhat different context that is primarily concerned with constructing identity as opposed to intercultural communication, interstitial space "is an open site that refuses the logic of binarism." She continues:

> [A]lthough this Third Space is unrepresentable because of its complexity and constantly shifting terrain, this is precisely why it ensures the conditions for enunciations to emerge. Such enunciations of symbols of culture have no primordial unity or fixity. Moreover, even the same signs can be appropriated, translated, rehistoricised, and read anew. This split-space, this Third Space

---

527. The term *third space* originates from the work of Homi Bhaba. See *The Location of Culture.*

528. For more on the development of the term *interstitial space* see Rabinow, *Reflections on Fieldwork in Morocco.* See also Reichel-Dolmatoff, *Amazonian Cosmos.*

529. Schreiter, *The New Catholicity,* 40–41. Schreiter specifically cites Matsuoka's "A Reflection on 'Teaching Theology from an Intercultural Perspective.'" This insight from intercultural hermeneutics is similar to Joh, who also discusses hybridity and interstitial third space (and also references Matsuoka). See *Heart of the Cross,* 53–55; 62–66

of enunciation, the in-between space, is the space that carries the 'burden of culture' by exploring hybridity.[530]

My envisioning of this dialogue as occurring within a third space of hybridity is an outgrowth of a particularist hermeneutic that respects the relative incommensurability of cultures. As Schreiter points out:

> Matsuoka's proposal may be particularly helpful in encounters of highly incommensurate cultures, of cultures that have been damaged badly by outside invaders, and of cultures that maintain a kind of *disciplina arcani*. An interstitial zone may protect important aspects of the culture's life. In any event, the proposal is also helpful in reminding us of the importance of finding ways to *imagine* the cultural encounter.[531]

My use of interstitial or third space to imagine the conversation in this chapter enables two structural elements. First, I can utilize the four elements of Schillebeeckx's soteriology as the organizing structure for this conversation. The purpose is to use Schillebeeckx's soteriology to unlock, receive, and interpret some of the theological meanings associated with *han* to help envision a more relatively adequate theological anthropology and soteriology for the sinned-against creature in the Roman Catholic Pastoral Constitution, *Gaudium et spes*. Second, it allows the dialogue between Schillebeeckx, Park, and Joh, although asymmetrical and occurring through the four soteriological points of Schillebeeckx, to unfold as mutually informing and mutually critical. That is, aspects of Schillebeeckx's soteriology may possibly challenge and/or augment Park's and Joh's while Park and Joh challenge and/or augment aspects of Schillebeeckx. As Schreiter points out, "Information is both lost and gained when crossing a cultural boundary. Aspects of a message that are obvious and transparent in the speaker's culture may become obscure and opaque in the hearer's culture. Hence, information is 'lost' to the hearer (lost in

---

530 Joh, *Heart of the Cross*, 62. This imagining of a third space in which intercultural communication occurs also is similar to Garcia-Rivera's observation that much destabilization and activity among signs, codes, and messages occurs at semiotic boundaries or between semiospheres. *Martin de Porres*, 36–37. One key difference, however, is that Garcia-Rivera focuses on the activity between binary oppositions that exist at these boundaries, whereas Joh's postcolonial, postmodern, and critical feminist hermeneutic views the very existence of binaries and binary opposites with suspicion.

531. Schreiter, *The New Catholicity*, 41.

the sense of not immediately understood though potentially retrievable at a later time)."[532]

Finally, although the heuristic device of interstitial space is helpful I must also point out that the ensuing dialogue is my own creation and interpretation.[533] This means that the conversation is bound within the limits of my own location as an outer hearer, as well as the relative adequacy of my interpretations of Schillebeeckx, Park, and Joh. To the best of my knowledge, Schillebeeckx never engaged with Korean *minjung* theology, *han,* or the theologies of Andrew Park or Wonhee Anne Joh. Similarly, to the best of my knowledge the interpreters of *han, minjung* theologians, and Park and Joh never engaged with the soteriology of Schillebeeckx.[534] Therefore, this is an imagined conversation (or perhaps thought experiment) among my interpretation of Schillebeeckx's soteriology and my interpretation of some of the meanings associated with *han* through the work of Park and Joh. Through this imagined conversation, the points of dialogue condensed from Schillebeeckx's soteriology (as a hearer or recipient of the message) can provide insight into the theologies of *han* in the attempt to bring *han* into a critical relationship with the relatively inadequate soteriology of *Gaudium et spes.*

Section Two: Intercultural Dialogue: Definition, Location, Foundation, Encounter

Definition of God's Salvation for Humankind: Salvation, Atonement, and Jeong

I will begin with the first point of dialogue condensed from Schillebeeckx's soteriology—definition—and bring it into conversation with Park's and Joh's anthropologies of woundedness and foci upon the cross as the site for reinterpreting God's salvation for humankind. This point

---

532. Ibid., 38.

533. I am indebted to the example of *conversation* as exhibited by Miguel Diaz in my formulation of this chapter. The method that Diaz adopts is a dialogue between elements of Karl Rahner's theology and elements of U.S. Hispanic theology is indebted to both David Tracy and Robert Schreiter. See Diaz, *On Being Human.* See also *Plurality and Ambiguity* and *The New Catholicity.*

534. The closest point of contact I have found, and this is not overly close, is Kim Chi-Ha's references of the political theology of J. B. Metz. Metz and Schillebeeckx had an influence upon each other, particularly through their work with the journal *Concilium.* For Kim's reference of Metz, see "Declaration of Conscience."

of dialogue will shed light upon the consonance and dissonance among the three thinkers.

The general definitions of God's salvation for humankind through Jesus the Christ that are articulated by Schillebeeckx, Park, and Joh show similarities. These include a focus upon liberation, forgiveness, healing, and wholeness in *this* world (*extra mundum nulla salus*), a focus on praxis in theologically articulating soteriology, and a fundamental concern with the problem of unwarranted human suffering. The theological languages employed by these thinkers, however, are disparate and are employed with specialized meanings. For example, Schillebeeckx discusses God's salvation for humankind through Jesus the Christ as the confluence of liberation for the sinned-against and redemption for sinners. *Salvation* is the broader term in Schillebeeckx's soteriology that points to human wholeness as seen in the always-threatened *humanum* as illustrated by the seven anthropological constants. To revisit a quote from chapter 2:

> Salvation cannot be identified exclusively with political liberation; exclusively with 'being nice to one another'; exclusively with ecological efforts; exclusively with identifying oneself either with micro-ethics or macro-ethics or with mysticism, liturgy and prayer; exclusively with concerning oneself with education or geriatric techniques, and so on. *All this* is part of the concept of *salvation* or *wholeness* of mankind, and is therefore also essentially concerned with salvation from God, which may be experienced as grace.[535]

In contrast, Park employs a different theological language to express a similar understanding. Park envisions God's action within history to resolve *han* and build up human beings bodily, mentally, and spiritually, as *atonement*. Park intentionally uses this traditional term, atonement, that has become problematic for much of contemporary theology. He interrogates the atonement tradition in order to reinterpret the cross. Park points to the literal meaning of the word—at-one-ment—which signifies the return to wholeness of all who are separated by sinning and being sinned-against. Similar to Schillebeeckx, Park also uses the term liberation to apply to the healing of the sinned-against, oppressed, and the victims. He uses the term salvation, however, to apply to the forgiveness and healing of sinners, oppressors and victimizers as symbolized by Jesus' bloody crucifixion. What Schillebeeckx terms salvation that is

---

535. Schillebeeckx, *Christ*, 779.

comprised of liberation and redemption Park terms atonement that is comprised of liberation and salvation.

Joh's terminology is distinct from both Schillebeeckx's and Park's while also remaining similar in her concern for concrete salvation for both sinner and sinned-against in this world. In contrast to Schillebeeckx and Park, she places her focus upon fragmented identity and the way that the cross can be interpreted by diversely oppressed communities. These are communities, she argues, whose experiences have been excluded from doctrinally interpreting Jesus' death on the cross and its connection to human salvation (Schillebeeckx) or atonement (Park). Joh retains this focus through using a critical hermeneutic based upon certain threads within feminist, postcolonial, and psychoanalytic theories.

Whereas Schillebeeckx speaks of salvation and Park speaks of atonement, Joh focuses upon *jeong*.[536] For Joh, salvation is rooted in the Christian symbol of the cross as an interstitial space in which both *han* and *jeong* exist together. Jesus shares in the *han* of the wounded while simultaneously manifesting the *jeong* of his lifestyle and ministry. She employs the terminology of *han*/sin/abjection and *jeong*/love/salvation as intermingling in the interstitial space of the cross for a new creation

---

536. I briefly introduced Joh's interpretation of the Korean understandings of *jeong* in chapter 4. To elaborate, she offers a constellation of signifiers in *Heart of the Cross* that unlock some of the meanings associated with *jeong*. For example, 1) *Jeong* is not identifiable with *love*. "Nor is it completely identifiable with compassion alone. Koreans understand that *jeong* is often much more powerful than even love. *Jeong* connotes agape, eros, and filial love with compassion, empathy, solidarity, and understanding that emerges between hearts of connectedness in relationality. *Jeong* is a supplement that comes into the interstitial site of relationalism. *Jeong* is rooted in relationalism. As it emerges in between connectedness, it works as a lubricant and as relentless faith that *han* does not have the final word" (120); 2) "*Jeong* is the in-between space created by the juxtaposition of *han* and love . . . Similar to eros's embodiment of both bitterness and sweetness, *jeong* creates indeterminacy within the unaccounted-for space between the oppressed and the oppressor, between hate and love, between the semiotic and the symbolic, and between the divine and this world" (121); 3) *Jeong* is a "stickiness" that "pervades the immanent reality of everyday relationships" and "is part of the divine reality." It is a "primal eros as the energy of God present in all things, all relationships, to sustain and cherish all that comes into contact. The primal eros that is present in all things, in all that comes into contact, is the presence of *jeong*" (121); 4) *Jeong's* power "lies in its ability to wedge itself into the smallest gaps between oppressed and oppressor" and *jeong* is "the divine presence that nudges us not only to perceive but also to accept the often negativized and shadowed parts of ourselves and thus ultimately to awaken to and practice the way of living in the fullness of *jeong*. The presence of *jeong* within and around relationality reveals us to ourselves" (122).

to emerge: one in which oppressed and oppressor, victim and victimizer, find transformed relationships as *jeong* overcomes *han*. As she writes:

> What is significant about the cross, then, is not that Jesus died on it but that because of his living out of *jeong*, he ends up de facto on the cross.
>
> *Jeong* is what is needed to bring wholeness and healing from abjection and *han*. The practice of *dan* is crucial in dismantling individual and collective experiences of *han*; however, healing can only come through the power of *jeong*. We might be able to wrestle some justice out of the unjust, but we cannot extract the profound transformation of the causes of injustice that come only through love/*jeong*.[537]

Several pages later, Joh continues with this reflection on God's work of achieving wholeness for oppressed and oppressor as interpreted through the cross:

> The cross is the interstitial space wherein both homage and mockery are embodied. It is the interstitial/hybrid site where abjection and agency are met. It is the site where the other and the self, while remaining autonomous, also recognize the presence of the both in the self. It is the site where death and life coexist, and where suffering/*han*/abjection, liberation/love, and *jeong* challenge one another . . . The cross embodies *han* and *jeong*, abjection and love. The cross signifies the logic of love that contests the logic of violence.[538]

If, as suggested above, Schillebeeckx's definition is *salvation* and Park's is *atonement*, then Joh's may be described as *jeong*. Joh thinks that God's salvation for humankind, through Jesus Christ, that includes liberation from being sinned-against and redemption from sinning, is the triumph of the meeting of divine and human *jeong* on the cross that transforms *han* into a new creation. *Jeong* embraces the wounds of *han*, heals them, and persuades sinners to repent and seek forgiveness and *metanoia*.

As these various definitions, with similar concerns but divergent theological articulations, interact they shed light upon nuances of *han* and raise at least one issue: the connection between *han* and the cross. The inner-speakers, Park and Joh, focus their theological articulations primarily, but not exclusively, upon the role of the cross and the

537. Joh, *Heart of the Cross*, 106.
538. Ibid., 111.

crucifixion in unveiling and resolving *han*. The cross is the center of the constellation of Christian symbols that they interrogate and re-envision through an encounter with *han* (and *jeong*). Does this mean that a relatively adequate reception, interpretation, and appropriation of *han* by an outer-hearer must also give priority to the symbol of the cross and the crucifixion when reflecting upon soteriology and theological anthropology through a thick description of *han*? In other words, must *han* be focused primarily upon the cross or does it hold the possibility of de-centering the cross while still giving it a location of great importance within the constellation of Christian symbols that inform theological anthropology and soteriology?

This is a particularly pressing question because a Roman Catholic outer hearer such as myself is greatly formed by a Schillebeeckxian notion that even though the cross is irreplaceable in soteriology, we must readjust our focus because we find salvation despite the cross. There is overlap, however, for Schillebeeckx writes:

> Only when someone opposed to injustice in all its forms has to suffer at the hands of others, can he do good for others: suffer for a good cause. In that case, his sacrifice for the good cause is so radical that the consequences for his own life are no longer important. It is here that we find the saving significance of Jesus' death: it points to the unconditional nature of his message and the life-style which accorded with it, to the unconditional character of his dedication and sacrifice, to the way in which his person, his message and his action were all of a piece.[539]

This question of reception, interpretation, *han,* and the cross will be explored in Section Three.

Location of God's Salvation for Humankind: Human Experience

The second point of dialogue condensed from Schillebeeckx's soteriology is that of location: human experience. In connection with location, I wish to explore its consonance with Park and Joh's preferential option for narrative and praxis and an anthropology of woundedness. As I stated in chapter 4, Park and Joh (within a broader theological trajectory) argue that *han* is intrinsically connected to human beings, individually and collectively, and is one cultural understanding through which to articulate

---

539. Schillebeeckx, *Interim Report*, 60.

the wounds inflicted upon humankind by personal, communal, and structural sinfulness. As one employs human experience as a fundamental theological source, then one also may cautiously employ *han* as an articulation of the experience of being human. The anthropology of woundedness and preferential option for narrative and praxis that are shared attributes of Park and Joh can converse with the location in which salvation from God arrives: *human experience*.

Chapter 2 clearly showed the importance of the category of human experience in Schillebeeckx's thought. After all, he focuses upon this when giving a concise statement of the origins of the Christian proclamation: "It began with an experience."[540] For Schillebeeckx, human experience is interpreted, developing due to the surprise, critique, and contrast of new experiences, best expressed in narrative, and is oriented towards the humanum as depicted by seven anthropological constants.

Schillebeeckx's emphasis on the importance of new experiences offers a fruitful location to engage with *han*. Schillebeeckx thinks that without Christianity's ability to accept, process, and articulate new experiences it will become irrelevant, at best, or may pass away, at worst. As Schillebeeckx points out

> Without constantly renewed experience a gulf develops between the content of the experience in on-going life and the expression in words of earlier experiences, a gulf between experience and doctrine and between people and the church. This already means that Christianity is not a message to be believed, but an experience of faith that becomes a message, and as an explicit message seeks to offer a new possibility of life-experience to others who hear it from within their own experience.[541]

This is because the historical foundation of Christianity is a new experience of God through the life, death, and resurrection of Jesus of Nazareth. It was an experience of contrast, conversion, and fragmentary salvation. As Schillebeeckx observes:

> Particular people experienced redemption and liberation in Jesus and began to communicate this experience to others. Their experience—for us—becomes a message. The beginning of the Christian tradition is therefore not a doctrine but a history of experience—not a neutral account of facts. In the New

---

540. Ibid., 10.
541. Ibid., 50.

Testament the disciples have given reflected expression to what they experienced.[542]

Park, Joh, and a thick description of *han* demonstrate that an anthropology of *han* is not a "new" experience. *Han*, however, can be interpreted cautiously as a resource for envisioning a new way to articulate and interpret diverse experiences within a globalized context characterized by continuous change and constant negotiation between the global and the local. Without such resources, the offer of salvation from God for humankind through Jesus the Christ can become unintelligible and difficult to articulate. An encounter with and reception and interpretation of *han*—when deemed relatively adequate by both inner speaker and outer hearer—may provide new avenues for articulating the human experience of salvation from God that is the foundation for the Christian proclamation.

Park's and Joh's anthropologies of woundedness and preferences for narrative and praxis provide a crucial insight into how *han* may be employed in such a way: it must be articulated in narrative, poetry, art, film, and music and its meaning must arise from and return to the lived experience of a people within a particular context. In other words, it is insufficient to conceptualize *han* in the Western, Kantian, philosophical sense. That would offer a relatively inadequate interpretation. Instead, if *han* is to be a means for a renewed articulation of the human experience of salvation from God, it must be framed in narrative, song, poetry, dance, liturgy, and other creative endeavors.

Schillebeeckx's thinking shows consonance with the underlying method of Park, Joh, *minjung* theology, and Shamanism; they all give preference to narrative and storytelling. Schillebeeckx shows this concern when reflecting upon the connection between suffering, explanation, and narrative. He writes,

> People do not *argue* against suffering, but tell a *story* and make statements on the basis of experience without giving an 'explanation': simply because as Christians they look to the suffering and death of *Jesus*. It must have meaning, even if no one knows how or why; the essential presupposition is that suffering should not be made light of. Faith in Jesus as Christ is an 'answer' without arguments: a 'nevertheless'. Christianity does not give any explanation for suffering, but demonstrates a way of life. Suffering is destructively *real*, but it does not have the last word.[543]

542. Ibid., 7–8.
543. Schillebeeckx, *Christ*, 698–99; italics original.

A renewed articulation of human experience is needed in order to understand more accurately the breadth and the depth of human woundedness, degradation, exploitation, and dehumanization. *Han* offers a reference point and a surplus of meaning that can enable Christians to articulate the connection between a barbarous excess of human degradation and the Christian experience of salvation.

In addition, a preference for praxis in theological articulations is a shared concern of Schillebeeckx, Park, and Joh. Park offers a concrete, fourfold process of compassionate confrontation for resolving *han* and Joh describes a praxis of *jeong* as following in the way that Jesus addressed *han*. Schillebeeckx's academic writings[544] are more theoretical and less concrete than Park's as to what this process entails. Nevertheless, praxis is at the heart of Schillebeeckx's theological work. Praxis, in Schillebeeckx's estimation, is the confluence of theory and practice that is mutually informing, mutually critical, and always developing. It involves a life embedded in the messiness of human history and in active ministry to the world while at the same time reflecting and challenging one's understanding of this through contemplation, study, and reflection. As Goergen points out, for Schillebeeckx "orthopraxis, rooted on one's experience of God, is a following of the praxis of Jesus."[545]

For an outer-hearer such as myself, this discussion surrounding location, anthropology of woundedness, and a preference for narrative and praxis raises an important fundamental question for attempting to receive, interpret, and appropriate some of the meanings associated with *han* to some degree of relative adequacy and intercultural communication competence: how can *han* be received and interpreted without distorting its meaning and deflating it from a thick description of woundedness to a mere "thin" synonym for suffering that is bereft of much of its meaning? In other words, how does an outer hearer deeply engage with some of the meanings associated with *han*, and interpret them into his or her semiotic domain, without reducing this exercise to little more than an orientalist theological tourism? This question will be addressed in Section Three.

---

544. I am not claiming that Schillebeeckx's works lack concrete pastoral application. Collections such as *God among Us,* among others, show this not to be true. Nevertheless, I am making a distinction between Schillebeeckx's and Park's general theological works.

545. Hilkert and Schreiter, *The Praxis of the Reign of God*, 122.

Foundation of God's Salvation for Humankind: God of Creation, the Paraclete of the Triune God, and a God of Jeong

Schillebeeckx writes, "Soteriology is the way to Christology—that is clear enough from the New Testament."[546] This is a location for further theological reflection when attempting to utilize *han* as an anthropological resource for Roman Catholic soteriology as articulated by *Gaudium et spes*. *Han*, as interpreted by Park, Joh, and *minjung* theologians such as Suh Nam-Dong, places the emphasis on resolving the wounds of *han*, preventing evil from spreading, and bringing about repentance by and atonement for sinners. This is a soteriological encounter that leads to the christological question: "who do you say that I am?" If one uses *han* as a tool in theological reflection, following the priority of salvation over Christology emphasized by Schillebeeckx, Park, and Joh (as well as Suh, Kim, and others), who is the God revealed in and through Jesus Christ? Who is the source, the foundation, upon which *han-pu-ri* ultimately is made available? How is this source experienced and named?

Chapter 2 provided one response that Schillebeeckx might give to these questions: the Creator God of pure positivity who does not want humankind to suffer. Or, as Kennedy described it, the Creator and creation that are the oxygen and lifeblood of Schillebeeckx's theology. Schillebeeckx points out that this Christian Creator God who is revealed definitively in the life, death, and resurrection of Jesus of Nazareth is One who is mindful of humanity and who does not want humankind to suffer. The one and the same God who is the God of creation is in solidarity with those who are poor, oppressed, and who suffer innocently. As he writes, "For the name of God is 'the one who shows solidarity with his people', and this people suffers."[547] I need not go further into this here.

Park's recent work provides a helpful interlocutor with Schillebeeckx's Creator God of pure positivity and who does not want humankind to suffer. As shown above, Park uses the term atonement as the focus of much of the soteriological meaning associated with *han*. In his definition, Park provides a fruitful supplement to the question about the foundation of God's salvation for humankind through Jesus Christ (and one aspect of God that Schillebeeckx was unable to address, for various reasons, in his massive *oeuvre*): the Trinitarian God.

---

546. Schillebeeckx, *Interim Report*, 12.
547 Schillebeeckx, *Christ*, 640.

Park uses the Triune God as the foundation upon which soteriology is constructed. For example, Park is concerned about the *han* that is too deeply saturated into creation to be perceived, let alone resolved, by humankind. Park suggests that the ultimate depths of *han* can only be addressed and resolved positively by God's own self, and in particular, the Paraclete. To quote Park at length:

> The Paraclete knows the depth of the wounds of the afflicted (*han*) because of his or her own experience of *han*. Some wounds within us are too deep to detect. Most of us are not fully aware of the wounds to our own soul. The Holy Spirit, the wounded healer, understands the magnitude of our *han*. The Paraclete searches our depths, knows our own unknowable and indescribable hurts of *han,* and heals them in us as we open ourselves to the Paraclete. The Paraclete alone is the Spirit that knows the deep inner groaning of suffering. 'Likewise the Spirit helps us in our weakness; for we do not know how to pray as we ought, but that very Spirit intercedes with sighs too deep for words' (Rom 8:26). The 'sighs too deep for words' are *han*. Such wounds within us are too deep to heal. The Paraclete who experienced the crucifixion and the resurrection with Jesus groans with us and heals us in compassion
>
> The Paraclete as the extension of Jesus' resurrection has concretized God's healing on earth. The Paraclete walks with victims and uplifts them every day. God's reign through the Paraclete has come in the midst of this world's troubles and tragedies. The Paraclete is the Spirit that is at work in the community.[548]

Moreover, one aspect of Park's understanding of God that may challenge Schillebeeckx is his claim that God has *han*. Again, Park is careful to point out that he is against the heresy of patripassionism. At the same time, Park argues that God indeed has *han* because God's love is too passionate, creative, and strong to keep God aloof from the barbarous excess of human misery. Park argues that *han* points to God's wounded heart that cries out with the victims. This is the God Park finds revealed in the Gospels and Hebrew Scriptures, as well as the works of Anselm of Canterbury, Martin Luther, Kazoh Kitamori, and Jürgen Moltmann.[549]

---

548. Park, *Triune Atonement*, 68.

549. Park, *The Wounded Heart of God*, 111–20. It is important to point out that Joh might question Park's engagement with Moltmann. This is because she dedicates an

Unlike the *han* manifest in human beings, such as *won-han*, *jeong-han*, and *hu-han*, which Jae Hoon Lee pointed out threaten the very existence of the human person, communities, and social structures through destructive and even nihilistic action, for Park *han* is not a threat to God's existence. God remains the Creator whose existence cannot be exterminated. Nevertheless, Park claims that God is inflicted with *han* by human beings. Park argues that God needs our salvation in the sense of human participation in resolving God's *han*. This is because, in the words of Schillebeeckx, God has chosen to be a God of and for men and women and not aloof from them. Human beings are of the utmost importance to God and as such human beings have a responsibility to participate in unraveling both God's *han* and the *han* festering within all of creation.

Joh's developing work thus far has not explored this foundation in depth. Nevertheless, she hints at an understanding of the Christian God as one of love/Eros/*jeong*. As she writes, "The love/Eros/*jeong* of God is incarnated within our lives. The cross signifies the semiotic oneness of the Godself with the neighbors, the created beings."[550] She continues, *jeong* is a "stickiness" that "pervades the immanent reality of everyday relationships" and "is part of the divine reality." It is a "primal eros as the energy of God present in all things, all relationships, to sustain and cherish all that comes into contact. The primal eros that is present in all things, in all that comes into contact, is the presence of *jeong*."[551] In addition, for Joh *jeong's* power "lies in its ability to wedge itself into the smallest gaps between oppressed and oppressor" and *jeong* is

> the divine presence that nudges us not only to perceive but also to accept the often negativized and shadowed parts of ourselves and thus ultimately to awaken to and practice the way of living

---

entire chapter in her monograph to a critique of Moltmann's theology of the cross and a crucified God. See *Heart of the Cross*, 71–90.

550. Joh, *Heart of the Cross*, 113. It is important to point out that the way in which Joh employs the term semiotic is quite different from the semiotic approach to culture that I have discussed. In short, Joh adopts a feminist, psychoanalytical approach to distinguish between two realms in which meaning, naming, identity, and the interpretation of symbols and doctrine occur: the symbolic and the semiotic. She argues that the symbolic is the realm of patriarchal interpretations in which any and all traces of hybridity or maternality are marginalized. She interprets the semiotic as the maternal, womb-like, interstitial space in which intersubjectivity and anti-patriarchal interpretations occur. In short, the maternal semiotic disrupts, resists, and transforms the patriarchal symbolic. See, for example, 109–11.

551. Joh, *Heart of the Cross*, 121.

in the fullness of *jeong*. The presence of *jeong* within and around relationality reveals us to ourselves.[552]

In short, for Joh the God revealed in Jesus Christ, both in ministry and execution, is the God of *Jeong*.

From this discussion among the foundation, focus on the cross, and anthropology of woundedness, yet another fundamental question emerges for an outer hearer to address: can *han* be infused with a robust theology of grace, creation, and sacramentality, all of which are foundational in Roman Catholic soteriology and anthropology, while remaining intelligible to the inner speakers? In other words, who is the God of Jesus Christ that is connected to *han* as an outer-hearer attempts to receive, interpret, and synthesize it from a Korean-Protestant semiotic domain to a Western, Roman Catholic semiotic domain? Are the God of Creation, the *han*-ful Paraclete of the Triune God, and the God of *Jeong*, fully incommensurate when receiving a theology of *han*? This question, too, will be explored in Section Three.

Encounter/Envisioning of God's Salvation for Humankind

As the above definitions showed, Schillebeeckx's understanding of *extra mundum nulla salus* that occurs fragmentarily within human history shows similarities with Park's and Joh's definitions. The language that each theologian employs is used with precision and in different ways, yet each definition points towards healing, liberation, forgiveness, and re-creation in this world. All three definitions show a soteriology that highlights the plight of the victims while not forgetting the sins of the victimizers.

Regarding the encounter and envisioning of God's salvation for humankind, there is dissonance when brought into dialogue with the three elements of Park's and Joh's theologies. Park offers a fourfold process for envisioning the resolution of *han*, as well as a claim that *han* is the site where the divine and human meet; the site of Christian religious experience. Joh offers the interstitial space of the cross as the location in which human and divine meet. Moreover, for Joh *jeong* is the ongoing experience in everyday life in which human beings encounter the Living God. *Jeong* is connected to the divine energy and God's ongoing actions for salvation, atonement, and *han-pu-ri* in this world.

552. Ibid., 122.

Nevertheless, there is dissonance between Park's and Joh's understandings and the mystical-political experience of *mediated immediacy* discussed by Schillebeeckx. This is the fundamentally religious experience of the finite and the infinite interrelating in what Schillebeeckx calls *mysticism* (and the *theologal life*) or what has become known in the contemporary U.S. context as *spirituality*.[553] As Schillebeeckx points out regarding salvation:

> Thus, real liberation, redemption, and salvation always diverge into *mysticism*, because for religious people, the ultimate source and foundation for the healing and salvation of mankind, living and dead, is to be found in God. His honor is man's salvation. We cannot set up any 'reasonable' expectation apart from him, since the only credentials that history can give us are in the event of Jesus the Christ.[554]

Schillebeeckx's soteriology that connects the location of human experience and the foundation of the Creator God of pure positivity takes form in what he calls the *mystical-political* dimension of Christianity. That is, the intrinsic connection between contemplation and action, prayer and protest, that is mutually informing, mutually critical, and always developing. This connection between fragments of salvation and the human experiences of God through *mediated immediacy* and *cognitive union with God* is an aspect of the human experience of salvation that, from my perspective, seems underdeveloped in the theologies of Park and Joh. As Schillebeeckx writes:

> The self-revelation of God does not manifest itself *from* our experiences but *in* them, as an inner pointer to what this experience and the interpretative language of faith have called into life. In the experience of a response of faith, being addressed by God becomes infinitely transparent, albeit in terms of our humanity.[555]

It is important to elaborate briefly upon how Schillebeeckx understands the term *mysticism*. In short, an authentic mysticism is not a

---

553 For various definitions of "spirituality" that are being debated in the academic literature, see the first five chapters in Dreyer and Burrows, *Minding the Spirit*, 1–78. For more contextual understandings, see Gutiérrez's *We Drink from Our Own Wells*; and Sobrino's *Spirituality of Liberation*.

554. Schillebeeckx, *Interim Report*, 60; italics added.

555. Ibid., 12.

detachment from life and the world. Instead, the human is also a political subject, which he thinks is the natural outgrowth of a particularly Christian spirituality.[556] Schillebeeckx describes this as "the art of making possible what is necessary for human salvation."[557] In other words, action on behalf of full human flourishing in the political realm is the natural extension and demand of the spiritual life.[558] The political Christian draws sustenance from her spirituality and is lead to exercise a prophetic or critical activity by calling powers and governments to responsibility for the suffering that they enable. This means that Christians must analyze and critique political plans with reference to the well-being of the downtrodden and to expose the faulty anthropologies of political parties. To wit, Schillebeeckx argues "belief in God radicalizes efforts for a better world" and that "Christian love is only possible when faith flows into social analysis and action."[559] He borrows the term *political holiness* from Jon Sobrino to describe this mystical-political praxis.

Schillebeeckx thinks that it is necessary that mysticism and politics interrelate, critique, and challenge one another in the ordinary lives of Christians. This is why he argues, "Without prayer or mysticism politics soon becomes cruel and barbaric; without political love, prayer or mysticism soon becomes sentimental or uncommitted interiority."[560] In Schillebeeckx's estimation, the political is the concrete action to oppose human suffering that is the natural extension of our mystical lives. It is rooted in a prayer life in which we encounter God's *mediated immediacy* and are emboldened to participate in God's work for justice.

Moreover, men and women are open to the new and surprising ways in which God's presence is found in the world and to the questions that are arising from human society. Schillebeeckx thinks that this practice involves an often surprising journey as one remains anchored to an unpredictable God in an enigmatic world. The foundation of this dual presence, the *mystical-political*, for Schillebeeckx is praxis. As Donald Goergen points out, "Indeed, one can say that spirituality for Schillebeeckx is praxis, and

---

556. Schillebeeckx, *Christ*, 815–17.
557. Ibid., 743.
558. Ibid., 815–17.
559. Ibid., 780–88.
560. Schillebeeckx, *On Christian Faith*, 75.

specifically orthopraxis, which Schillebeeckx defines as action in accord with the reign of God, or action on behalf of humankind."[561]

The language of a mystical-political dimension of Christianity is somewhat foreign to Park and Joh, let alone the ways in which *han* has been articulated. Joh focuses upon the experience of a fragmented Asian-American hybrid identity, the relationality of *jeong* and its soteriological implications, and the cross as a site of *han* and *jeong*. At this point in time, the articulation of a daily mystical experience of relationship with God is not part of her theological project. She undoubtedly is concerned with the political realm, the realm that Schillebeeckx calls "the art of making possible what is necessary for salvation." But investigating and articulating one's relationship with God is not at the forefront of her project. Schillebeeckx's concern for the mystical-political offers a possible growing edge for Joh's theology. Similarly, Park's theologies of *han*, his call for doctrinally articulating a soteriology for the sinned-against creature, his concern with resolving *han* creatively and not destructively, and his work on re-envisioning the cross as a site for Triune Atonement, also is not yet immediately concerned with articulating the mystical aspect of daily life.

Therefore, one more fundamental question emerges from this dialogue between encounter/envisioning and Park's and Joh's understandings of anthropology of woundedness, preference for narrative and praxis, and focus upon a crucifixion soteriology: can *han* carry both the political *and* the mystical dimensions of Christianity? In other words, chapter 4 clearly showed that that Park, Joh, and the broader tradition to which they are indebted, have embraced and articulated the political dimension of Christianity. But their articulation of a mystical aspect of Christianity, or a spirituality associated with *han*, is less clear and perhaps underdeveloped.

Section Three: Discussion of the Four Questions

Having envisioned a brief dialogue between Schillebeeckx, Park, and Joh, I now turn to the four questions raised by the dialogue. Respectively, these questions are centered upon: the cross, human experience, grace/creation, and mysticism:

561. Hilkert and Schreiter, *The Praxis of the Reign of God*, 122.

1. Must an outer-hearer give priority to the symbol and theology of the cross and the crucifixion when reflecting upon soteriology and theological anthropology through a thick description of *han*?

2. How can *han* be received and interpreted as an articulation of human experience without distorting its meaning and deflating it from a thick description of the human experience of woundedness to a mere "thin" synonym for suffering that is bereft of much of its meaning?

3. Can *han* be infused with a robust theology of grace, creation, and sacramentality, all of which are foundational in Roman Catholic soteriology and anthropology, while remaining intelligible to the inner speakers?

4. Can *han* carry or account for both the political *and* the mystical dimensions of Christianity?

These four questions are fundamental for enabling an outer hearer to engage, interpret, and appropriate the surplus of meaning carried by *han* into a differing semiotic domain: that of Roman Catholic soteriology as represented by *Gaudium et spes*. There are neither clear nor simple answers to these questions and addressing each with full adequacy would require many more chapters. For the purposes of this present work, it must suffice to briefly address each question and offer cautious responses.

My response to the first question is "yes." When an outer hearer receives and appropriates *han* as an anthropology for theological reflection, the symbol of the cross should remain at the center. At the same time, a relatively adequate theological reflection upon *han* cannot be limited to the cross. Park and Joh demonstrate this non-exclusive focus upon the cross in theological reflection. Each theologian has focused much of his and her work upon interpreting this primary symbol of the Christian tradition. Park and Joh seek to embrace the cross as the center of soteriological discourse but in a revised way. For example, each theologian interrogates traditional atonement theory in order to seek a more relatively adequate understanding of the role of the cross and crucifixion in God's salvation for humankind. At the same time, Park focuses on the cross as the site of liberation and healing from *han* for the victims and salvation from sinning for the violators. The Triune God, particularly through the work of the Paraclete, works out atonement for humankind and all of creation through, but not limited to, this primary Christian symbol. This is similar to Schillebeeckx's claim that although the cross is a necessary Christian symbol that must play a role in soteriology humankind is saved despite the cross and not because of the cross. Joh's re-interpretation of the cross as an interstitial space of *han* and *jeong*, sin and salvation, also focuses upon the cross in a theological reflection upon *han*. Joh thinks that the cross is of great importance even though (like Schillebeeckx) she argues that the cross cannot be interpreted apart from the life-praxis of Jesus of Nazareth.

In short, when *han* is reflected upon theologically, and interculturally, it must retain a focus upon the symbol of the cross. Its soteriology is not limited to the cross and includes the entire life-praxis of Jesus, as well as the Incarnation and Resurrection. But the wounds signified by *han* are illuminated primarily through the cross. The unjust execution of Jesus of Nazareth is a *contrast experience* that unveils and protests against all the barbarous excess of unwarranted suffering. Without an intrinsic connection between *han* and the cross, *han* would lose much of its meaning and value as a resource for supplementing the theological anthropology and soteriology of *Gaudium et spes*.

Regarding the second question, I respond with a cautious "yes." It is indeed possible to receive, interpret, and appropriate a human experience of *han* without distorting its meaning beyond recognition or rendering it little but a thin synonym for suffering and woundedness that is bereft of its rich surplus of meaning. The hermeneutical safeguard is a preference for praxis, narrative, poetry, and art when attempting to employ *han* as an intercultural resource for soteriological reflection. As theologians of *han* such as Suh, Park and Joh point out, as well as Schillebeeckx, human experience is best communicated through stories and other artistic creations that arise from a contextual human experience and speak soteriologically to that context. Within the Western intellectual and theological tradition, abstract conceptualization clearly has a role to play. But it must remain secondary to, and perhaps an elaboration upon, the narrative through which *han* is articulated and given flesh.

In short, when *han* is received to some degree of relative adequacy it provides a rich resource for articulating human experience in the twenty-first century. As Schillebeeckx pointed out, it is the new, the surprising, and the contrast experiences that give rise to new ways of thinking and new ways of articulating the salvation offered by God through Jesus the Christ. *Han* offers one particular cultural interpretation of human experience that may give rise to such new thinking. Again, *han* is not a "new" experience and it must not be relegated to the orientalist realm of theological tourism in which it becomes an interesting, exotic, anthropology that is little more than a multicultural accessory to what remains essentially Euro-centric and Western articulations of God's offer of salvation for humankind, through Jesus Christ. To employ it successfully, one must provide a thick description of a human experience of *han* and the Christian theological reflections upon it within its native context and correlate it to a thick description of human experience within a different context.

My response to the third question is more complex. Although a theological reflection that uses *han* as a resource must retain an important place for the cross, as addressed above, the surplus of theological meaning imbued into *han* must be reconfigured as it crosses the cultural boundary from a Korean and Korean-American Protestant context to a more Western, Roman Catholic semiotic domain. *Han* must be enriched and supplemented with a robust theology of creation, grace, and sacramentality in order to adequately function among the signs, codes, and messages within Roman Catholicism. A rigid focus upon the cross, even within a larger context, is insufficient. There must be a reconfiguring of its theology through a *sacramental* or *analogical* imagination.

Schillebeeckx's early work offers an insight into the importance of sacramentality and sacrament for Roman Catholicism. He describes the broad idea of sacramentality—the immanent yet invisible presence of God as grace saturated into all of creation—as an "intrinsic requirement of the Christian religion."[562] Furthermore, he writes that sacramentality bridges the gap between the glorified Christ and unglorified humanity "and makes possible a reciprocal human encounter of Christ and men, even after the ascension."[563] He describes the ritual sacraments as "the face of redemption turned visibly towards us, so that in them we truly encounter the living Christ. The heavenly saving activity, invisible to us, becomes visible in the sacraments."[564]

To elaborate briefly upon Schillebeeckx's basic understanding, it is helpful to focus upon two of the defining codes within a Roman Catholic semiotic-theological domain: a doctrine of creation and an analogical imagination. Regarding the former, much of the Catholic tradition[565] has

---

562. Schillebeeckx, *Christ: The Sacrament of the Encounter with God*, 44.

563. Ibid.

564. Ibid., 43–44.

565. Among a vast amount of literature attesting to the importance of creation in Roman Catholic theology, see the following: Augustine, *De Libero Arbitrio* and

a focus upon a theology of creation due to its connection to God's ever-present grace in the world around us. God's creation is inherently good and is saturated with God's presence.[566] Sin, evil, and suffering are indeed part of the reality in which human beings reside and in which they participate. Nevertheless, there is a primacy of grace and original goodness at the core of creation and this means that the God of Life, and not evil and the idols that bring death, will have the final word. In Augustine of Hippo's famous dictum, ". . . evil has no existence except as the privation of the good, down to that level which is altogether without being."[567] This means that evil is a kind of parasite that is reliant upon the goodness intrinsic in creation and that feeds upon it and perverts it. The grace infused into creation precedes all else. So, as *han* is interpreted into the Roman Catholic semiotic domain, it must account for this code and its signs while also retaining its deep connection to the cross and crucifixion.

Regarding the latter—an analogical imagination—this has been articulated most definitively by David Tracy. In short, an analogical imagination searches for the similarities within even greater dissimilarities and in doing so highlights God's presence in creation. Referencing Bonaventure and Francis of Assisi, Tracy writes, "The entire world, the ordinary in all its variety, is now theologically envisioned as sacrament—a sacrament emanating from Jesus Christ as the paradigmatic sacrament of God, the paradigmatic clue to humanity and nature alike."[568] This analogical imagination, however, does not rest on easy and facile similarities. The greater dissimilarities remain in the forefront and cause the analogical imagination to remain in tension between the very real similarity that can be encountered and experienced as presence and the very real dissimilarity

---

Confessions; Aquinas's *Summa Theologica*; Rahner's *Foundations of Christian Faith*; and Hayes, *The Gift of Being*. See also Greeley's *The Catholic Imagination*.

566. This omnipresence of God within creation Rahner links to grace, which he defines as God's always, already available self-communication and gift of self to humankind. See *Foundations of Christian Faith*.

567. Augustine, *Confessions* 3.7.12 (Chadwick, p. 43).

568. *The Analogical Imagination*, 413. One interpretation of the task at hand in receiving and interpreting *han* may include Tracy's framework of manifestation-proclamation-historical action as important and non-negotiable moments in theological discourse. In this schema, the creation-focus and analogical imagination of Roman Catholicism would be challenged and augmented by the proclamations and historical actions represented by Park and Joh, among others. Tracy argues that the core of Roman Catholicism takes form as a religion of manifestation; that is, a religion that gives greater emphasis to God's glorious presence within creation that can be encountered as an event.

that can be encountered and experienced as absence or negation. As Tracy remarks, this imagination "recognizes that each of us understands each other through analogies to our own experience or not at all."[569]

Tracy explains that the underlying foundation for an analogical imagination is an analogical[570] understanding of God that is based in an apophatic sensibility, the purpose of which is to safeguard the radical mystery of God.[571] That is, in Tracy's paraphrasing of the First Vatican Council, a language that is "'partial, incomplete, analogous but real understanding of the mysteries of the Catholic faith.'"[572] This apophatic, analogical language traditionally begins with an analogy from nature (otherwise known as *analogia entis*) then proceeds to make connections between the main mysteries of faith and finally relates this composite understanding towards the horizon of the eschaton.[573] For Tracy, this apophatic underpinning means that religious language should be understood as a *limit language*.[574] As a limit language, analogy is a tool that

569. Ibid., 451.

570. The principle of analogical language when speaking of God was defined most clearly by Thomas Aquinas. See, for example, *Summa Theolgica*, I, q. 13, a. 5. For a concise summary of Aquinas' theory of analogy, see Johnson, *She Who Is*, 113–20.

571. Tracy, *The Analogical Imagination*, 409.

572. Tracy, "The Analogical Imagination in Catholic Theology," 18.

573. Ibid. As is well documented, in the twentieth century there was a long debate between Protestants and Catholics as to the suitability of the *analogia entis* as adequate theological discourse. Karl Barth famously called this movement as being of the "Antichrist" because in his view it was supplanting God's revelation as the foundation for faith. In response, Catholic theologian Hans Urs von Balthasar corrected Barth and argued that the Catholic *analogia entis* was alive and functioning within Barth's *analogia fidei*. For more on this complicated argument, see Guarino's discussion of Barth and Balthasar on this topic in *Foundations of Systematic Theology*, 218–34; See also McFague, *Metaphorical Theology*, 3.

574. The term *limit language* is adopted by Tracy to refer to the religious dimension of human experience. He makes a distinction between scientific, moral, and everyday limit experiences and questions and explores each of these dimensions. Focusing upon the "everyday," however, Tracy writes: "[T]he concept fundamentally refers to those human situations wherein a human being ineluctably finds manifest a certain ultimate limit or horizon to his or her existence. The concept itself is mediated by 'showing' the implications of certain crucial positive and negative experiential limit-situations. More exactly, limit-situations refer to two basic kinds of existential situation: either those 'boundary' situations of guilt, anxiety, sickness, and the recognition of death as one's destiny, or those situations called 'ecstatic experiences'—intense joy, love, reassurance, creation. All genuine limit-situations refer to those experiences, both positive and negative, wherein we both experience our own human limits (limits-to) as well as recognize, however haltingly, some disclosure of a limit-of of experience." See *Blessed*

creates a system out of other images and usages. It provides the limits of a vision of the whole of reality into which is woven God's radical incomprehensibility.[575]

In light of the importance of creation, sacramentality, and the analogical imagination for Roman Catholic theology, there are three theological ideas discussed above that can assist with a reconfiguration of some of the meanings associated with *han*: Schillebeeckx's Creator God, Park's Paraclete of the Triune God, and Joh's God of *Jeong*. These three understandings of God show at least one important commonality: they focus upon the immanence of God and God's Spirit within all of creation. God as Creator, Paraclete, and being present in *Jeong* all indicate that the Christian God is not aloof from creation. God remains transcendent but God's immanence within creation becomes the focus. As Schillebeeckx described this in one of his earliest works:

> For God through his revelation personally intervenes on behalf of mankind, not merely as the Creator who guides history in creative transcendence, but as someone who himself takes part in the unfolding play of history and comes to take his place at our side. Because grace is a personal encounter with God, it "makes history," and precisely for this reason it is also "sacramental."[576]

The divine immanence that accompanies these three images of God can enable *han* to be imbued with a robust understanding of grace and sacramentality as it is received and interpreted into the Roman Catholic theological anthropology and soteriology of *Gaudium et spes*.[577]

Rage for Order, 105. See also *Analogical Imagination*, 160–61.

575. There remains, however, a strong critique within Tracy's continuing work against any comprehensive system arising from this vision. It would seem that theological language in Tracy's work is more for the purpose of creating fragments that call meta-narratives into question. In his more recent work he is more interested in the latent fragments within the tradition, such as the apocalyptic and the apophatic. See Tracy's "Form and Fragment," 98–114.

576. Schillebeeckx, *Christ: The Sacrament of the Encounter with God*, 5.

577. For the purposes of this present work, I cannot address the similarities of divine immanence and a subsequent relative commensurability/incommensurability among Schillebeeckx's Creator God, Park's Paraclete of the Triune God, and Joh's God of *Jeong*. This is an important topic for further study in understanding the ways in which *han* can enter and be lodged within the Roman Catholic semiotic-theological domain to some degree of relative adequacy. I hope to delve deeper into this and other topics in a further study of *han*.

Regarding the fourth question, the politics and activism already deeply associated with a theological reflection upon *han* must be complemented by an understanding of the mystical aspect of it; a Christian mystical-political praxis of *han-pu-ri* that includes what can be cautiously termed a mysticism of *han*. This points to the problems of articulating one's experience of God—that Schillebeeckx calls mediated immediacy and cognitive union—in a way appropriate to the meanings imbued in *han*. What exactly is a *han*-centered mysticism or theologal life? What kind of encounter with and experience of God does this entail?

Park offers a partial answer in his statement that *han* is where God and humankind meet. God and humans both carry *han*—to varying degrees—and thus *han* and *han-pu-ri* become privileged sites for encountering the God of Jesus Christ. Similarly, Joh observes that it is in *jeong* that we truly encounter the Living God. This is particularly true in the interstitial space created by the cross in which human and divine, *jeong* and *han*, meet and intermingle. Joh has yet to indicate what the mystical dimension of a praxis of *jeong* entails and how God is truly encountered in one's daily life. But *jeong* remains a site, or "energy," in which to encounter the God of Jesus Christ.

In further envisioning a 'mysticism' to balance and complement the political aspect of *han*, it is helpful to re-visit the story of Chun Tae-Il. Chun's story, as related by Suh Nam-Dong, shows both mysticism and politics. Chun's contrast experience of working in the Peace Market garment factories led to the sharpening of his political consciousness. His eventual response was to go on retreat in the mountains to a church. Once there, he prayed, reflected, and encountered God—what can be loosely referred to as mysticism. It is through this time of mystical encounter with God that Chun undergoes a true *metanoia* and decides to return to the garment factory and offer his very self as a sacrifice for the betterment of the oppressed and abused workers. Jae-Hoon Lee's incisive and persuasive critique of Chun as a man of *hu-han* notwithstanding, the story as interpreted by Suh and Andrew Park show a political *and* mystical dimension to the *han*-filled life of Chun. Chun embraces his own *han* and that of his coworkers through encountering God and attempting to discern the best course of action to resolve the *han* of the exploited workers.

A Resource: The Minjung Writings of Kim Chi-Ha[578]

The *minjung* writings of Kim Chi-Ha provide another example of a mystical encounter with God that can be part and parcel of a theological reflection upon *han*. Thus, it is helpful to elaborate upon Kim's work with more depth. As I mentioned in chapter 4, Kim acts as a "priest of *han*" who returns to and retrieves original deeds and memories of violence and suffering—which have created *han*— in order to bring them into the present. His purpose is to create room for the *han*-ridden people, living and dead, to experience justice, healing, and peace. In some of his writings after converting to Catholicism in 1971 he shows how an experience of God, or mysticism, accompanies a praxis of *han-pu-ri*. Today, Kim no longer considers himself a Roman Catholic or a Christian, per se,[579] but in some his writings of the 1970s he envisions a connection among an experience of *han*, an experience of the Christian God, and an experience of salvation.

When engaging Kim and his work more closely than in chapter 4, it is helpful to point out that he already considers himself as part of the *han*-filled *minjung* and employs this experience in his writings. He is willing to be further inflicted with *han* but he is not a man of nihilistic and self-destructive *hu-han*; he seeks neither destruction for himself nor for others. His constructive philosophy of *dan* (as discussed in chapter 4) precludes a devolution into *hu-han*. Rather, Kim is a man who is compelled to write provocative works against the violence of the Park regime regardless of the consequences. As he states:

---

578. I elaborate upon this topic in Considine, "Kim Chi Ha's *Han* Anthropology and its Challenge to Catholic Thought."

579. As scholar Won-Chung Kim points out, the vast majority of English translations and collections of Kim Chi-Ha's poetry were published before his release from prison in 1980. See *Heart's Agony: Selected Poems of Chi-Ha Kim*, 11–12. Regarding Kim's later development, I defer to literary scholar Chan J. Wu who points out that much of Kim's recent poetry shows more of a Buddhist and Shamanistic sensibility, particularly after the end of the Cold War. Wu argues that Kim's writings show a *poetics of full-emptiness*. As Kim's poetry develops after the change in the political situation in South Korea, Wu argues that Kim's writings take an interior turn. See ibid., 15–16; 29–33. For example, in the poem "My Home" Kim longs for communion with the cosmos rather than explicitly with the God of Jesus Christ. One additional illustration of this development is the poem "A New Church," in which Kim's vision of church becomes the ecological environment and the cosmos. In more recent decades, as Volker Küster points out, Kim explicitly has turned his back on Roman Catholic Christianity. This is because he now interprets it as a gateway to the cultural and economic neo-colonialism of Korea by the West. See Küster, *A Protestant Theology of Passion*, 148n46.

> I want to explain why I wrote *Five Bandits, Groundless Rumors, Chang Il-Tam, Maltuk,* and other works. So they could be used by someone? No. Because *I* wanted to write them. I had no choice. They were deep inside of me, stirring, swirling. I had to let them burst out. I wrote because I had to. That was the only reason.[580]

Through offering his body and mind in solidarity with the oppressed, even unto torture and death, Kim seeks to voice the cries of the tortured, the exploited, the dehumanized—the *han*-filled masses. Furthermore, he connects his embrace of the *han* of the *minjung* to his vocation as a poet. He writes,

> I am a poet. And the poet is the man who stands in the midst of the miserable lives of the poor, shares their agony and suffering, and expresses it in poetry. He should give hope to the poor by finding the cause of their unhappiness and trying to remove it and by dreaming a better future and presenting its fruits to them. Hence, we call the true poet the flower of the common people.[581]

Kim offers two helpful suggestions for how one might envision such a *han* mysticism: encountering God in the wounds of *han* and the preferential option for the *minjung* in authentically experiencing God.[582] Two works that illustrate Kim's contribution to envisioning a '*han* mysticism' in this way include "Torture Road—1974" and *The Gold-Crowned Jesus*.

In "Torture Road," Kim reflects upon his time in prison, being tortured, and being sentenced to death. Chong-Sun Kim and Shelly Killen characterize this work, as "A mixture of prose, poetry, and incantation, *Torture Road* testifies to the poet's alchemic wedding of Korean shamanism with Christian liberation theology."[583] Kim characterizes his

---

580. Kim Chi-Ha, "Declaration of Conscience," 34.

581. Kim quoted in "Preface," *Heart's Agony*, 10.

582. In truth, there is at least one other important contribution that Kim's work can make to envisioning a kind of *han* mysticism: what he calls the unity of God and revolution. This is Kim's synthesis of Roman Catholicism, Korean *Tonghak* religion, and Shamanism. This is an aspect of a *han* mysticism that holds great potential for addressing the problem of the *mystical-political* dimension of an interculturally constructed Roman Catholic soteriology for the sinned-against creature. For example, this unity implies that God is Incarnate among the people and working for justice, healing, liberation, and redemption. This presents a robustly immanent aspect to a *han* mysticism that resonates with the sacramental mysticism of Roman Catholicism. Unfortunately, I am unable to explore this aspect of Kim's theology, philosophy, and poetry here. My tentative suggestions in this footnote must suffice.

583. Kim Chi-Ha and Killen, preface to *The Gold-Crowned Jesus*, xxx.

incarceration and torture as an ongoing struggle with death. He is in the crucible of *han* and it is here that he encounters God. This occurs, however, through what Kim and Killen characterize as his 'dark night of the soul' and *via crucis*.[584] They observe, "Kim Chi Ha frequently uses the image of a fire that purifies, and like the Christian mystics he perceives the light within the darkness."[585] Furthermore, they write:

> Unlike mystics who have travelled the dark night of the soul in solitude, Kim Chi Ha's spiritual journey [in "Torture Road"] was made in the company of others who like himself chose truth rather than the lie that could save their life. The mystery of the spirit flashes in the poet's mind as a moment of religious, artistic, and political insight. All of the questions he had asked himself were answered in the brilliant 'flame of truthful life,' which burned inside the chained flesh. This spiritual ecstasy and wholeness that Kim Chi Ha experiences when overcoming death cannot be verbalized, and he states quite simply, 'I began to feel as if I were in touch with the mystery of the spirit.'[586]

Paradoxically, Kim encounters the God of Life through the contrast experiences of abandonment, pain, emptiness, and darkness of prison life. Here, in the depths of despair and pain, Kim somehow experiences God in the proclamation of the birth of his son. He is surprised to discover that new life was still possible through (or despite) this hellish place. Kim enters more deeply into the mystery of the torture road. For example, Kim writes:

> Mysterious torture road of candlelight, paradox of overcoming death by choosing death. This was our task: to comprehend this mysterious torture road. In the death room, where the question

---

584. For the authoritative understanding of *dark night of the soul*, see John of the Cross, *Ascent of Mount Carmel* and *The Dark Night*, in *John of the Cross: Selected Writings*. See also the work of Pseudo-Dionysius, and in particular his work *The Mystical Theology*. As the hymn that begins this treatise states, "Trinity . . . /Lead us up beyond unknowing and light,/ up to the farthest, highest peak/ of mystic scripture,/ where the mysteries of God's Word/ lie simple, absolute and unchangeable/ in the brilliant darkness of a hidden silence./ Amid the deepest shadow/ they pour overwhelming light/ on what is most manifest./ Amid the wholly unsensed and unseen/ they completely fill our sightless minds/ with treasure beyond all beauty. See *The Mystical Theology* 997a–997b, in *Pseudo-Dionysius: The Complete Works*, 135. For a liturgical example of *via crucis*, see Pope John Paul II, "Way of the Cross at the Coliseum, Meditations by His Holiness Pope John Paul II, Good Friday 2003."

585. Kim Chi-Ha and Killen, preface to *The Gold-Crowned Jesus*, xiv.

586. Ibid., xxii–xxiii.

of death clung to us, I learned of the birth of my son. Oh, God, for the first time I understood your will.[587]

The mysticism that Kim lives out is encountering God in the strange, hellish places within his daily predicament. He finds the God of Life by embracing death. He experiences the Spirit of God through this paradox and mystery. Through letting-go of hope, entering more deeply into the *han* of this empty space (perhaps similar to the *nada* of St. John of the Cross), he encounters the presence of God. He describes the divine presence through a mystical-political insight. Kim writes:

> By choosing death, we collectively gained eternity. With deep feeling, we gazed into the brilliant flame of truthful life, which began to burn inside our collectively-chained flesh. It was our historical moment. No, it was not something of this world. It was religious inspiration. But it was not only that. It was the height of artistic vision. No, it cannot be expressed in words. It was a glittering zenith of wholeness and of all human values and sublimities. *I began to feel as if I were in touch with the mystery of the spirit* . . . At that time, for some reason, the word—"the power of political imagination"—suddenly flashed back into my mind. I felt these words were deeply carved into the bottom of my heart like red-blue hot brands. Yes, "the power of political imagination": the wedding of politics and art in the highest sense of the words . . . The definitive answer to this enigma has been presented to me through the torture road. An extravagant, extravagant moment. At the time, I muttered to myself, "I thank you," and those almost unspeakable words, "I am honored."[588]

Kim's gratefulness towards his imprisonment and torture is difficult to understand. He clearly describes that this prison is a place of darkness, terror, and despair. Surprisingly, Kim envisions his time of imprisonment and torture being a road in which he finds purification and enlightenment of some sort. Kim's connection between his experience of *han* and his experience of God shows a similarity with Park's claim that often we encounter God in *han*. This is one possible aspect of a *han* mysticism.

The second of Kim's insights into a *han* mysticism is God's preferential self-revelation to the *minjung*. This is shown in Kim's play *The Gold-Crowned Jesus*. Here, Kim shows how the rich, the powerful, and the clergy have imprisoned the Risen Christ into a concrete statue

---

587. Kim Chi-Ha, "Torture Road—1974," 72.
588. Ibid., 76–77; iItalics added.

adorned with a golden crown of thorns. The statue was created to celebrate their own piousness as "good" Christians but is a manifestation of their misunderstanding of Jesus. They have an insufficient experience with and understanding of the Christian God. This misunderstanding has consequences for those pondering Christianity in the larger society. As the character of the Leper declares in Act III, "Once I was a believer. But it's the clean, rich, educated people who *believe* in Jesus."[589] The leper points out how these "believers" run from him, abuse him, destroy his home, and then claim it is God's will and that he should accept it and turn the other cheek. He goes on to exhort,

> "Go ahead, take all the goodies, all you rich, respectable, Jesus people and make him of concrete or a mass of gold, strong as a fortress if you want, so he'll last you a thousand years. Sell your Jesus and take your goodies forever and ever if you want, I don't care."[590]

Later, the leper notices the solid-gold crown of thorns on the statue's head, removes it, and ponders its worth. By selling it, he could get food and medical attention as well as take care of his friends who are prostitutes. This act awakens the statue of Jesus, who immediately says, "Why don't you take it with you? You may have it."[591] Jesus goes on to tell the leper that he has been imprisoned within the concrete statue for ages due to the insincere worship and idolatry of the wealthy and powerful. They have imprisoned him through their false religiosity and it is the leper lifting the gold crown from his head that has allowed him to speak again.

In short, a false mysticism of the powerful has imprisoned Jesus and has led to a distorted politics within society. As Jesus tells the leper:

> They locked me up for their own gain. They pray using my name in a way that prevents my reaching out to poor people like yourself. In my own name, they nailed me down to the cross again . . . They shun the poor and hungry, ignore the cries of the suffering, and dwell only on the acquisition of material gain, wealth, power, and glory.[592]

Kim shows that it is the Leper, an outcast even within the *minjung*, who authentically experiences God through Jesus Christ. Due to his

589. Kim Chi-Ha, "The Gold Crowned Jesus," 119; italics original.
590. Ibid., 120.
591. Ibid., 121.
592. Ibid., 123.

lowliness, he has an authentic encounter with God through Jesus rather than with an idol of him. The Leper's mystical experience of God through this statue of Jesus reveals the Living God's compassion and desire for justice. This mystical experience also shows the leper that Jesus must be freed from the false mysticism that imprisoned him. When the leper asks what can be done to free Jesus from this concrete statue, Jesus tells him:

> My power alone is not enough. People like you must help to liberate me . . . Only those, though very poor and suffering like yourself, who are generous in spirit and seek to help the poor and the wretched can give me life again. You have helped give me life again. You removed the gold crown from my head and so freed my lips to speak. People like you will be my liberators.[593]

Then, a priest, police officer, and wealthy businessman return to the scene, snatch the golden crown of thorns from the leper, and place it back on the head of the statue of Jesus. Jesus becomes inert and again is imprisoned. In Act IV, these three men explain to the leper how they are good Christians and how the leper is not. The play ends with the leper lamenting in front of the inert statue of Jesus. For the time being, the false mysticism of the powerful has triumphed over the true mysticism of the *minjung*. Nevertheless, Kim suggests God's preferential option for self-revelation among the *minjung* and the *minjung's* more adequate attunement to the spirit, life, and desires of the Christian God. The true mysticism of the Leper is what holds the possibility of emancipatory politics (what Schillebeeckx calls "the art of making possible what is necessary for salvation") and of human healing. This illustrates Kim's claim that in Catholicism he intuited a religion that could lead to universal salvation for both oppressed and oppressor.[594]

The theological sketches of Park and Joh regarding mysticism, as well as the illustrations of Chun Tae-Il and two of the works of Kim Chi-Ha, provide tentative suggestions for what may be termed a *han* mysticism. I have elaborated upon this topic at some length due to the complexity of this question. The above discussion of the four questions

---

593. Ibid., 123–24.

594. Kim, "Declaration of Conscience," 19. As quoted from the same page of Kim's "Declaration" in chapter 4: "I became a Catholic because Catholicism conveys a universal message. Not only the spiritual and material burdens could be lifted from people but also oppression itself could be ended by the salvation of *both* the oppressor and the oppressed. Catholicism is capable of assimilating and synthesizing these contradictory and conflicting ideologies, theories, and value standards into a universal truth."

is meant to lay a foundation for a relatively adequate reception, interpretation, and appropriation of *han* from its original semiotic domain to that of Roman Catholicism as illustrated by *Gaudium et spes*. These points of discussion do not exhaust the possibilities for addressing *han*, but they do offer fundamentals for employing *han* as a theological resource to engage, challenge, and supplement the theological anthropology and soteriology of *Gaudium et spes* as discussed in chapter 1. This discussion is meant to enable the appropriation of the excess of meaning carried by *han* to envision a Roman Catholic soteriology for the sinned-against creature that supplements its relatively inadequate theological anthropology and soteriology.

Summary and Conclusion

In this chapter, I have attempted to bring Schillebeeckx, Park, and Joh into conversation in a third space. My purpose was to envision the possibilities and limitations of employing *han* as a resource and reference point for developing a more relatively adequate theological anthropology and soteriology for the sinned-against creature in the Roman Catholic semiotic-theological domain as articulated by *Gaudium et spes*.

From the conversation above, I have arrived at four guidelines by which to embrace and reinterpret Korean and Korean-American understandings of *han* with reference to the signs, codes, and messages of Roman Catholic theology:

1. A necessity for the cross to be the primary (but not the only) Christian symbol for understanding and articulating *han*.

2. A possibility of interpreting *han* as a resource for re-articulating human experiences of God's salvation for humankind, through Jesus Christ, despite a barbarous excess of human degradation and within a twenty-first-century globalizing context of ongoing and more profound intercultural encounters as well as greater cultural hybridity. This may be attempted through a mutually-critical correlation between a thick description of Korean and Korean-American understandings of *han* and a thick description of an analogous human experience within a different culture and context.[595]

---

595. Two such possibilities are the understandings of *affliction* and the *blues*. Regarding affliction, it is a term and a concept of that is attributed to Simone Weil. Among her many writings, see *Waiting for God*. Regarding the blues, Andrew Sung

3. A necessity for imbuing *han* with a robust understanding of sacramentality and creation, as well as the perspective of an analogical imagination, in order to function more adequately among the signs, codes, and messages of Roman Catholicism. With respect to guideline number one, the cross can remain the center and the primary symbol for understanding some of the meanings associated with *han*. At the same time, this primary symbol can be augmented and supplemented through its inclusion within a constellation of signifiers based upon creation, sacramentality, and an analogical imagination.

4. A possibility for articulating a *han* mysticism to complement and critique the concrete political and social action for justice, healing, and *han-pu-ri* in this world.

Chapter 5 concludes my argument. I have shown that these four guidelines can constitute a foundation for a subsequent articulation and vision of a Roman Catholic soteriology for the sinned-against creature. They provide a skeleton to be fleshed out by the subsequent work of articulating the content of this kind of an intercultural soteriology and how it supplements the relatively inadequate soteriology illustrated by *Gaudium et spes*. Again, this study has been preliminary and cautious in nature. I have conducted my study through five chapters and there are many more avenues that are necessary to pursue for further investigation and development of this topic, however, I am unable to adequately address these areas within the narrow scope of this study.[596]

Instead, I must reiterate that the purpose of this study is to *point towards* a Roman Catholic soteriology for the sinned-against creature.

Park offers this as a possible intercultural correlate to *han*. He has the work of James Cone in mind. See Park, *Triune Atonement*. See also Cone, *The Spirituals and the Blues*. Nevertheless, *han* may be better approached as a cultural anthropology (and perhaps even cosmology) whose surplus of meaning cannot be fully unpacked as it crosses a cultural boundary.

596. Much of this work includes integrating a theology and anthropology of *han* within the theological-semiotic domain of *Gaudium et spes*. In other words, what is the content of a relatively adequate Roman Catholic soteriology for the sinned-against creature that uses an anthropology of *han* as a fundamental theological source? How is it articulated in order to remain the Good News of God's offer of salvation for humankind through Jesus the Christ? What signs, codes, and messages—not to mention religious rituals, symbols, and practices—enable this soteriology to become authentic and effective Christian praxis? These are but a few of the questions in need of engagement and further study.

This study has been an exercise in beginning to envision an intercultural soteriology that uses *han* as a fundamental theological source. My intention has been to lay a foundation upon which it is possible, subsequently, to more adequately envision and articulate an intercultural soteriology. Through investigating and articulating a thick description of *han* and bringing it into critical and constructive intercultural dialogue with the soteriology of Edward Schillebeeckx, the relatively inadequate theological anthropology and soteriology of *Gaudium et spes* can be supplemented and re-articulated to a greater degree of relative adequacy.

Han compels Roman Catholic soteriology to focus not only upon the healing needed between sinning creature and Sinned-Against Creator, but also between the sinning and sinned-against creatures. By referring to and remaining in conversation with the four guidelines above, the theological anthropology and soteriology of *Gaudium et spes* indeed may be supplemented to account for the wounds inflicted upon the sinned-against creature in the presence of the Living God of Jesus Christ. To paraphrase Schillebeeckx, this is living in the presence of a God of pure positivity who does not want humankind to suffer and who is new each moment. That is, a God of Life who guarantees that good, and not evil, will have the final word.

Bibliography

Abraham, Susan. "What Does Mumbai Have to Do with Rome? Postcolonial Perspectives on Globalization and Theology." *Theological Studies* 69 (2008) 376–93.
Aeterni Patris (1879). Pope Leo XIII. The Holy See. http://www.vatican.va/holy_father/leo_xiii/encyclicals/documents/hf_l-xiii_enc_04081879_aeterni-patris_en.html.
Ahn, Byung-Mu. *Jesus of Galilee*. Hong Kong: Christian Conference of Asia, 2004.
Alberigo, Giuseppe. *A Brief History of Vatican II*. Translated by Matthew Sherry. Maryknoll, NY: Orbis, 2006.
Alberigo, Giuseppe, and Joseph Komanchak. *The History of Vatican II*. 5 vols. Maryknoll, NY: Orbis, 1996–2006.
Anderson, Victor. *Beyond Ontological Blackness: An Essay in African-American Religious and Cultural Criticism*. New York: Continuum, 1995.
Anselm of Canterbury. *Anselm of Canterbury: The Major Works*. Edited by Brian Davies and G. R. Evans. Oxford: Oxford University Press, 2008.
Aquinas, Thomas. *The Summa Theologica*. In *Introduction to Thomas Aquinas*. Edited by Anton C. Pegis. Modern Library College Editions. New York: Random House, 1948.
Arbuckle, Gerald A. *Culture, Inculturation, and Theologians: A Post-Modern Critique*. Collegeville, MN: Liturgical, 2010.
Asante, Molef, and William Gudykunst. *Handbook of International and Intercultural Communication*. London: Sage, 1989.
Augustine of Hippo. *Confessions*. Translated by Henry Chadwick. Oxford World's Classics. Oxford: Oxford University Press, 1991.
———. *De Libero Arbitrio*. In *Augustine: Earlier Writings*, edited by J. H. S. Burleigh, 102–217. Library of Christian Classics: Ichthus Edition. Philadelphia: Westminster, 1953.
Balthasar, Hans Urs von. *The Glory of the Lord: A Theological Aesthetics*. Vol. 1, *Seeing the Form*. Edited by John Riches and Joseph Fessio. 2nd ed. San Francisco: Ignatius, 2009.
Barth, Karl. "The Humanity of God." In *Karl Barth: Theologian of Freedom*, edited by Clifford Green, 46–66. Minneapolis: Fortress, 1991.
Baum, Gregory. *The Twentieth Century: A Theological Overview*. Maryknoll, NY: Orbis, 1999.
Bevans, Stephen B. *Models of Contextual Theology*. Rev. and exp. ed. Maryknoll, NY: Orbis, 2002.
Bhabha, Homi. *The Location of Culture*. London: Routledge, 1994.
Bibliography: 1936–1996 of Edward Schillebeeckx, O.P. Compiled by Ted Schoof and Jan van de Westelaken. Baarn: Nelissen, 1997.

Boeve, Lieven, et al. *Edward Schillebeeckx and Contemporary Theology*. New York: T. & T. Clark, 2010.

Borgman, Erik. *Edward Schillebeeckx: A Theologian in His History*. Vol. 1, *A Catholic Theology of Culture (1914–1965)*. Translated by John Bowden. New York: Continuum, 2003.

Brock, Rita Nakashima, et al., eds. *Off the Menu: Asian and Asian North American Women's Religion and Theology*. Louisville: Westminster John Knox, 2007.

Carter, J. Kameron. *Race: A Theological Account*. Oxford: Oxford University Press, 2008.

Cartledge, Mark, and David Cheetham. *Intercultural Theology: Approaches and Themes*. London: SCM, 2011.

Chen, Guo-Ming, and William J. Starosta. "Intercultural Communication Competence: A Synthesis." In *The Global Intercultural Communication Reader*, edited by Molefi Kete Asante et al., 215–38. New York: Routledge, 2008.

Choi, Hoon. "Brothers in Arms and Brothers in Christ? The Military and the Catholic Church as Sources for Modern Korean Masculinity." *Journal of the Society of Christian Ethics* 32 (2012) 75–92.

Chung, Hyun Kyung. "*Han-Pu-Ri*: Doing Theology from Korean Women's Perspective." *Ecumenical Review* (1988) 27–36.

———. "*Han-Pu-Ri*: Doing Theology from Korean Women's Perspective." In *Frontiers in Asian Christian Theology*, edited by R. S. Sugirtharaja, 52–62. Maryknoll, NY: Orbis, 1994.

———. *Struggle to Be the Sun Again: Introducing Asian Women's Theology*. Maryknoll, NY: Orbis, 1991.

Chung, Paul S. *Constructing Irregular Theology: Bamboo and Minjung in East Asian Perspective*. Leiden: Brill, 2009.

———. *Hermeneutical Theology and the Imperative of Public Ethics: Confessing Christ in Post-Colonial World Christianity*. Missional Church, Public Theology, World Christianity. Eugene, OR: Pickwick, 2013.

———. *Postcolonial Imagination: Archaeological Hermeneutics and Comparative Religious Theology*. Hong Kong: Chinese University Press, forthcoming.

Chung, Paul S., et al., eds. *Asian Contextual Theology for the Third Millennium: Theology of Minjung in Fourth Eye Formation*. Princeton Theological Monograph 70. Eugene, OR: Pickwick, 2007.

The Church in the Present-Day Transformation of Latin America in the Light of the Council: Second General Conference of Latin American Bishops, Bogotá, 24 August, Medellin, 26 August–6 September, Colombia, 1968. 2 vols. Edited by Louis Michael Colonnese. Bogota: General Secretariat of CELAM, 1970.

Colberg, Kristin. "The Hermeneutics of Vatican II: Reception, Authority, and Debate over the Council's Interpretation." *Horizons* 8 (2011) 230–52.

Compendium of the Social Doctrine of the Church. Pontifical Council for Justice and Peace. Libreria Editrice Vaticana, 2004.

Cone, James H. *Black Theology and Black Power*. Maryknoll, NY: Orbis, 1997.

———. *God of the Oppressed*. Rev. ed. Maryknoll, NY: Orbis, 1997.

———. *The Spirituals and the Blues: An Interpretation*. Maryknoll, NY: Orbis, 1992.

Congar, Yves. *My Journal of the Council*. Collegeville, MN: Liturgical, 2012.

Considine, Kevin P. "*Han* and Salvation for the 'Sinned Against.'" *New Theology Review* 26 (2013) 87–89.

———. "Kim Chi-Ha's *Han* Anthropology and Its Challenge to Catholic Thought." *Horizons* 41 (2014) 49–73.

"The Constitution on the Sacred Liturgy, *Sacrosanctum concilium*." The Holy See. http://www.vatican.va/archive/hist_councils/ii_vatican_council/documents/vat-ii_const_19631204_sacrosanctum-concilium_en.html.

Cooper, Jennifer. *Humanity in the Mystery of God: The Theological Anthropology of Edward Schillebeeckx.* T. & T. Clark Studies in Systematic Theology. New York: T. & T. Clark, 2009.

Copeland, M. Shawn. *Enfleshing Freedom: Body, Race, and Being.* Minneapolis: Fortress, 2009.

Cruz, Gemma Talmud. "Between Identity and Security: Theological Implications of Migration in the Context of Globalization." *Theological Studies* 69 (2008) 357–75.

Day, Dorothy. *Dorothy Day, Selected Writings: By Little and By Little.* Edited by Robert Ellsberg. Maryknoll, NY: Orbis, 2005

"Declaration on the Relationship of the Church to Non-Christian Religions, *Nostra Aetate*." The Holy See. http://www.vatican.va/archive/hist_councils/ii_vatican_council/documents/vat-ii_decl_19651028_nostra-aetate_en.html.

"Declaration on Religious Freedom, *Dignitatis humanae*." The Holy See. http://www.vatican.va/archive/hist_councils/ii_vatican_council/documents/vat-ii_decl_19651207_dignitatis-humanae_en.html.

"Decree on Ecumenism, *Unitatis redintegratio*." The Holy See. http://www.vatican.va/archive/hist_councils/ii_vatican_council/documents/vat-ii_decree_19641121_unitatis-redintegratio_en.html.

Deuchler, Martina. *The Confucian Transformation of Korea: A Study of Society and Ideology.* Cambridge, MA: Harvard University Press, 1992.

Diaz, Miguel. *On Being Human: U.S. Hispanic and Rahnerian Perspectives.* Maryknoll, NY: Orbis, 2001.

"The Dogmatic Constitution on the Church, *Lumen Gentium*." The Holy See. http://www.vatican.va/archive/hist_councils/ii_vatican_council/documents/vat-ii_const_19641121_lumen-gentium_en.html.

"The Dogmatic Constitution on Divine Revelation, *Dei verbum*." The Holy See. http://www.vatican.va/archive/hist_councils/ii_vatican_council/documents/vat-ii_const_19651118_dei-verbum_en.html.

Dolphin, Kathleen J. "Spirituality and Practical Theology: Edward Schillebeeckx as Resource for Faith Communities." PhD diss., University of Chicago, 1998.

Dreyer, Elizabeth, and Mark Burrows. *Minding the Spirit: The Study of Christian Spirituality.* Baltimore: Johns Hopkins University Press, 2004.

Elizondo, Virgilio. "Emergence of a World Church and the Irruption of the Poor." In *The Twentieth Century: A Theological Overview,* edited by Gregory Baum, 104–17. Maryknoll, NY: Orbis, 1999.

———. *The Future Is Mestizo: Life Where Cultures Meet.* Rev. ed. Boulder: University of Colorado Press, 2000.

———.*The Galilean Journey: The Mexican-American Promise.* Rev. and exp. ed. Maryknoll, NY: Orbis, 2000.

Espin, Orlando. *Grace and Humanness: Theological Reflections because of Culture.* Maryknoll, NY: Orbis, 2007.

Faggioli, Massimo. *Vatican II: The Battle for Meaning.* Mahwah, NJ: Paulist, 2012.

Fung, Raymond. "Compassion for the Sinned Against." *Theology Today* 37 (1980) 162–69.

Gadamar, Hans-Georg. *Truth and Method*. Translated and revised by Joel Weinsheimer and Donald Marshall. 2nd rev. ed. New York: Continuum, 2004.

Gaillardetz, Richard, and Catherine E. Clifford. *Keys to the Council: Unlocking the Teaching of Vatican II*. Collegeville, MN: Liturgical, 2012.

Garcia-Rivera, Alejandro. *The Garden of God: A Theological Cosmology*. Theology and the Sciences. Minneapolis: Fortress, 2009.

———. *St. Martin de Porres: The "Little Stories" and the Semiotics of Culture*. Maryknoll, NY: Orbis 1995.

Geertz, Clifford. *The Interpretation of Cultures*. New York: Basic, 1973.

The Great Queen Seondeok (*Seondeok Yeowang*). Directed by Geun-hong Kim and Hong Kyun Park, 2009. Seoul, South Korea: MBC-TV Korea. 2010. DVD.

Greeley, Andrew. *The Catholic Imagination*. Berkeley: University of California Press, 2000.

Gremillion, Joseph. "Pastoral Constitution on the Church in the Modern World, *Gaudium et spes*, 7 December, 1965." In *Vatican II and Its Documents: An American Reappraisal*, edited by Timothy W. O'Connell, 216–36. Wilmington, DE: Glazier, 1986.

Guarino, Thomas. *Foundations of Systematic Theology*. New York: T. & T. Clark, 2005.

Guisso, R. L. W., and Chai-Shin Yu. *Shamanism: The Spirit World of Korea*. Studies in Korean Religions and Culture 1. Fremont, CA: Asian Humanities, 2003.

Gutiérrez, Gustavo. *The God of Life*. Translated by Matthew J. O'Connell. Maryknoll, NY: Orbis, 1991.

———. *A Theology of Liberation*. 15th anniv. ed. Rev ed. with new introduction. Translated by Sister Caridad Inda and John Eagleson. Maryknoll, NY: Orbis, 1988.

———. *We Drink from Our Own Wells: The Spiritual Journey of a People*. Translated by Matthew J. O'Connell. Maryknoll, NY: Orbis, 1984.

Ham, Sok-Hon. *The Queen of Suffering: A Spiritual History of Korea*. London: Friends World Committee for Consultation, 1985.

Hayes, Zachary. *The Gift of Being: A Theology of Creation*. New Theology Studies 10. Collegeville, MN: Liturgical, 2001.

Headland, Thomas N., et al., eds. *Emics and Etics: The Insider/Outsider Debate*. London: Sage, 1990.

Hicks, George. *The Comfort Women: Japan's Brutal Regime of Enforced Prostitution during the Second World War*. New York: Norton, 1997.

Higgins, George. "The Church in the Modern World." In *The Church in the World*, edited by Charles P. O'Donnell, 8–25. Milwaukee: Bruce, 1967.

Hilkert, Mary Catherine. "Edward Schillebeeckx: Encountering God in a Secular and Suffering World." *Theology Today* 62 (2005) 376–87.

———. "'Grace-Optimism': The Spirituality at the Heart of Schillebeeckx's Theology." *Spirituality Today* 44 (1991) 220–39.

Hilkert, Mary Catherine, and Robert J. Schreiter. *The Praxis of the Reign of God: An Introduction to the Theology of Edward Schillebeeckx*. New York: Fordham University Press, 2002.

Hopkins, Dwight. *Being Human: Religion, Race, and Culture*. Minneapolis: Fortress, 2005.

Hopkins, Dwight, et al., eds. *Religions/Globalizations: Theories and Cases*. Durham, NC: Duke University Press, 2001.

Hwang, Kyung-Moon. *A History of Korea: An Episodic Narrative*. New York: Palgrave Macmillan, 2010.

Jeanrond, Werner G., and Aasulv Lande. *The Concept of God in Global Dialogue*. Maryknoll, NY: Orbis, 2005.

Jennings, Willie James. *The Christian Imagination: Theology and the Origins of Race*. New Haven: Yale University Press, 2010.

Joh, Wonhee Anne. "Grief and Grievability: A Postcolonial Spectrality of the Cross." *Concilium* 2 (2013) 41–50.

———. *Heart of the Cross: A Postcolonial Christology*. Louisville: Westminster John Knox, 2006.

———. *In Proximity to the Other: Materiality, Affect, and Postcolonial Planetarity*. Louisville: Westminster John Knox, forthcoming.

———. "Loves' Multiplicity: *Jeong* and Spivak's Notes toward Planetary Love." In *Planetary Loves: Gayatri Spivak, Postcoloniality, and Theology*, edited by Stephen Moore and Mayra Rivera, 169–90. New York: Fordham University Press, 2010.

———. *Terror, Trauma and Hope: A Postcolonial Spectrality of the Cross*. Louisville: Westminster John Knox, in progress.

———. "The Transgressive Power of *Jeong*: A Postcolonial Hybridization of Christology." In *Postcolonial Theologies: Divinity and Empire*, edited by Catherine Keller et al., 149–63. St. Louis: Chalice, 2004.

———. "Violence and Asian American Experience: From Abjection to *Jeong*." In *Off the Menu: Asian and Asian North American Women's Theology and Religion*, edited by Kwok Pui-lan et al., 145–62. Louisville: Westminster John Knox, 2007.

John of the Cross. *John of the Cross: Selected Writings*. Edited by Kieran Kavanaugh. Classics of Western Spirituality. New York: Paulist, 1987.

John Paul II. "Only Christ Can Fulfill Man's Hopes." *Communio* 23 (1996) 122–28.

———. "Way of the Cross at the Coliseum, Meditations by His Holiness Pope John Paul II, Good Friday 2003." The Holy See. http://www.vatican.va/news_services/liturgy/2003/documents/ns_lit_doc_20030418_viacrucis_en.html.

Johnson, Elizabeth. *She Who Is: The Mystery of God in Feminist Theological Discourse*. 10th anniv. ed. New York: Herder & Herder, 2002.

Kaspar, Walter. "The Theological Anthropology of *Gaudium et spes*." *Communio* 23 (1996) 129–40.

Keller, Catherine, et al., eds. *Postcolonial Theologies: Divinity and Empire*. St. Louis: Chalice, 2004.

Keller, Norah Okja. *Comfort Woman*. New York: Penguin, 1998.

Kennedy, Philip. *Deus Humanissimus: The Knowability of God in the Theology of Edward Schillebeeckx*. Fribourg: Fribourg University Press, 1993.

———. *Schillebeeckx*. Outstanding Christian Thinkers. Collegeville, MN: Liturgical, 1994.

Kerr, Fergus. "Rebels with a Cause: Twentieth-Century Roman Catholic Theologians." *Theology Today* 62 (2005) 297–304.

Kim Chi-Ha. "Declaration of Conscience." *Bulletin of Concerned Asian Scholars* 9 (1977) 8–15.

———. *The Gold Crowned Jesus and Other Writings*. Preface by Chong-sun Kim and Shelly Killen. Maryknoll, NY: Orbis, 1978.

———. *Heart's Agony: Selected Poems of Kim Chi-Ha*. Translated by Won-Chung Kim and James Han. Fredonia, NY: White Pine, 1998.

———. *The Middle Hour: Selected Poems of Kim Chi-Ha*. Stanfordville, NY: Human Rights, 1980.

———. "The Story of a Sound." In *Contemporary Literature of Asia*, edited by Arthur Biddle et al., 466–75. Upper Saddle River, NJ: Prentice Hall, 1996.

———. "Twelve Poems of Kim Chi-Ha." Translated by Susie Jie Young Kim. *Korea Journal* (1995) 67–84.

Kim, Chong-Ho. *Korean Shamanism: The Cultural Paradox*. Burlington, VT: Ashgate, 2003.

Kim, Grace Ji-Sun. *Colonialism, "Han," and the Transformative Spirit*. New York: Palgrave Macmillan, 2013.

———. *The Grace of Sophia: A Korean North-American Woman's Christology*. Cleveland: Pilgrim, 2002.

———. *The Holy Spirit, Ch'i, and the Other: A Model of Global and Intercultural Pneumatology*. New York: Palgrave Macmillan, 2011.

———. "Oppression and *Han*: Korean Women's Historical Context." *Journal of Asian and Asian-American Theology* 3 (1999) 55–70.

Kim, Jeong-Soo. *Telling the Stories of Han*. Gender, Theology, and Spirituality. London: Equinox, 2011.

Kim, Sang-Yil. "Han and *Han*: Phenomenological Interpretation of Hanism." *Acta Koreana* 1 (1998) 19–25.

———. *Hanism as Korean Mind: An Interpretation of Han Philosophy*. Los Angeles: Eastern Academy of Human Sciences, 1984.

———. "Hanism: Korean Concept of Ultimacy." *Ultimate Reality and Meaning* 9 (1986) 17–36.

Kim, Sung-Soo. *Ham Sok Hon, Voice of the People and Pioneer of Religious Pluralism in Twentieth-Century Korea: A Biography of a Korean Quaker*. Seoul: Saman, 2001.

Kim, Ui-Chol, and Sang-Chin Choi. "Indigenous Form of Lamentation, *Han*: Conceptual and Philosophical Analysis." In *Korean Cultural Roots: Religion and Social Thought*, edited by Ho-Youn Kwon, 245–66. Chicago: Integrated Technical Resources, 1995.

Küster, Volker. *The Many Faces of Jesus Christ: Intercultural Christology*. Maryknoll, NY: Orbis, 2001.

———. *A Protestant Theology of Passsion: Korean Minjung Theology Revisited*. Studies in Systematic Theology. Leiden: Brill, 2010.

Lamentabili Sane Exitu (1907). Pope Pius X. Papal Encyclicals Online, http://papalencyclicals.net/Pius10/p10lamen.htm.

Langan, John. "Political Hopes and Political Tasks: A Reading of *Gaudium et Spes* after Twenty Years." In *"Questions of Special Urgency": The Church and the Modern World after Vatican II*, edited by Judith A. Dwyer, 99–122. Washington, DC: Georgetown University Press, 1986.

Lee, Jae-Hoon. *The Exploration of the Inner Wounds—Han*. American Academy of Religion Academy Series 86. Atlanta: Scholars, 1994.

Lee, Jung-Young. *An Emerging Theology in World Perspective: Commentary on Korean Minjung Theology*. New London, CT: Twenty-Third, 1988.

———. *Marginality: The Key to Multicultural Theology*. Minneapolis: Augsburg Fortress, 1995.

Lee, Peter H., et al. *Sources of Korean Tradition*. Vol. 1, *From Early Times to the Sixteenth Century*. New York: Columbia University Press, 1997.

———. *Sources of Korean Tradition*. Vol. 2, *From the Sixteenth to the Twentieth Centuries*. New York: Columbia University Press, 2000.

Lonergan, Bernard. *Method in Theology*. Toronto: University of Toronto Press, 1990.

———. "Transition from a Classicist Worldview to Historical-Mindedness." In *Second Collection*, edited by William F. J. Ryan and Bernard J. Tyrrell, 1–10. Toronto: University of Toronto Press, 1996.

Lotman, Juri. "On the Semiosphere." Translated by Wilma Clark. *Sign System Studies* 33 (2005) 205–29.

Lustig, Myron W., and Jolene Koester. *Intercultural Competence: Interpersonal Communication across Cultures*. 6th ed. Boston: Allyn & Bacon, 2009.

Marchetto, Agostino. *The Second Vatican Council: A Counterpoint for the History of the Council*. Scranton, PA: University of Scranton Press, 2010.

McFague, Sallie. *Metaphorical Theology: Models of God in Religious Language*. Minneapolis: Fortress, 1982.

McGuckin, John. *Saint Cyril of Alexandria and the Christological Controversy*. Crestwood, NY: St. Vladimir's Seminary Press, 2004.

McManus, Kathleen. "Reconciling the Cross in the Theologies of Edward Schillebeeckx and Ivone Gebara." *Theological Studies* 66 (2005) 638–50.

———. "Suffering in the Theology of Edward Schillebeeckx." *Theological Studies* 60 (1999) 476–91.

———. *Unbroken Communion: The Place and Meaning of Suffering in the Theology of Edward Schillebeeckx*. New York: Rowman and Littlefield, 2003.

Matsuoka, Fumitaka. "A Reflection on 'Teaching Theology from an Intercultural Perspective.'" *Theological Education* 36 (1989) 35–42.

Maximus the Confessor. *On the Cosmic Mystery of Jesus Christ*. Translated by Paul M. Blowers and Robert Louis Wilken. Crestwood, NY: St. Vladimir's Seminary Press, 2003.

Metz, Johannes Baptist. *The Emergent Church*. Translated by Peter Mann. New York: Crossroad, 1981.

———. *Faith in History and Society: Towards a Practical Fundamental Theology*. Translated by David Smith. New York: Seabury, 1980.

———. *A Passion for God: The Mystical-Political Dimension of Christianity*. Edited and translated by J. Matthew Ashley. Mahwah, NJ: Paulist, 1998.

Miller, Vincent. "Where Is the Church? Globalization and Catholicity." *Theological Studies* 69 (2008) 412–32.

Minjung Theology: People as the Subjects of History. Edited by The Commission on Theological Concerns of the Christian Conference of Asia. Rev. ed. Maryknoll, NY: Orbis, 1983.

Mosley, LaReine-Marie. "Negative Contrast Experience: An Ignatian Appraisal." *Horizons* 41 (2014) 74–95.

———. "Salvation Despite the Death of Jesus? The Cross in the Soteriology of Edward Schillebeeckx: An African American Christian Female Perspective." PhD diss., University of Notre Dame, 2006.

Moss, David, and Edward T. Oakes. "Introduction." In *The Cambridge Companion to Hans Urs von Balthasar*, edited by Edward T. Oakes and David Moss, 1–10. Cambridge: Cambridge University Press, 2004.

O'Malley, John W. *What Happened at Vatican II*. Cambridge, MA: Belknap, 2010.

O'Malley, John W., et. al. *Vatican II: Did Anything Happen?* Edited by David G. Schultenover. New York: Continuum, 2007.

Ormerod, Neil. "Vatican II: Continuity or Discontinuity? Towards an Ontology of Meaning." *Theological Studies* 71 (2010) 606–39.

Ormerod, Neil and Shane Clifton, eds. *Globalization and the Mission of the Church*. NY: T. & T. Clark, 2009.

Pagden, Anthony. *Peoples and Empires: A Short History of European Migration, Exploration, and Conquest from Greece to the Present*. New York: Random House, 2001.

Park, Andrew Sung. *From Hurt to Healing: A Theology of the Wounded*. Nashville: Abingdon, 2004.

———. "God Who Needs Our Salvation." In *The Changing Face of God*, edited by Frederick W. Schmidt, 81–94. Harrisburg, PA: Morehouse, 2000.

———. "Minjung and P'ungryu Theologies in Contemporary Korea: A Critical and Comparative Examination." PhD diss., Graduate Theological Union, 1986.

———. "Minjung Theology: A Korean Contextual Theology." *Indian Journal of Theology* 33 (1984) 1–11.

———. *Racial Conflict and Healing: An Asian-American Perspective*. Maryknoll, NY: Orbis, 1996.

———. "Theology of Han (the Abyss of Pain)." *Quarterly Review* 9 (1989) 48–62.

———. "A Theology of the Way (Dao)." *Interpretation* 55 (2001) 389–99.

———. *Triune Atonement: Christ's Healing for Sinners, Victims, and the Whole of Creation*. Louisville: Westminster John Knox, 2009.

———. *The Wounded Heart of God: The Asian Concept of Han and the Christian Doctrine of Sin*. Nashville: Abingdon, 1993.

Park, Andrew Sung, and Susan Nelson. *The Other Side of Sin: Woundedness from the Perspective of the Sinned-Against*. Albany: State University of New York Press, 2001.

Park, Jung Eun Sophia. *A Hermeneutics of Dislocation as Experience: Creating a Borderland, Constructing a Hybrid Identity*. Studies in Biblical Literature. New York: Lang, 2011.

———. "Jesus of Minjung on the Road to Emmaus (Luke 24:13–32): Envisioning a Post-Minjung theology." In *Jesus of Galilee: Contextual Theology for the 21st Century*, edited by Robert Lassalle-Klein, 149–59. Maryknoll, NY: Orbis, 2011.

"*Pascendi Dominici Gregis*" (1907). Pope Pius X. The Holy See. http://www.vatican.va/holy_father/pius_x/encyclicals/documents/hf_p-x_enc_19070908_pascendi-dominici-gregis_en.html.

"Pastoral Constitution on the Church in the Modern World, *Gaudium et spes*. The Holy See. http://www.vatican.va/archive/hist_councils/ii_vatican_council/documents/vat-ii_cons_19651207_gaudium-et-spes_en.html.

Phan, Peter. *Christianity with an Asian Face: Asian American Theology in the Making*. Maryknoll, NY: Orbis, 2003.

———. "Jesus Christ with an Asian Face." *Theological Studies* 57 (1996) 399–430.

Phan, Peter, and Diana Hayes, eds. *Many Faces, One Church: Cultural Diversity and the American Catholic Experience*. Lanham, MD: Rowman & Littlefield, 2005.

Phan, Peter, and Jung Young Lee. *Journeys at the Margin: Towards an Autobiographical Theology in American-Asian Perspective*. Collegeville, MN: Liturgical, 1999.

Pieris, Aloysius. *An Asian Theology of Liberation*. New York: T. & T. Clark, 1988.
Plato. *Five Dialogues*. Translated by G. M. A. Grube and revised by John M. Cooper. 2nd ed. Indianapolis: Hackett, 2002.
———. *The Republic*. Translated by G. M. A. Grube and revised by C. D. C. Greeve. Indianapolis: Hackett, 1992.
Premnath, D. N. *Border Crossings: Cross Cultural Hermeneutics*. Maryknoll, NY: Orbis, 2007.
Pseudo-Dionysius. *The Mystical Theology* in *Pseudo-Dionysius: The Complete Works*. Classics of Western Spirituality. Mahwah, NJ: Paulist, 1987.
Quanta cura and its *Syllabus of Errors* (Pius IX, 1864). Papal Encyclicals Online. http://www.papalencyclicals.net/Pius09/p9quanta.htm; http://www.papalencyclicals.net/Pius09/p9syll.htm
Rabinow, Paul. *Reflections on Fieldwork in Morocco*. 30th anniv. ed. Berkeley: University of California Press, 1997.
Rahner, Karl. "The Abiding Significance of Vatican II." In *Theological Investigations XX: Concern for the Church*, translated by Edward Quinn, 90–103. New York: Crossroad, 1981.
———. "Basic Theological Interpretation of Vatican II." In *Theological Investigations XX: Concern for the Church*, translated by Edward Quinn, 77–89. New York: Crossroad, 1981.
———. *Foundations of Christian Faith: An Introduction to the Idea of Christianity*. Translated by William V. Dych. New York: Crossroad, 1978.
Ratzinger, Joseph. *Theological Highlights of Vatican II*. Mahwah, NJ: Paulist, 2009.
Rego, Aloysius. *Suffering and Salvation: The Salvific Meaning of Suffering in the Later Theology of Edward Schillebeeckx*. Louvain Pastoral and Theological Monographs 33. Louvain: Peeters, 2006.
Reichel-Dolmatoff, Gerardo. *Amazonian Cosmos: The Sexual and Religious Symbolism of the Tukano Indians*. Chicago: University of Chicago Press, 1974.
Rynne, Xavier. *Vatican Council II*. Maryknoll, NY: Orbis, 1999.
Said, Edward. *Orientalism*. New York: Pantheon, 1978.
Samovar, Larry, et. al., eds. *Intercultural Communication: A Reader*. 13th ed. Boston: Wadsworth, 2012.
The Sandglass (Moraesigye). Directed by Jong-Hak Kim. 1995. Seoul, South Korea: SBS-TV Korea. 2006. DVD.
Schelkens, Karim. *The Council Diaries of Edward Schillebeeckx, 1962–1963*. Critically annotated bilingual ed. Louvain: Peeters, 2010.
The Schillebeeckx Case: Official Exchange of Letters and Documents in the Investigation of Fr. Edward Schillebeeckx by the Sacred Congregation for the Doctrine of the Faith, 1976–1980. Edited with introduction and notes by Ted Schoof. New York: Crossroad, 1984.
Schillebeeckx, Edward. *Christ: The Experience of Jesus as Lord*. Translated by John Bowden. New York: Crossroad, 1981.
———. *Christ: The Sacrament of the Encounter with God*. Kansas City: Sheed & Ward, 1963.
———. *For the Sake of the Gospel*. Translated by John Bowden. New York: Crossroad, 1990.
———. *God among Us: The Gospel Proclaimed*. Translated by John Bowden. New York: Crossroad, 1988.

―――. *God Is New Each Moment: In Conversation with Huub Oosterhuis and Piet Hoogeveen.* Translated by David Smith. London: Continuum, 2004.

―――. *I Am a Happy Theologian: Conversations with Francisco Strazzari.* Translated by John Bowden. New York: Crossroad, 1994.

―――. *Interim Report on the Books Jesus and Christ.* Translated by Hubert Hoskins. New York: Crossroad, 1981.

―――. *Jesus: An Experiment in Christology.* Translated by Hubert Hoskins. New York: Seabury, 1979.

―――. *The Language of Faith: Essays on Jesus, Theology, and the Church.* Maryknoll, NY: Orbis 1995.

―――. *On Christian Faith: The Spiritual, Ethical and Political Dimensions.* Translated by John Bowden. New York: Crossroad, 1987.

―――. "Prologue: Human God-Talk and God's Silence." In *The Praxis of the Reign of God: An Introduction to the Theology of Edward Schillebeeckx,* edited by Mary Catherine Hilkert and Robert Schreiter, ix–xviii. New York: Fordham University Press, 2002.

―――. *The Schillebeeckx Reader.* Edited by Robert J. Schreiter. New York: Crossroad, 1983.

Schillebeeckx, Edward, and Johann Baptist Metz. *No Heaven without Earth.* Concilium. London: SCM, 1991.

Schreiter, Robert. "Christian Witness in a 'New Modernity': Trajectories in Intercultural Theology." *Concilium* 1 (2011) 27–36.

―――. *Constructing Local Theologies.* Maryknoll, NY: Orbis, 1985.

―――. "Edward Schillebeeckx." In *The Modern Theologians,* edited by David Ford, 152–61. 2nd ed. Oxford: Blackwell, 1997.

―――. "The Impact of Vatican II." In *The Twentieth Century: A Theological Overview,* edited by Gregory Baum, 158–72. Maryknoll, NY: Orbis, 1999.

―――. *The New Catholicity: Theology between the Global and Local.* Maryknoll, NY: Orbis, 1997.

―――. "The Possibilities (and Limitations) of an Intercultural Dialogue on God." In *The Concept of God in Global Dialogue,* edited by Werner Jeanrond and Aasulv Lande, 19–31. Maryknoll, NY: Orbis, 2005.

―――. "The Relevance of Professor Edward Schillebeeckx, O.P. for the 21st Century." The Kathleen and John F. Bricker Memorial Lecture. Tulane University, New Orleans, Louisiana, October 8, 2009. http://schillebeeckx.nl/wp-content/uploads/2008/11/Lecture-on-relevance-Schillebeeckx.pdf.

Schüssler-Fiorenza, Elisabeth. *In Memory of Her: A Feminist Reconstruction of Christian Origins.* New York: Crossroad, 1983.

Seth, Michael J. *Concise History of Modern Korea: From the Late Nineteenth Century to the Present.* Lanham, MD: Rowman & Littlefield, 2010.

―――. *A History of Korea: From Antiquity to the Present.* Lanham, MD: Rowman & Littlefield, 2011.

Shorter, Aylward. *Toward a Theology of Inculturation.* Maryknoll, NY: Orbis, 1988. Reprint, Eugene, OR: Wipf & Stock, 2006.

Simon, Derek. "Provisional Liberations, Fragments of Salvation: The Practical-Critical Soteriology of Edward Schillebeeckx." PhD diss., University of Ottawa, 2001.

―――. "Salvation and Liberation in the Practical-Critical Soteriology of Edward Schillebeeckx." *Theological Studies* 63 (2002) 494–520.

Sobrino, Jon. *Jesus the Liberator: A Historical-Theological View.* Translated by Paul Burns and Francis McDonagh. Maryknoll, NY: Orbis, 1993.

———. *Spirituality of Liberation: Towards Political Holiness.* Translated by Robert R. Barr. Maryknoll, NY: Orbis, 1988.

Son, Chang-Hee. *Haan of Minjung Theology and Han of Han Philosophy: In the Paradigm of Process Philosophy and Metaphysics of Relatedness.* Lanham, MD: University Press of America, 2000.

Speyr, Adrienne von. *Erde und Himmel: Ein Tagebuch.* Part II, *Die Zeit der grossen Diktate.* Einsiedeln: Johannes, 1975.

Spivak, Gayatri Chakravorty. *The Spivak Reader: Selected Works of Gayatri Chakravorty Spivak.* Edited by Donna Landry and Gerald MacLean. New York: Routledge, 1996.

Steele, D. "Creation and Cross in the Later Soteriology of Edward Schillebeeckx." PhD diss., University of Notre Dame, 2000.

Suh, David Kwang-Sun. "Foreword." In *A Protestant Theology of Passion: Korean Minjung Theology Revisited*, xi–xviii. Studies in Systematic Theology. Leiden: Brill, 2010.

———. *The Korean Minjung in Christ.* Eugene, OR: Wipf & Stock, 2001.

———. "The Priesthood of Han." *Reformed World* 39 (1986) 597–607.

Sympathy for Lady Vengeance (Chinjeolhan geumjassi). Directed by Park Chan-Wook. 2005. Seoul, South Korea: CJ Entertainment. 2006. DVD.

Tanner, Kathryn. *Theories of Culture: A New Agenda for Theology.* Minneapolis: Fortress, 1997.

Thangaraj, M. Thomas. "Let God be God: Crossing Boundaries as a Theological Perspective." In *Border Crossings: Cross-Cultural Hermeneutics*, edited by D. M. Premnath, 89–102. Maryknoll, NY: Orbis, 2005.

Tillar, Elizabeth K. "Critical Remembrance and Eschatological Hope in Edward Schillebeeckx's Theology of Suffering for Others." *Heythrop Journal* 44 (2003) 15–42.

Tracy, David. *The Analogical Imagination: Christian Theology and the Culture of Pluralism.* New York: Crossroad, 1981.

———. "The Analogical Imagination in Catholic Theology." In *Talking about God: Doing Theology in the Context of Modern Pluralism*, by John Cobb and David Tracy, 17–28. San Francisco: Harper & Row, 1984.

———. *Blessed Rage for Order: The New Pluralism in Theology.* Chicago: University of Chicago Press, 1996.

———. *Dialogue with the Other: The Inter-Religious Dialogue.* Louvain Theological and Pastoral Monographs 1. Louvain: Peeters, 1991.

———. "Form and Fragment: The Recovery of the Hidden and Incomprehensible God." In *The Concept of God in Global Dialogue*, edited by Werner Jeanrond and Aasulv Lande, 98–114. Maryknoll, NY: Orbis, 2005.

———. *Plurality and Ambiguity: Hermeneutics, Religion, Hope.* San Francisco: Harper & Row, 1987.

———. "The Uneasy Alliance Reconsidered." *Theological Studies* 50 (1989) 548–70.

Vatican Council II: The Conciliar and Post-Conciliar Documents. Edited by Austin Flannery. Rev. ed. Northport, NY: Costello, 1988.

Weil, Simone. *Waiting for God.* Translated by Emma Craufurd. 1955. Reprint, New York: HarperCollins, 2001.

Wright, John J. "The Thrust of the Council." In *The Church in the World*, edited by Charles P. O'Donnell, 1–7. Milwaukee: Bruce, 1967.

Yi, Sang-Taek. *Religion and Social Formation in Korea: Minjung and Milennarianism*. New York: de Gruyter, 1996.

Yoo, Yani. "*Han*-Laden Women: Korean 'Comfort Women' and Women in Judges 19–21." *Semeia* 78 (1997) 37–46.

Yoshimi, Yoshiaki. *Comfort Women: Sexual Slavery in the Japanese Military during World War II*. Translated by Suzanne O'Brien. New York: Columbia University Press, 2002.

Youn, Il-Sun. "Toward Authentic Partnership for Mutual Ministry in the Korean Catholic Context: A Dialogue between a Catholic Feminist and Korean Folk Religions." DMin thesis, Catholic Theological Union, 2002.

Yu, Chai-Shin. *The Founding of Catholic Tradition in Korea*. Studies in Korean Religion and Culture 7. Fremont, CA: Asian Humanities, 2004.

———. *Korea and Christianity*. Studies in Korean Religion and Culture 8. Fremont, CA: Asian Humanities, 2004.

———. *Korean Thought and Culture: A New Introduction*. Bloomington, IN: Trafford, 2011.

Index of Authors

Abraham, Susan, 87n284
Ahn, Byung-Mu, 107, 114n361,
Alberigo, Giuseppe, 1n1, 3n4, 4n8, 5, 6, 6n11n12n14, 8, 8n19
Anderson, Victor, 69n217
Anselm of Canterbury, 152, 152n502, 153n502
Arbuckle, Gerald, 68, 72–73, 75nn237-38
Aquinas, Thomas, 117, 185n565, 186n570,
Augustine of Hippo, 184n565, 185, 185n567

Balthasar, Hans Urs von, 34n77, 37n90, 58n177, 186n573
Barth, Karl, 53n154, 186n573
Baum, Gregory, 9n24,
Bevans, Stephen B., 84n270,
Bhabha, Homi, 87n284, 154
Boeve, Lieven, 33n71, 53n155, 64n209
Borgman, Erik, 29, 30n63, 31n66, 35n79, 39, 39n97
Burrows, Mark, 179n553

Carter, J. Kameron, 69n217
CELAM, 6n15, 20n49
Chen, Guo-Ming, 92n299
Chenu, Marie-Dominique, 33, 33n73, 34n77, 35n78, 36n88,
Choi, Hoon, 130n424
Chung, Hyun-Kyung,
  critique of *minjung* theology, 123–25
  on *han-pu-ri* and salvation, 124–25
  on shamanism, 111–12
  on women's *han*, 123

Chung, Paul, 163n524
Cone, James H., 23n53, 70n217, 196n595,
Congar, Yves, 8n20, 31, 33, 34n77, 36n88, 37
Cooper, Jennifer, 35n78, 39n96, 44n117,
Copeland, M. Shawn, 56n169, 70n217
Cruz, Gemma Talmud, 78n253
Cyril of Alexandria, 139–40n458

Day, Dorothy, xxiii*n*10
Deuchler, Martina, 103n324
De Lubac, Henri, 31, 36n88, 37n90,
De Petter, Dominicus, 32–33, 34n77, 53n78
De Smedt, Emile, 8
Diaz, Miguel, 167n533
Dolphin, Kathleen, 35n78
Dreyer, Elizabeth, 179n553

Elizondo, Virgilio, 2n3, 6n15, 7, 22–23, 79n257
Erp, Stephan van, 33n71
Espin, Orlando, 76n242

Faggioli, Massimo, 3n4,
Fung, Raymond, xvii n2

Garcia-Rivera, Alejandro, xxiv, 82–83, 88n288, 89, 90–91, 93, 166n530
Geertz, Clifford, 68–69, 82, 94
Godzieba, Anthony, 53n158
Goergen, Donald, 174, 180
Greeley, Andrew, 185n565
Gremillion, Joseph, 13

Guisso, R. L. W.
    on shamanism, 109n342, 110n345, 111n352
Guarino, Thomas, 186n573
Gutierrez, Gustavo, 22–23, 30

Hahm, Pyong-Choon
    on shamanism, 109–10
Ham, Sok-Hon, 106–108
Hayes, Zachary, 185n565
Hicks, George, 104n327
Higgins, George, 10, 11
Hilkert, Mary Catherine
    on contrast experiences, 45
    on Schillebeeckx and narrative, 46
    on Schillebeeckx and spirituality, 35n78, 53n155
    on Schillebeeckx and suffering, 35n83
Hill, William J., 32n67
Hopkins, Dwight, 70n217
Hwang, Kyung-Moon, 102n321, 124n403
    on Tonghak Rebellion, 104n326
Hyun, Young-Hak, 113, 114n361, 136n443

Jennings, Willie James, 78n252
Joh, Wonhee Anne
    on Anselmian atonement theory, 152–53
    on *han*, 146–48
    on interstitial space/third space, 153–54, 165–66
    on *jeong*, 149–151, 156–157, 169n536
    on Kim Chi-Ha, 151
    on salvation, 154–56
    on theology of the cross, 152–56

John of the Cross, 191n584
John XXIII (pope), 2–8,
John Paul II (pope), 13, 19–20, 191n584
Johnson, Elizabeth, 186n570

Kaspar, Walter, 12
Kennedy, Phillip, 52, 53, 55, 59, 175
Kerr, Fergus, 37n90

Killen, Shelly, 115, 117n375,
    on Kim Chi Ha's *Torture Road*, 190–91
Kim, Chi-Ha
    on "agonized violence of love", 117
    on *Chang Il-Dam*, 118
    on conversion to Roman Catholicism, 114, 194n594
    on *dan* philosophy, 116–18
    on *Declaration of Conscience*, 114–15, 117
    on *Gold-Crowned Jesus*, 192–94
    on *Groundless Rumours*, 115
    on *han*, 114–18, 189–95
    on *minjung*, 115
    on poetry, 189–90
    on rejecting Roman Catholicism, 189n579
    on religion, revolution, and social change, 117, 119
    on *Torture Road*, 190–92
Kim, Chong-Ho,
    on shamanism, 112n356
Kim, Chong-Sun, 115, 117n375,
    on Kim Chi Ha's *Torture Road*, 190–91
Kim, Grace Ji-Sun, 103n323, 110, 124n403, 130n424
Kim, Sang-Yil
    on philosophy of hanism, 99–101,
Kim Sung-Soo, 102n321
    on Ham Sok-Hon, 106
Kim, Won-Chung, 189n579
Kim, Yong-Bock, 114n361, 122n397
Keller, Catherine, 87n284
Keller, Norah Okja, 104n327
Kuster, Volker, 109n344, 113n359n360, 114n361
    on Chung Hyun-Kyung, 123
    on Kim Chi-Ha and Suh Nam-Dong, 119, 189n579
    on shamanism's *kut*, 111
    on women's roles in Yi Dynasty, 103

Langan, John, 5, 10, 11, 12n29,
Lee, Jae-Hoon
    on Chun Tae-Il, 128
    on *hu-han*, 128–29

on *jeong-han*, 127
on *minjung theology*, 126
on *won-han*, 127
Lee, Jung-Young, 117n376, 118n380, 153n505
on *silhwa* and *mindam*, 121
Leo XIII (pope), 32n69
Lonergan, Bernard, 70n219, 71n226, 72
Lotman, Juri, 83n267

Matsuoka, Fumitaka, 165–66,
Maximus the Confesssor, 140n458
McManus, Kathleen, 40, 43n116, 46, 47n134
Metz, Johannes Baptist, 2n3, 37, 139n458, 167n534
on "dangerous memory," 46n130
Miller, Vincent, 76n242, 77n244
Mosely, LaReine-Marie, 56n169
Moss, David, 34n77

Oakes, Edward, 34n77
O'Malley, John, 3n4, 4n7, 5n10, 6n13, 7, 8,
on interpreting the Second Vatican Council, 7,8
on *Gaudium et spes*, 9
Ormerod, Neil, 3n4, 71n226, 89n292

Pagden, Anthony, 80n260
Park, Andrew Sung
on atonement, 141–44
on God, 139
on *han*, 131–36
on original sin, 138
on the Paraclete, 176
on resolution of *han*, 135, 137–38
on sin and evil, 136–140
on Tong-Shik Ryu and *Pungryu* theology, 99n307
Park, Jung-Eun Sophia, 130n424
Paul VI (pope), 1
Phan, Peter, 123n400
Pieris, Aloysius, 7n15
Plato, 71n222
Pius X (pope), 9n24, 32n69,
Portier, William, 34, 38–39
Premnath, D. N. , 87n283

Pseudo-Dionysius, 191n584

Rabinow, Paul, 165n528
Rahner, Karl, 7, 31, 36n88, 37, 59, 139n458, 184n565, 185n566
Ratzinger, Joseph, 3n4, 31, 36n88, 37n90
Rego, Aloysius, 47
Reichel-Dolmatoff, Gerardo, 165n528
Rochford, Dennis, 44n117

Said, Edward, 87n284, 92n300,
Schillebeeckx, Edward
on anthropological constants, 50–52
on contrast experiences and innocent suffering, 47–50
on the Dominicans and the Jesuits, 32n68
on God and creation, xxiii, 52–58
on human experience, xviii, 44–52
on Marie-Dominique Chenu, 33n73
on mediated immediacy, 59–61
on mysticism, 179–81
on salvation, xix, 40–43, 61–64, 168
Schreiter, Robert
on the concept of "religion," 70n218
on the concept of "third space," 165–66
on "globalized" understanding of culture, 76–80
on intercultural communication competence, 92–95
on intercultural hermeneutics, 85–91
on Schillebeeckx's continuing significance, 64n209
on Schillebeeckx and human experience, 43n116, 45, 51
on semiotics of culture, 82–84
on theological method, xix
Speyr, Adrienne von, 34n77
Spivak, Gayatri, 87n284
Shorter, Aylward, 70n219, 71n226, 72n227
Simon, Derek, 42n109, 43n114, 57, 61–64,
Sobrino, Jon, 23n53, 179n553, 180

Son, Chang-Hee
  on *haan* and *han,* 99–102
Suh, David Kwang-sun, 114n361
  on *minjung* definition, 113
  on shamanism, 112
Suh, Nam-Dong, 119–23,
  on Chun Tae-Il, 121–22
  on *han,* sin, and salvation, 119–20
  on the Millennium vs. God's Kingdom, 120–21
  on storytelling and *mindam,* 121–22

Tanner, Kathryn, 70–74
Thangaraj, M. Thomas, 75n238
Tillar, Elizabeth, 42

Tracy, David, 37n90, 67n210, 71n225
  on Catholic Analogical imagination, 185–87

Weil, Simone, 195n595
Wu, Chan J., 189n579

Youn, Il-Sun
  on Neo-Confucianism and women, 103
  on shamanism, 109–12
Yoo, Yani, 123n399
Yoshimi, Yoshiaki, 104n327
Yu, Chai-Shin, 100n310, 105n329
  On *Hwarang-do,* 109n342
  on shamanism, 111n352
  on Tonghak Rebellion, 104n326

www.ingramcontent.com/pod-product-compliance
Lightning Source LLC
Chambersburg PA
CBHW051640230426
43669CB00013B/2380